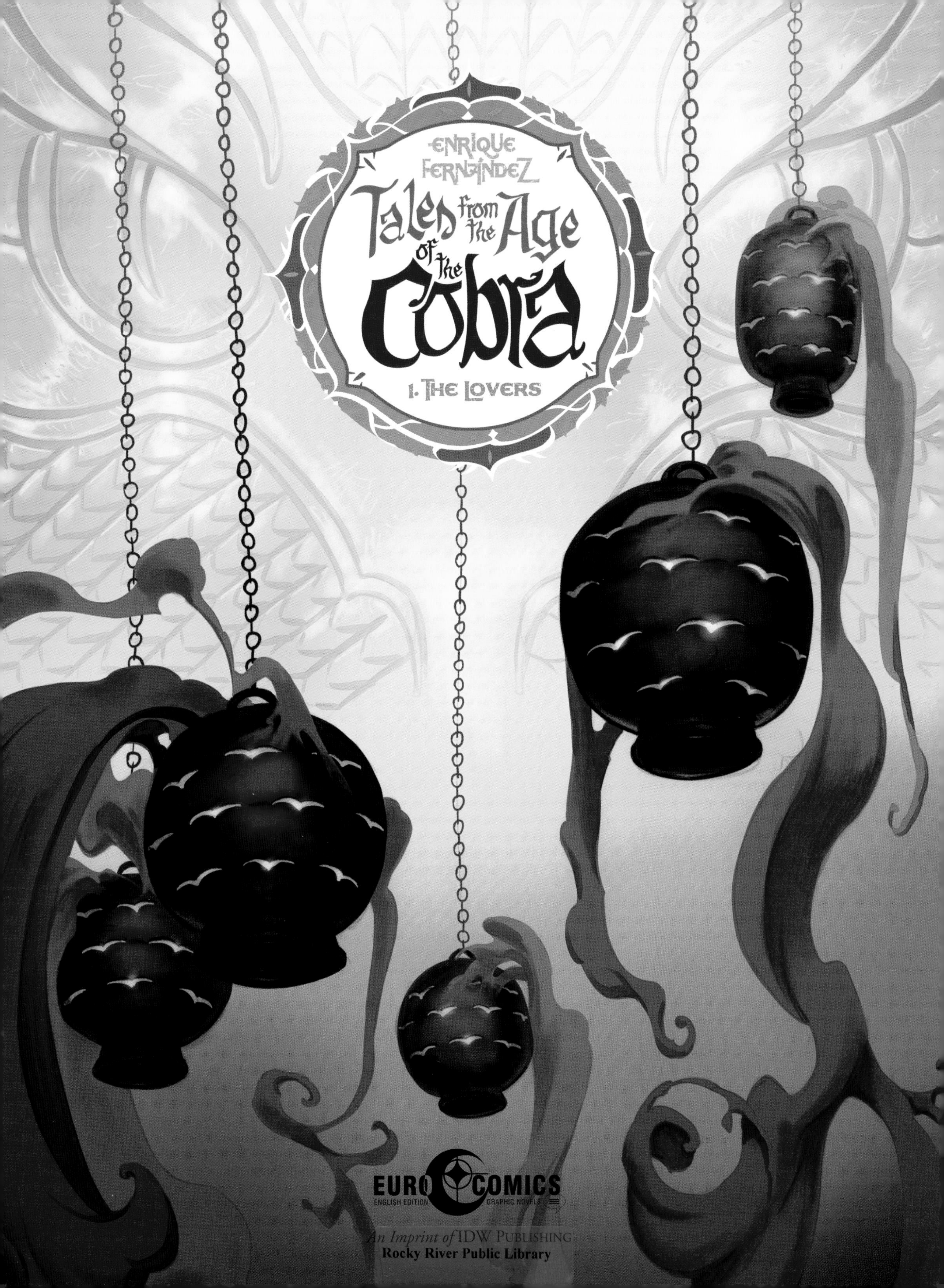
Enrique Fernández
Tales from the Age of the Cobra
1. The Lovers
EURO COMICS
ENGLISH EDITION GRAPHIC NOVELS
An Imprint of IDW Publishing

For my dear friends Antonio and Tania, Dela, Javi & Carol, Marc and Ara,
Ramon & Mabel, Sam & Karla, Sergio & Sonia — E.F.

EDITOR Dean Mullaney
ART DIRECTOR Lorraine Turner
TRANSLATION Edward Gauvin

EuroComics.us

EuroComics is an imprint of
IDW Publishing
a Division of Idea and Design Works, LLC
2765 Truxtun Road
San Diego, CA 92106
www.idwpublishing.com

ISBN: 978-1-68405-063-5 • First Printing, December 2017

Distributed to the book trade by Penguin Random House
Distributed to the comic book trade by Diamond Book Distributors

IDW Publishing
Ted Adams, Chief Executive Officer/Publisher
Greg Goldstein, Chief Operating Officer/President
Robbie Robbins, EVP/Sr. Graphic Artist
Chris Ryall, Chief Creative Officer
David Hedgecock, Editor-in-Chief
Matthew Ruzicka, CPA, Chief Financial Officer
Laurie Windrow, Senior VP of Sales and Marketing
Lorelei Bunjes, VP of Digital Services
Jerry Bennington, VP of New Product Development

Special thanks to Germund von Wowern, Justin Eisinger, and Alonzo Simon.

Originally published in French as *Les contes de L'ere du Cobra*, in two volumes.
Author : Enrique Fernandez
© 2012, Editions Glénat– ALL RIGHTS RESERVED

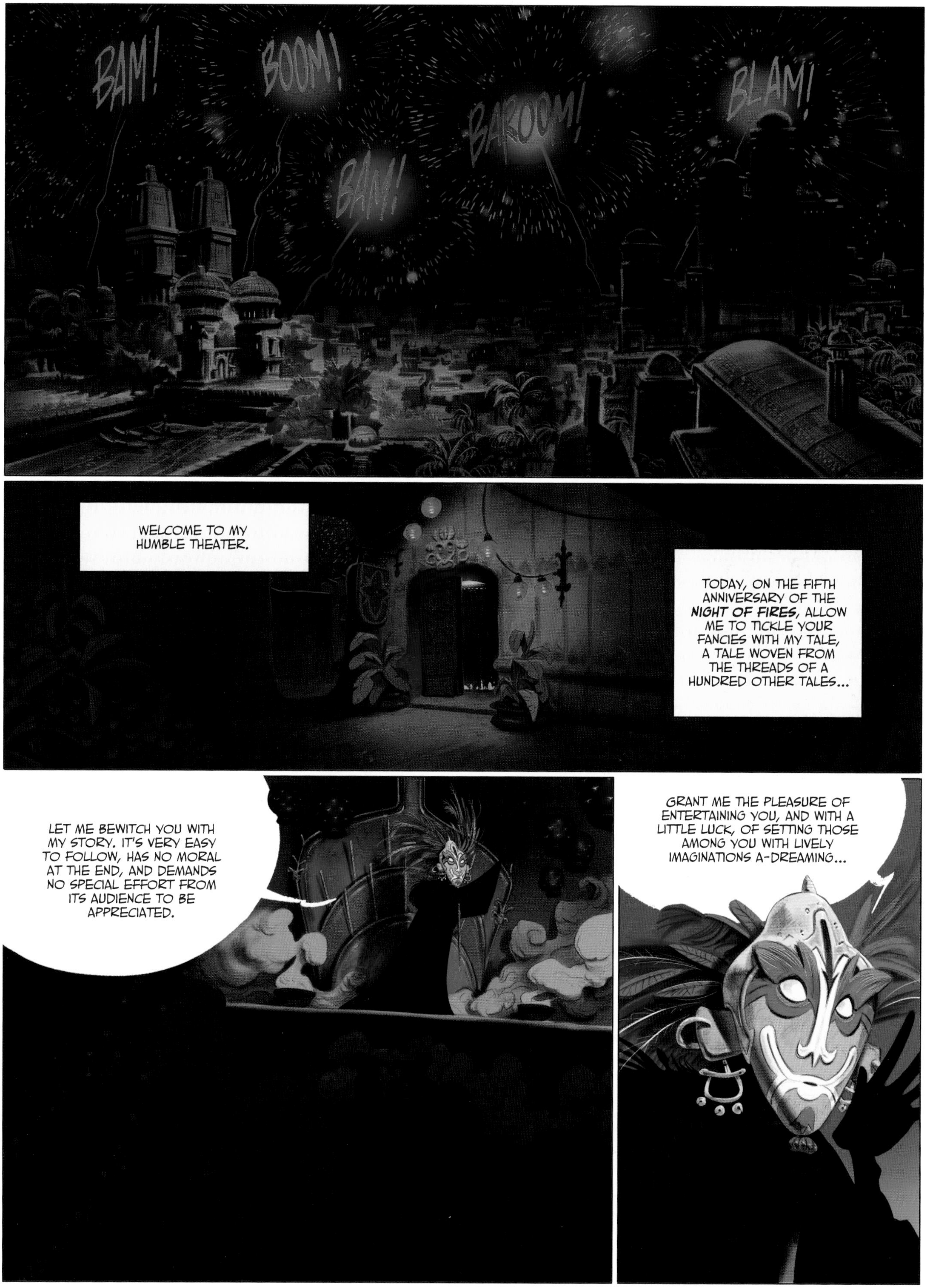
BAM!
BOOM!
BAROOM!
BLAM!
BAM!
WELCOME TO MY HUMBLE THEATER.
TODAY, ON THE FIFTH ANNIVERSARY OF THE **NIGHT OF FIRES**, ALLOW ME TO TICKLE YOUR FANCIES WITH MY TALE, A TALE WOVEN FROM THE THREADS OF A HUNDRED OTHER TALES...
LET ME BEWITCH YOU WITH MY STORY. IT'S VERY EASY TO FOLLOW, HAS NO MORAL AT THE END, AND DEMANDS NO SPECIAL EFFORT FROM ITS AUDIENCE TO BE APPRECIATED.
GRANT ME THE PLEASURE OF ENTERTAINING YOU, AND WITH A LITTLE LUCK, OF SETTING THOSE AMONG YOU WITH LIVELY IMAGINATIONS A-DREAMING...

THIS STORY INVOLVES QUITE A FEW CHARACTERS, STARTING WITH THE BEAUTIFUL **SIAN**, A FLOWER BORN ON A DUNGHILL.

HER FAMILY, HUMBLE MERCHANTS ONE AND ALL, JOURNEYED FOR GENERATIONS SEEKING THE FINEST MERCHANDISE TO TRADE IN THEIR LAND.

OVER TIME, HER ANCESTRAL TREE PUT DOWN ROOTS HERE, THERE, AND EVERYWHERE, IN EVERY KNOWN LAND, AND FROM SUCH CROSS-FERTILIZING OF SOILS FINALLY AROSE THIS RAVISHING EXOTIC BLOSSOM.

BUT MUCH TO SIAN'S DISMAY, HER BEAUTY EARNED HER NO GREATER LOVE FROM HER PARENTS, WHO SAW IN HER ONLY AN EXCELLENT BARGAIN, THE KIND OF WHICH THE FAMILY HAD ALWAYS DREAMED.

THEY WISHED TO MAKE A FORTUNE BY SELLING HER TO THE HOUSE OF PRINCESSES. A DESPICABLE RELIC FROM OUR PAST, THAT BAZAAR OF YOUNG VIRGINS HAS FOR YEARS BROUGHT IN THE MOST TAINTED GOLD OUR LAND HAD EVER SEEN.

SIAN'S PARENTS CONVINCED THEMSELVES SHE WAS SO BEAUTIFUL THAT A NOBLEMAN, OR EVEN A PRINCE, WOULD PURCHASE HER, THUS INCREASING ALL THE MORE ANY PROFITS FROM HER SALE.

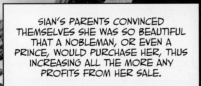

BUT THEY HADN'T COUNTED ON THE YOUNG LADY HAVING OTHER PLANS IN MIND FOR HER FUTURE...

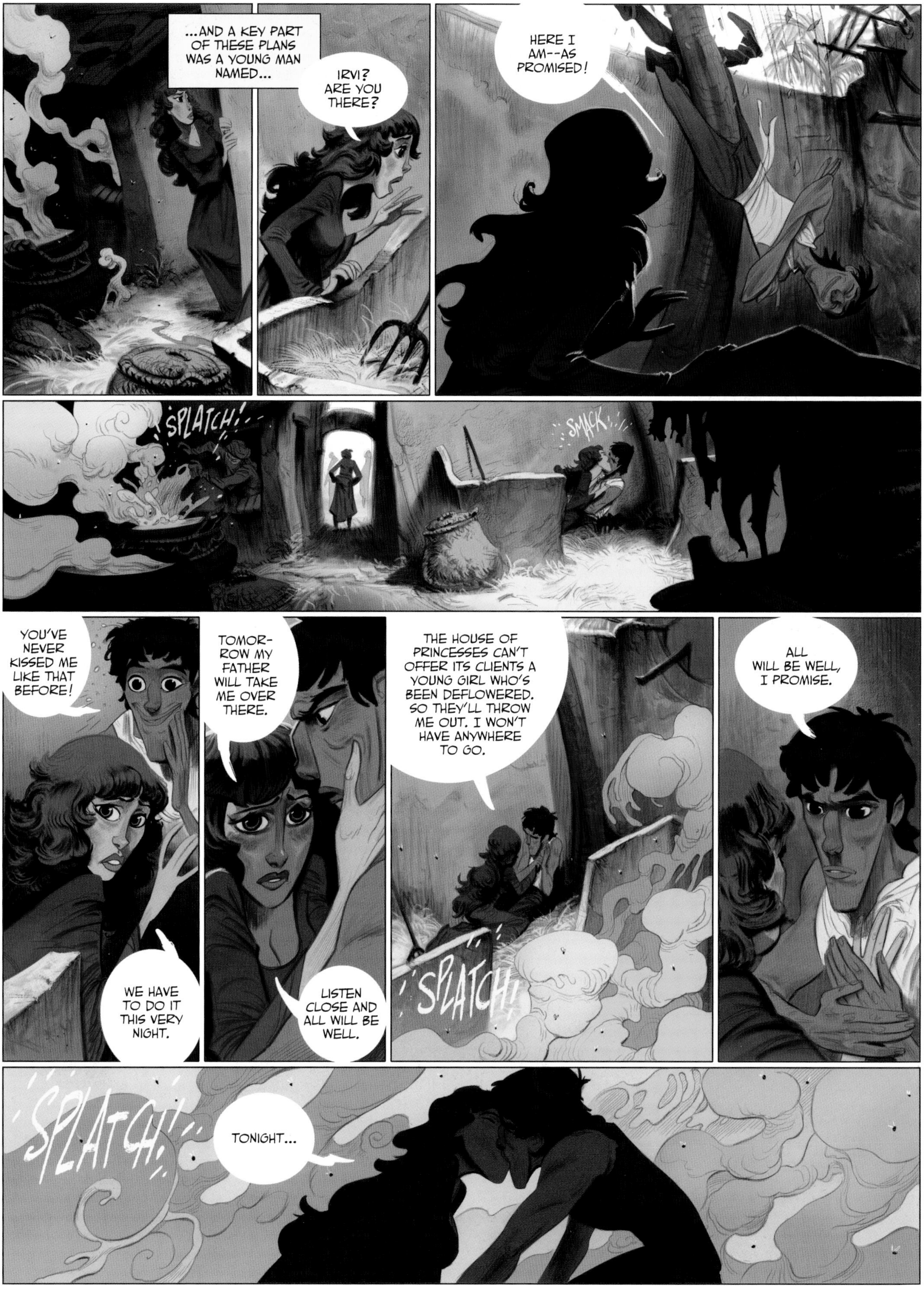
...AND A KEY PART OF THESE PLANS WAS A YOUNG MAN NAMED...
IRVI? ARE YOU THERE?
HERE I AM--AS PROMISED!
SPLATCH!
SMACK
YOU'VE NEVER KISSED ME LIKE THAT BEFORE!
WE HAVE TO DO IT THIS VERY NIGHT.
TOMOR-ROW MY FATHER WILL TAKE ME OVER THERE.
LISTEN CLOSE AND ALL WILL BE WELL.
THE HOUSE OF PRINCESSES CAN'T OFFER ITS CLIENTS A YOUNG GIRL WHO'S BEEN DEFLOWERED. SO THEY'LL THROW ME OUT. I WON'T HAVE ANYWHERE TO GO.
SPLATCH!
ALL WILL BE WELL, I PROMISE.
SPLATCH!
TONIGHT...

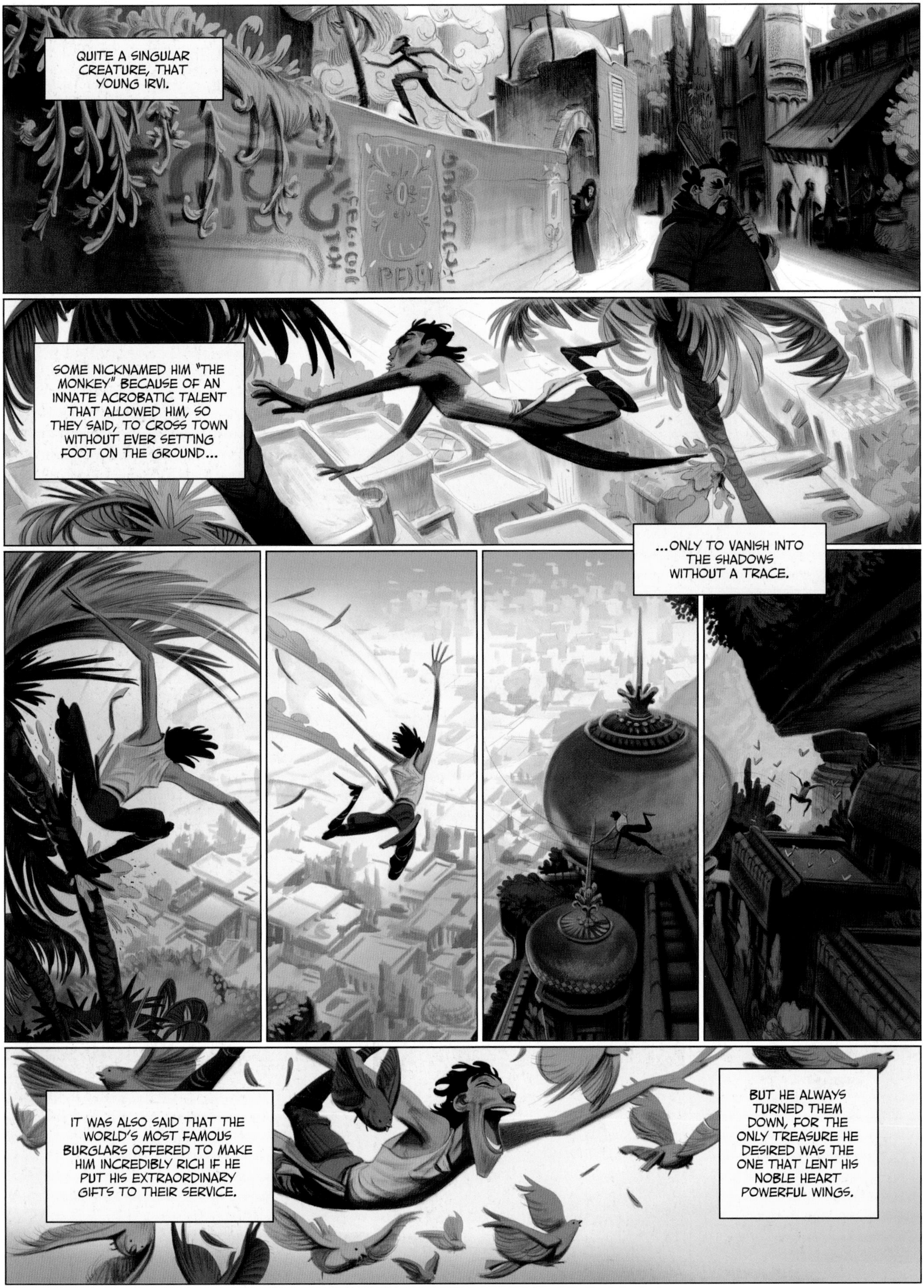
QUITE A SINGULAR CREATURE, THAT YOUNG IRVI.
SOME NICKNAMED HIM "THE MONKEY" BECAUSE OF AN INNATE ACROBATIC TALENT THAT ALLOWED HIM, SO THEY SAID, TO CROSS TOWN WITHOUT EVER SETTING FOOT ON THE GROUND...
...ONLY TO VANISH INTO THE SHADOWS WITHOUT A TRACE.
IT WAS ALSO SAID THAT THE WORLD'S MOST FAMOUS BURGLARS OFFERED TO MAKE HIM INCREDIBLY RICH IF HE PUT HIS EXTRAORDINARY GIFTS TO THEIR SERVICE.
BUT HE ALWAYS TURNED THEM DOWN, FOR THE ONLY TREASURE HE DESIRED WAS THE ONE THAT LENT HIS NOBLE HEART POWERFUL WINGS.

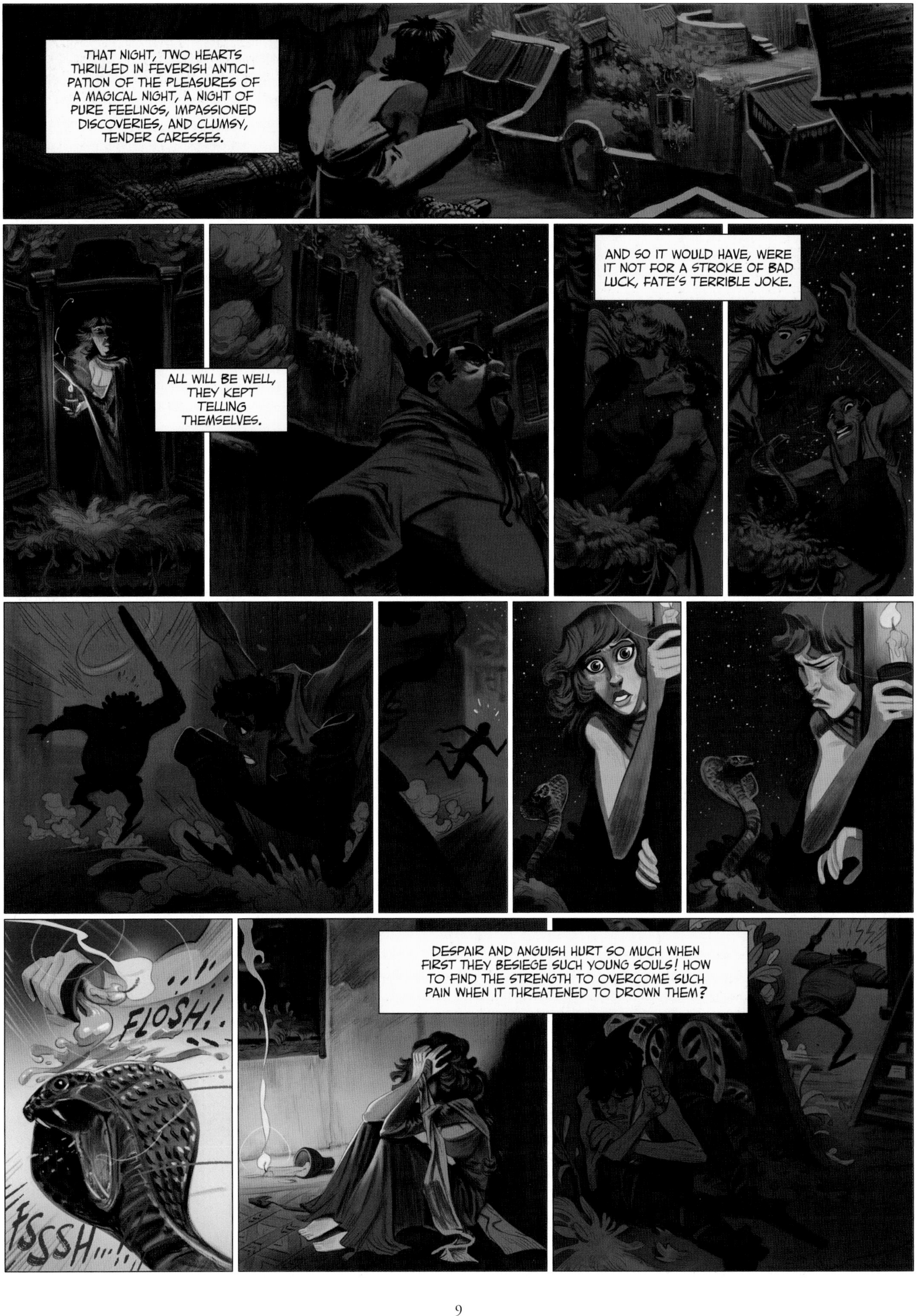
THAT NIGHT, TWO HEARTS THRILLED IN FEVERISH ANTICIPATION OF THE PLEASURES OF A MAGICAL NIGHT, A NIGHT OF PURE FEELINGS, IMPASSIONED DISCOVERIES, AND CLUMSY, TENDER CARESSES.
ALL WILL BE WELL, THEY KEPT TELLING THEMSELVES.
AND SO IT WOULD HAVE, WERE IT NOT FOR A STROKE OF BAD LUCK, FATE'S TERRIBLE JOKE.
FLOSH!
FSSSH
DESPAIR AND ANGUISH HURT SO MUCH WHEN FIRST THEY BESIEGE SUCH YOUNG SOULS! HOW TO FIND THE STRENGTH TO OVERCOME SUCH PAIN WHEN IT THREATENED TO DROWN THEM?

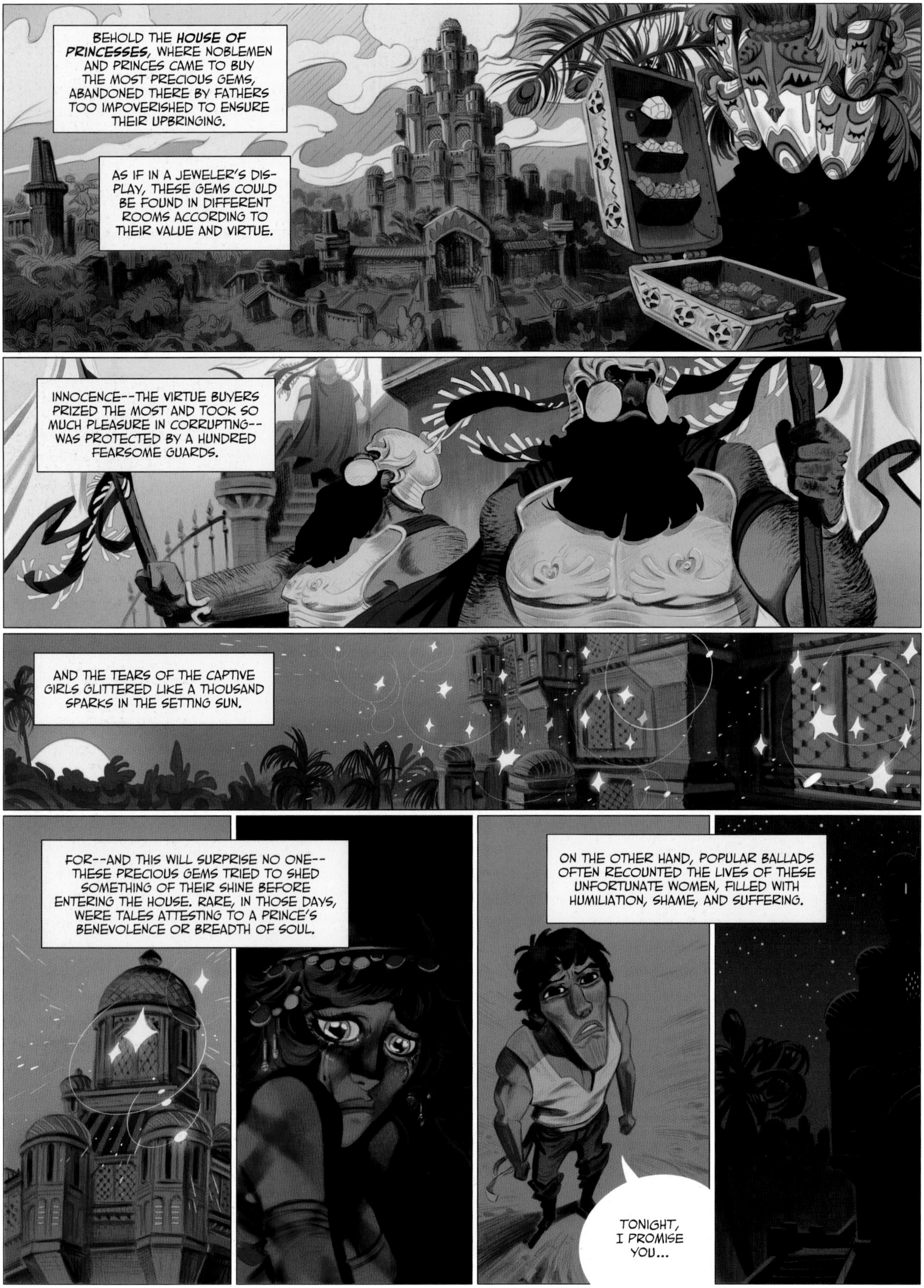
BEHOLD THE HOUSE OF PRINCESSES, WHERE NOBLEMEN AND PRINCES CAME TO BUY THE MOST PRECIOUS GEMS, ABANDONED THERE BY FATHERS TOO IMPOVERISHED TO ENSURE THEIR UPBRINGING.
AS IF IN A JEWELER'S DISPLAY, THESE GEMS COULD BE FOUND IN DIFFERENT ROOMS ACCORDING TO THEIR VALUE AND VIRTUE.
INNOCENCE--THE VIRTUE BUYERS PRIZED THE MOST AND TOOK SO MUCH PLEASURE IN CORRUPTING--WAS PROTECTED BY A HUNDRED FEARSOME GUARDS.
AND THE TEARS OF THE CAPTIVE GIRLS GLITTERED LIKE A THOUSAND SPARKS IN THE SETTING SUN.
FOR--AND THIS WILL SURPRISE NO ONE--THESE PRECIOUS GEMS TRIED TO SHED SOMETHING OF THEIR SHINE BEFORE ENTERING THE HOUSE. RARE, IN THOSE DAYS, WERE TALES ATTESTING TO A PRINCE'S BENEVOLENCE OR BREADTH OF SOUL.
ON THE OTHER HAND, POPULAR BALLADS OFTEN RECOUNTED THE LIVES OF THESE UNFORTUNATE WOMEN, FILLED WITH HUMILIATION, SHAME, AND SUFFERING.
TONIGHT, I PROMISE YOU...

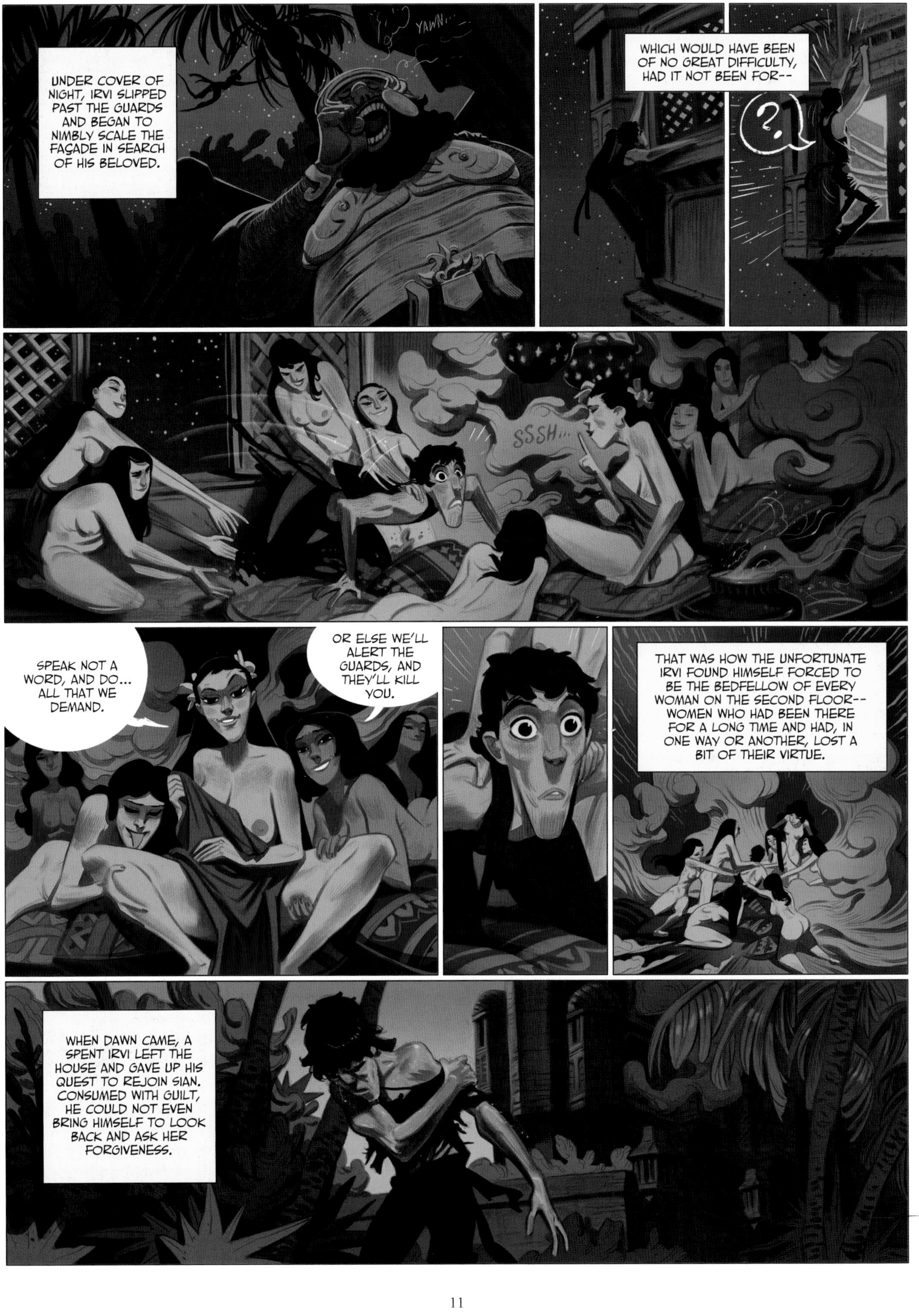
YAWN...
UNDER COVER OF NIGHT, IRVI SLIPPED PAST THE GUARDS AND BEGAN TO NIMBLY SCALE THE FAÇADE IN SEARCH OF HIS BELOVED.
WHICH WOULD HAVE BEEN OF NO GREAT DIFFICULTY, HAD IT NOT BEEN FOR--
?
SSSH...
SPEAK NOT A WORD, AND DO... ALL THAT WE DEMAND.
OR ELSE WE'LL ALERT THE GUARDS, AND THEY'LL KILL YOU.
THAT WAS HOW THE UNFORTUNATE IRVI FOUND HIMSELF FORCED TO BE THE BEDFELLOW OF EVERY WOMAN ON THE SECOND FLOOR--WOMEN WHO HAD BEEN THERE FOR A LONG TIME AND HAD, IN ONE WAY OR ANOTHER, LOST A BIT OF THEIR VIRTUE.
WHEN DAWN CAME, A SPENT IRVI LEFT THE HOUSE AND GAVE UP HIS QUEST TO REJOIN SIAN. CONSUMED WITH GUILT, HE COULD NOT EVEN BRING HIMSELF TO LOOK BACK AND ASK HER FORGIVENESS.

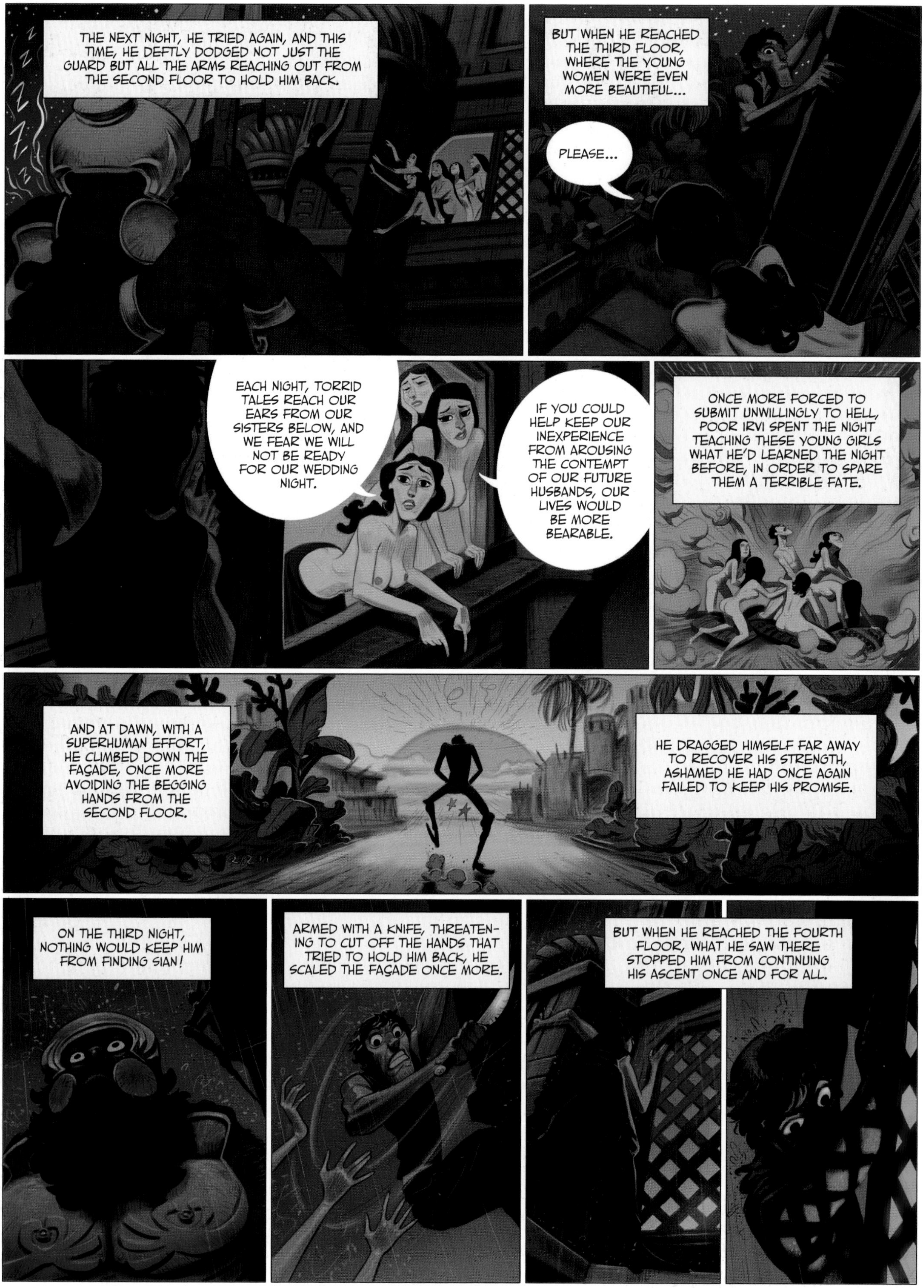

THE NEXT NIGHT, HE TRIED AGAIN, AND THIS TIME, HE DEFTLY DODGED NOT JUST THE GUARD BUT ALL THE ARMS REACHING OUT FROM THE SECOND FLOOR TO HOLD HIM BACK.
BUT WHEN HE REACHED THE THIRD FLOOR, WHERE THE YOUNG WOMEN WERE EVEN MORE BEAUTIFUL...
PLEASE...
EACH NIGHT, TORRID TALES REACH OUR EARS FROM OUR SISTERS BELOW, AND WE FEAR WE WILL NOT BE READY FOR OUR WEDDING NIGHT.
IF YOU COULD HELP KEEP OUR INEXPERIENCE FROM AROUSING THE CONTEMPT OF OUR FUTURE HUSBANDS, OUR LIVES WOULD BE MORE BEARABLE.
ONCE MORE FORCED TO SUBMIT UNWILLINGLY TO HELL, POOR IRVI SPENT THE NIGHT TEACHING THESE YOUNG GIRLS WHAT HE'D LEARNED THE NIGHT BEFORE, IN ORDER TO SPARE THEM A TERRIBLE FATE.
AND AT DAWN, WITH A SUPERHUMAN EFFORT, HE CLIMBED DOWN THE FAÇADE, ONCE MORE AVOIDING THE BEGGING HANDS FROM THE SECOND FLOOR.
HE DRAGGED HIMSELF FAR AWAY TO RECOVER HIS STRENGTH, ASHAMED HE HAD ONCE AGAIN FAILED TO KEEP HIS PROMISE.
ON THE THIRD NIGHT, NOTHING WOULD KEEP HIM FROM FINDING SIAN!
ARMED WITH A KNIFE, THREATENING TO CUT OFF THE HANDS THAT TRIED TO HOLD HIM BACK, HE SCALED THE FAÇADE ONCE MORE.
BUT WHEN HE REACHED THE FOURTH FLOOR, WHAT HE SAW THERE STOPPED HIM FROM CONTINUING HIS ASCENT ONCE AND FOR ALL.

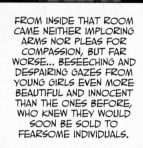

FROM INSIDE THAT ROOM CAME NEITHER IMPLORING ARMS NOR PLEAS FOR COMPASSION, BUT FAR WORSE... BESEECHING AND DESPAIRING GAZES FROM YOUNG GIRLS EVEN MORE BEAUTIFUL AND INNOCENT THAN THE ONES BEFORE, WHO KNEW THEY WOULD SOON BE SOLD TO FEARSOME INDIVIDUALS.

DID THEY, TOO, NOT DESERVE TO BE LOVED TENDERLY, IF EVEN FOR THE FIRST AND ONLY TIME IN THEIR LIVES?

THUS DID IRVI SPEND A GOOD PART OF THE THIRD NIGHT GIVING A GREAT LESSON IN DISINTERESTED GENEROSITY.

IN TRUTH, FEW MEN WOULD HAVE BEEN CAPABLE OF SUCH A SACRIFICE!

AND WITH THE DAWN, HIS BODY EXHAUSTED FROM THIS SHOW OF ALTRUISM, HE CLIMBED TO THE FINAL FLOOR TO FIND SIAN, HIS BELOVED. HOW DIFFERENT THEIR ENCOUNTER WOULD NOW BE!

THE DIFFIDENT, HESI-TANT BOY BELONGED TO THE PAST. A MAN OF EXPERIENCE WOULD NOW LEAD HER TO ECSTASY!

THERE SHE WAS, AS BEAUTIFUL AS EVER. TEARS OF JOY SPRANG FROM HER EYES IN TORRENTS.

THE GUARDS WERE THERE TOO, LYING IN WAIT TO GET THEIR HANDS ON THE PRODIGY WHO'D MANAGED TO RUIN ALL THE GOODS IN THE HOUSE IN UNDER THREE NIGHTS.

HEY, STALLION, WE'RE GONNA CUT THOSE JEWELS OFF AND HANG THEM FROM THE WALL!

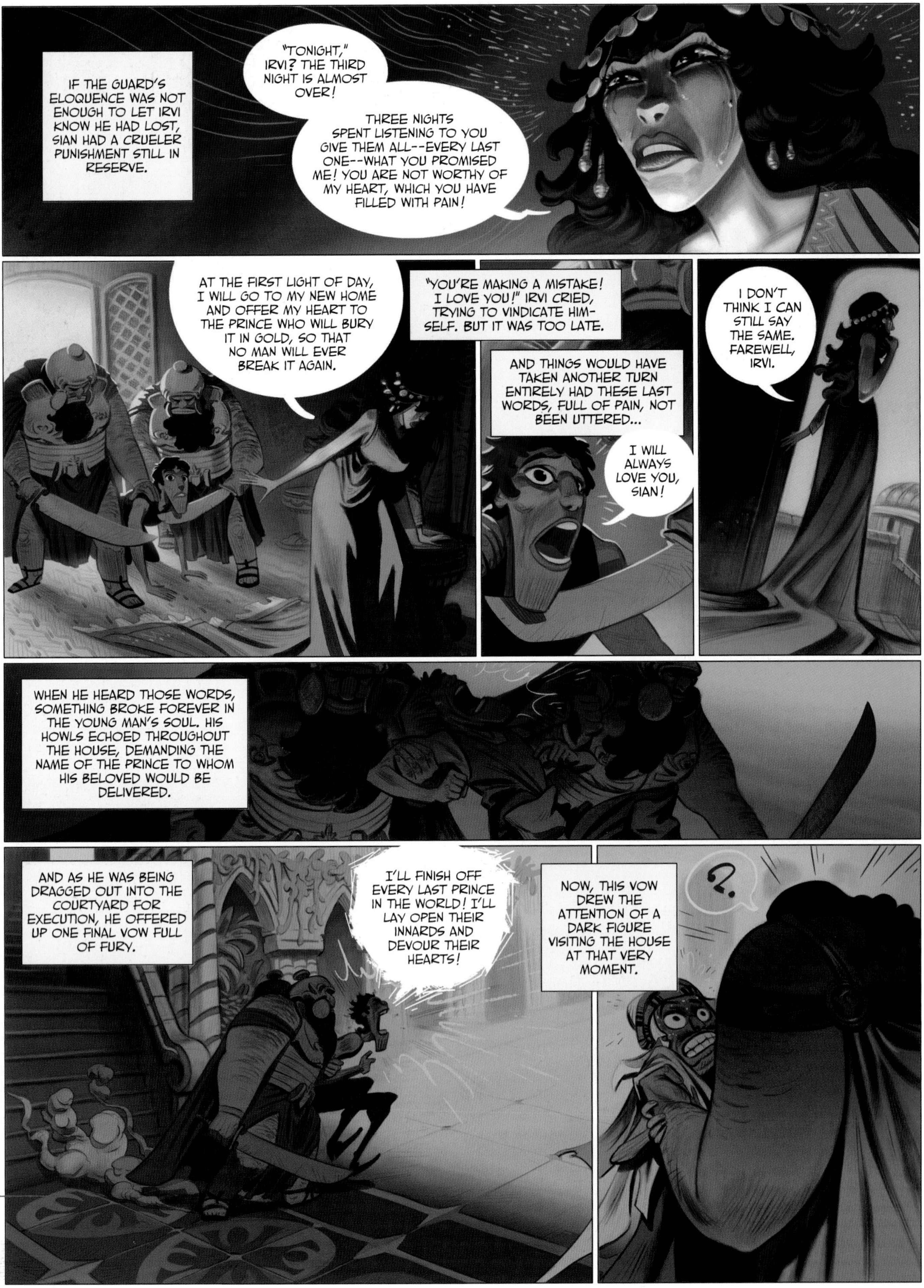
IF THE GUARD'S ELOQUENCE WAS NOT ENOUGH TO LET IRVI KNOW HE HAD LOST, SIAN HAD A CRUELER PUNISHMENT STILL IN RESERVE.
"TONIGHT," IRVI? THE THIRD NIGHT IS ALMOST OVER!
THREE NIGHTS SPENT LISTENING TO YOU GIVE THEM ALL--EVERY LAST ONE--WHAT YOU PROMISED ME! YOU ARE NOT WORTHY OF MY HEART, WHICH YOU HAVE FILLED WITH PAIN!
AT THE FIRST LIGHT OF DAY, I WILL GO TO MY NEW HOME AND OFFER MY HEART TO THE PRINCE WHO WILL BURY IT IN GOLD, SO THAT NO MAN WILL EVER BREAK IT AGAIN.
"YOU'RE MAKING A MISTAKE! I LOVE YOU!" IRVI CRIED, TRYING TO VINDICATE HIMSELF. BUT IT WAS TOO LATE.
AND THINGS WOULD HAVE TAKEN ANOTHER TURN ENTIRELY HAD THESE LAST WORDS, FULL OF PAIN, NOT BEEN UTTERED...
I WILL ALWAYS LOVE YOU, SIAN!
I DON'T THINK I CAN STILL SAY THE SAME. FAREWELL, IRVI.
WHEN HE HEARD THOSE WORDS, SOMETHING BROKE FOREVER IN THE YOUNG MAN'S SOUL. HIS HOWLS ECHOED THROUGHOUT THE HOUSE, DEMANDING THE NAME OF THE PRINCE TO WHOM HIS BELOVED WOULD BE DELIVERED.
AND AS HE WAS BEING DRAGGED OUT INTO THE COURTYARD FOR EXECUTION, HE OFFERED UP ONE FINAL VOW FULL OF FURY.
I'LL FINISH OFF EVERY LAST PRINCE IN THE WORLD! I'LL LAY OPEN THEIR INNARDS AND DEVOUR THEIR HEARTS!
NOW, THIS VOW DREW THE ATTENTION OF A DARK FIGURE VISITING THE HOUSE AT THAT VERY MOMENT.
?

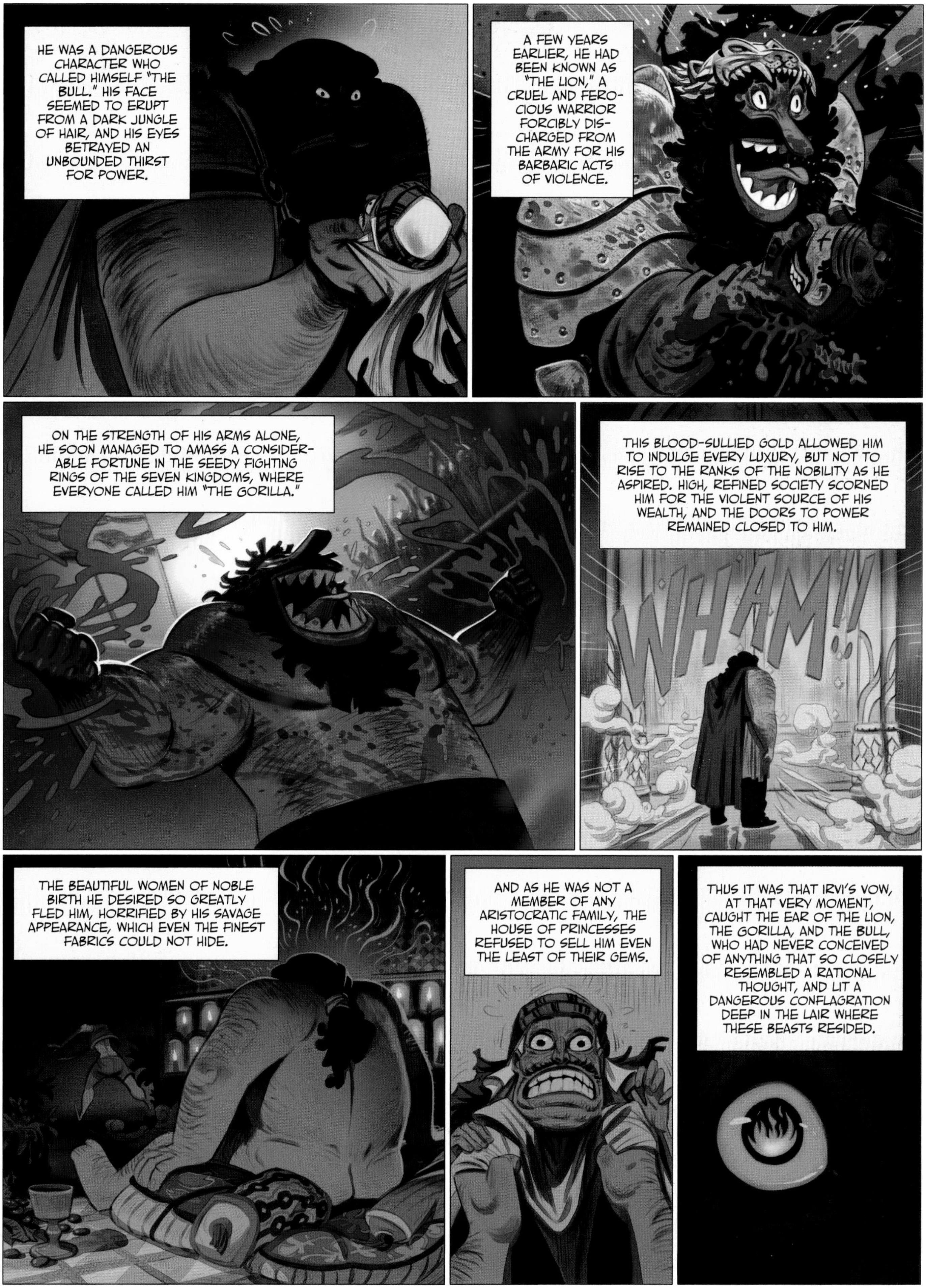
HE WAS A DANGEROUS CHARACTER WHO CALLED HIMSELF "THE BULL." HIS FACE SEEMED TO ERUPT FROM A DARK JUNGLE OF HAIR, AND HIS EYES BETRAYED AN UNBOUNDED THIRST FOR POWER.
A FEW YEARS EARLIER, HE HAD BEEN KNOWN AS "THE LION," A CRUEL AND FEROCIOUS WARRIOR FORCIBLY DISCHARGED FROM THE ARMY FOR HIS BARBARIC ACTS OF VIOLENCE.
ON THE STRENGTH OF HIS ARMS ALONE, HE SOON MANAGED TO AMASS A CONSIDERABLE FORTUNE IN THE SEEDY FIGHTING RINGS OF THE SEVEN KINGDOMS, WHERE EVERYONE CALLED HIM "THE GORILLA."
THIS BLOOD-SULLIED GOLD ALLOWED HIM TO INDULGE EVERY LUXURY, BUT NOT TO RISE TO THE RANKS OF THE NOBILITY AS HE ASPIRED. HIGH, REFINED SOCIETY SCORNED HIM FOR THE VIOLENT SOURCE OF HIS WEALTH, AND THE DOORS TO POWER REMAINED CLOSED TO HIM.
WHAM!!
THE BEAUTIFUL WOMEN OF NOBLE BIRTH HE DESIRED SO GREATLY FLED HIM, HORRIFIED BY HIS SAVAGE APPEARANCE, WHICH EVEN THE FINEST FABRICS COULD NOT HIDE.
AND AS HE WAS NOT A MEMBER OF ANY ARISTOCRATIC FAMILY, THE HOUSE OF PRINCESSES REFUSED TO SELL HIM EVEN THE LEAST OF THEIR GEMS.
THUS IT WAS THAT IRVI'S VOW, AT THAT VERY MOMENT, CAUGHT THE EAR OF THE LION, THE GORILLA, AND THE BULL, WHO HAD NEVER CONCEIVED OF ANYTHING THAT SO CLOSELY RESEMBLED A RATIONAL THOUGHT, AND LIT A DANGEROUS CONFLAGRATION DEEP IN THE LAIR WHERE THESE BEASTS RESIDED.

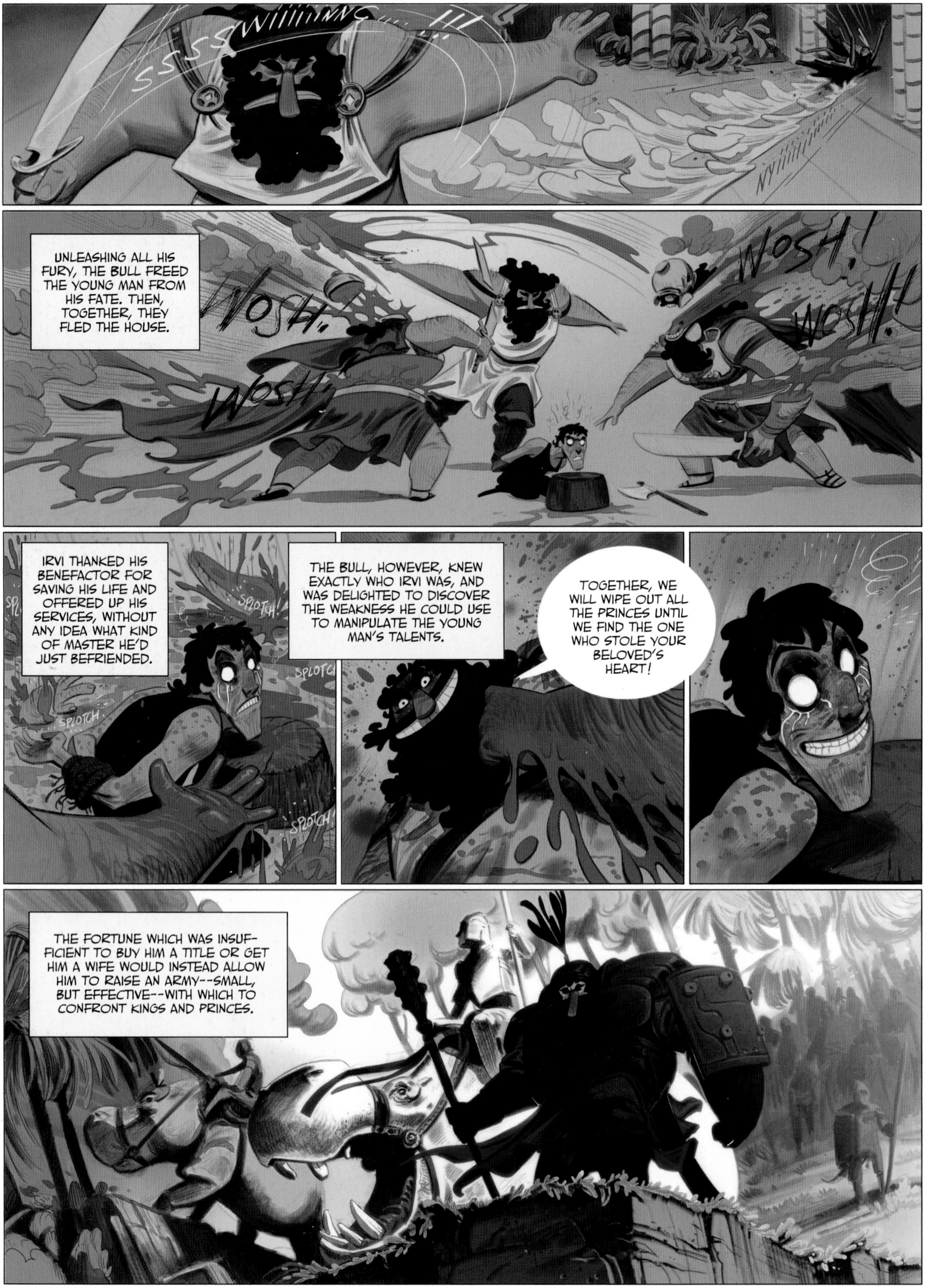
SSSSWIIIIIINNG...!!
NYIIIIIIIII
UNLEASHING ALL HIS FURY, THE BULL FREED THE YOUNG MAN FROM HIS FATE. THEN, TOGETHER, THEY FLED THE HOUSE.
WOSH!
WOSH!
WOSH!
WOSH!
IRVI THANKED HIS BENEFACTOR FOR SAVING HIS LIFE AND OFFERED UP HIS SERVICES, WITHOUT ANY IDEA WHAT KIND OF MASTER HE'D JUST BEFRIENDED.
SPLOTCH!
SPLOTCH
SPLOTCH
SPLOTCH!
THE BULL, HOWEVER, KNEW EXACTLY WHO IRVI WAS, AND WAS DELIGHTED TO DISCOVER THE WEAKNESS HE COULD USE TO MANIPULATE THE YOUNG MAN'S TALENTS.
TOGETHER, WE WILL WIPE OUT ALL THE PRINCES UNTIL WE FIND THE ONE WHO STOLE YOUR BELOVED'S HEART!
THE FORTUNE WHICH WAS INSUFFICIENT TO BUY HIM A TITLE OR GET HIM A WIFE WOULD INSTEAD ALLOW HIM TO RAISE AN ARMY--SMALL, BUT EFFECTIVE--WITH WHICH TO CONFRONT KINGS AND PRINCES.

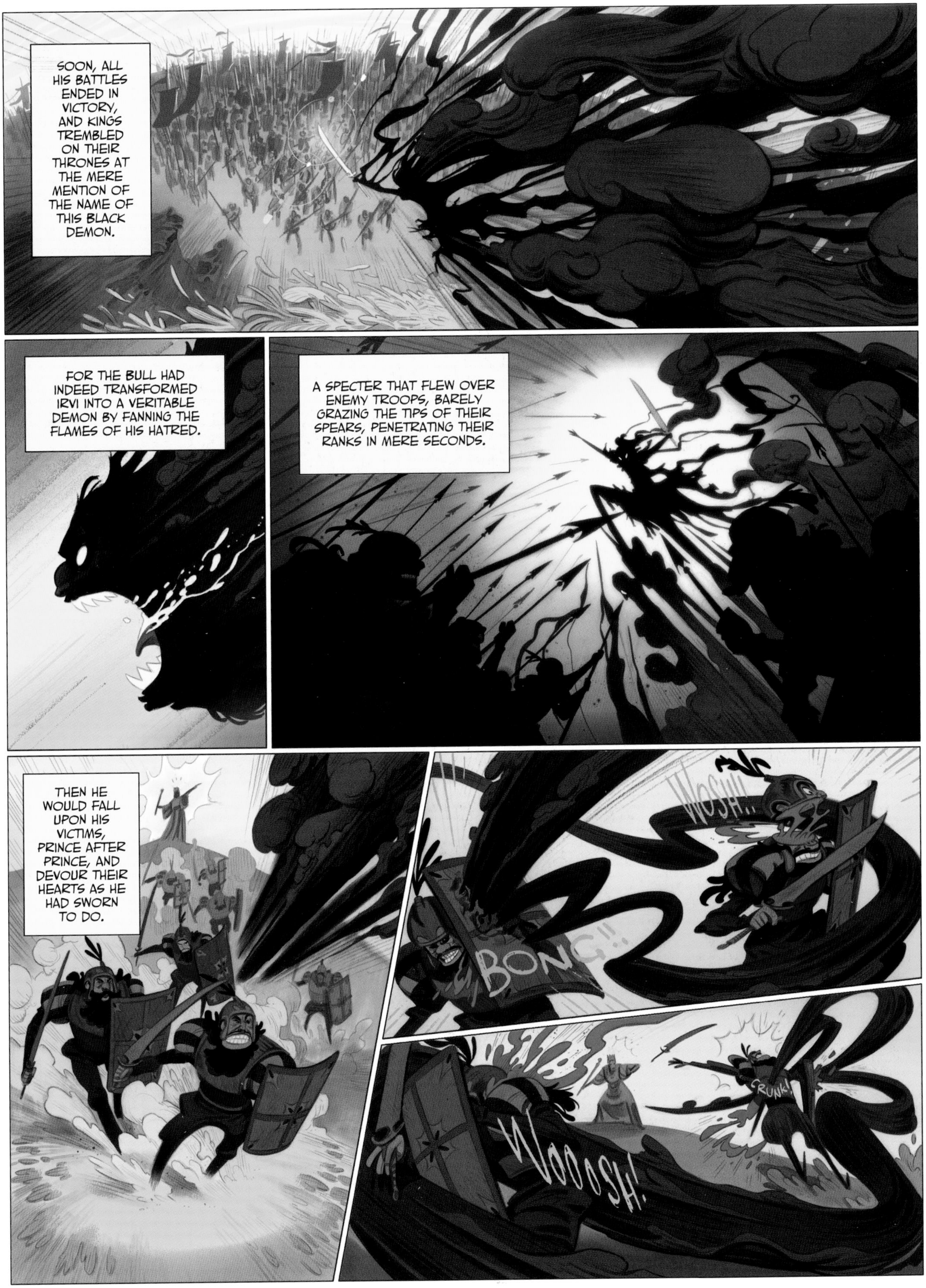
SOON, ALL HIS BATTLES ENDED IN VICTORY, AND KINGS TREMBLED ON THEIR THRONES AT THE MERE MENTION OF THE NAME OF THIS BLACK DEMON.
FOR THE BULL HAD INDEED TRANSFORMED IRVI INTO A VERITABLE DEMON BY FANNING THE FLAMES OF HIS HATRED.
A SPECTER THAT FLEW OVER ENEMY TROOPS, BARELY GRAZING THE TIPS OF THEIR SPEARS, PENETRATING THEIR RANKS IN MERE SECONDS.
THEN HE WOULD FALL UPON HIS VICTIMS, PRINCE AFTER PRINCE, AND DEVOUR THEIR HEARTS AS HE HAD SWORN TO DO.
WOSH!!
BONG!!
CRUNK!
WOOOOSH!

"SIAN"

NOOO!!

CHOMP CHOMP

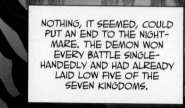

NOTHING, IT SEEMED, COULD PUT AN END TO THE NIGHT-MARE. THE DEMON WON EVERY BATTLE SINGLE-HANDEDLY AND HAD ALREADY LAID LOW FIVE OF THE SEVEN KINGDOMS.

CLOC

IN THE SIXTH KINGDOM, HE WAS ALL THE GENERALS TALKED ABOUT, BUT ALL THEIR STRATEGIES SEEMED IN VAIN.

AND SO, THE PRINCE BELIEVED HIS FATE WAS INEVITABLE.

ON THE EVE OF THE BATTLE, HIS WIFE OF-FERED HIM A STRANGE GLASS VIAL.

IF I AM TO LOSE YOUR HEART, MAY IT AT LEAST SERVE TO DESTROY THE CREATURE WHO WILL STEAL IT FROM ME.

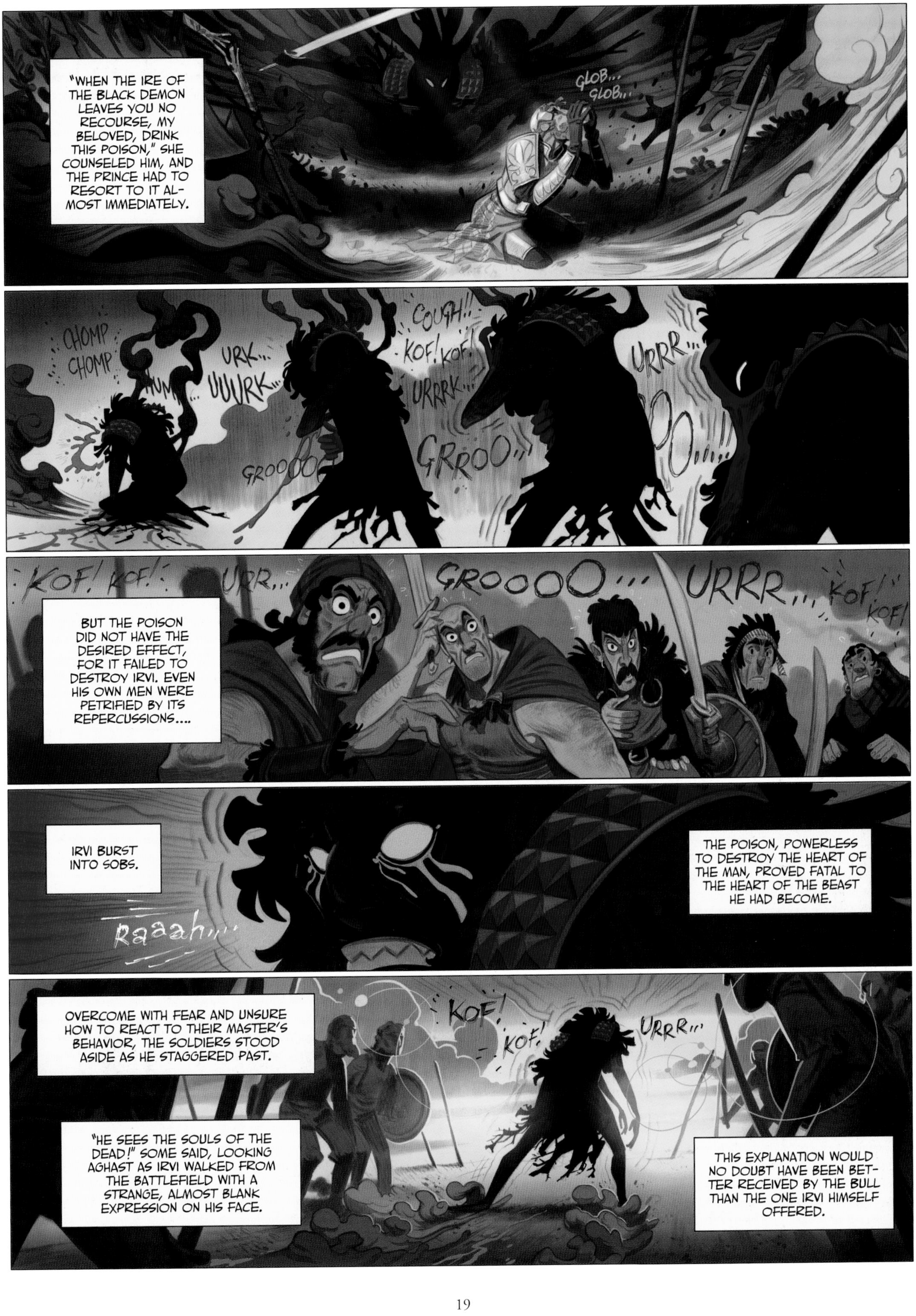
"WHEN THE IRE OF THE BLACK DEMON LEAVES YOU NO RECOURSE, MY BELOVED, DRINK THIS POISON," SHE COUNSELED HIM, AND THE PRINCE HAD TO RESORT TO IT ALMOST IMMEDIATELY.
GLOB... GLOB...
CHOMP CHOMP
URK... UUURK...
COUGH!! KOF! KOF!
URRRK...
URRR...
GRROO
GROOOO
KOF! KOF!
URR...
GROOOO...
URRR...
KOF! KOF!
BUT THE POISON DID NOT HAVE THE DESIRED EFFECT, FOR IT FAILED TO DESTROY IRVI. EVEN HIS OWN MEN WERE PETRIFIED BY ITS REPERCUSSIONS....
IRVI BURST INTO SOBS.
Raaah...
THE POISON, POWERLESS TO DESTROY THE HEART OF THE MAN, PROVED FATAL TO THE HEART OF THE BEAST HE HAD BECOME.
OVERCOME WITH FEAR AND UNSURE HOW TO REACT TO THEIR MASTER'S BEHAVIOR, THE SOLDIERS STOOD ASIDE AS HE STAGGERED PAST.
KOF! KOF!
URRR...
"HE SEES THE SOULS OF THE DEAD!" SOME SAID, LOOKING AGHAST AS IRVI WALKED FROM THE BATTLEFIELD WITH A STRANGE, ALMOST BLANK EXPRESSION ON HIS FACE.
THIS EXPLANATION WOULD NO DOUBT HAVE BEEN BETTER RECEIVED BY THE BULL THAN THE ONE IRVI HIMSELF OFFERED.

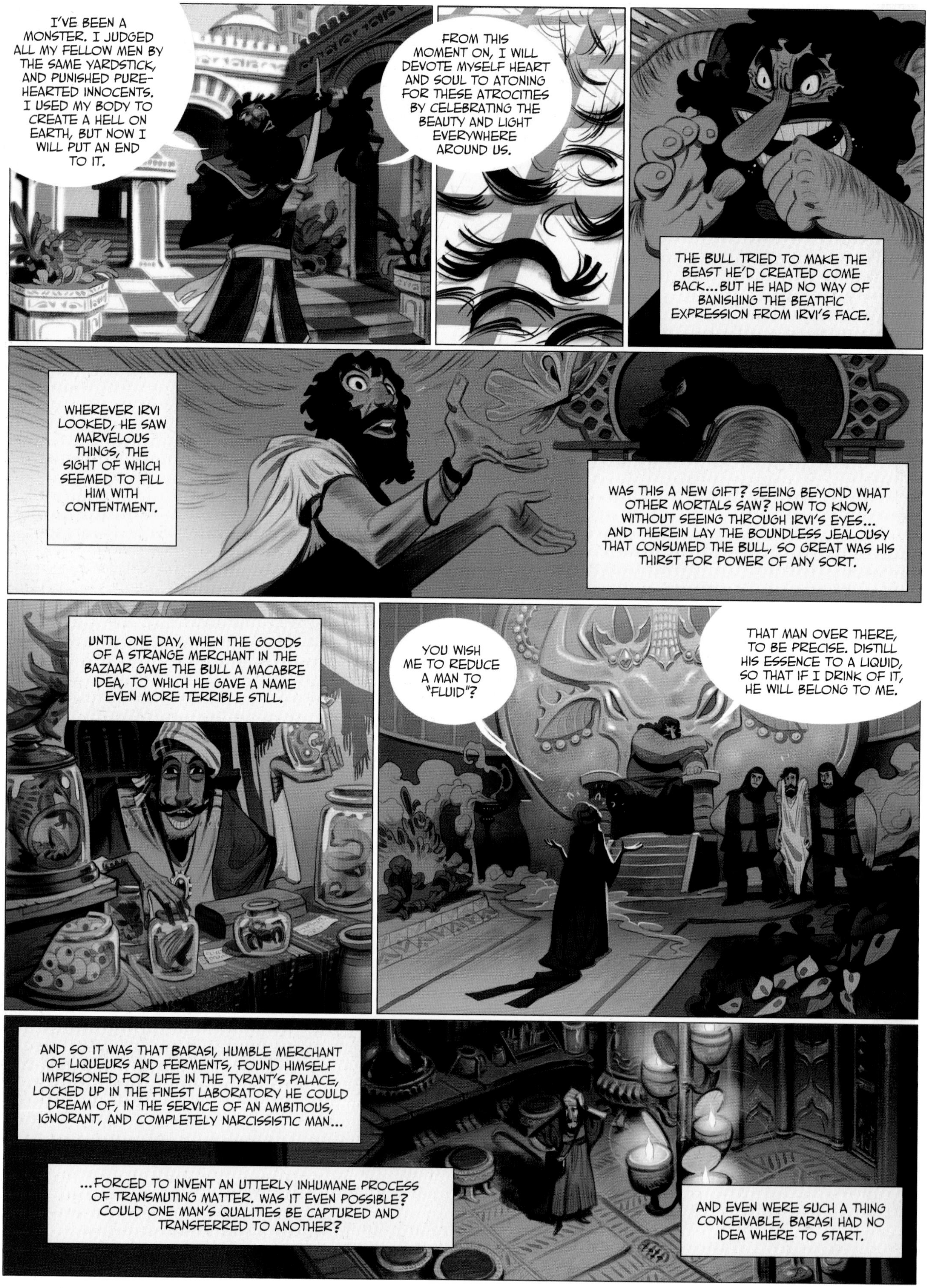
I'VE BEEN A MONSTER. I JUDGED ALL MY FELLOW MEN BY THE SAME YARDSTICK, AND PUNISHED PURE-HEARTED INNOCENTS. I USED MY BODY TO CREATE A HELL ON EARTH, BUT NOW I WILL PUT AN END TO IT.
FROM THIS MOMENT ON, I WILL DEVOTE MYSELF HEART AND SOUL TO ATONING FOR THESE ATROCITIES BY CELEBRATING THE BEAUTY AND LIGHT EVERYWHERE AROUND US.
THE BULL TRIED TO MAKE THE BEAST HE'D CREATED COME BACK...BUT HE HAD NO WAY OF BANISHING THE BEATIFIC EXPRESSION FROM IRVI'S FACE.
WHEREVER IRVI LOOKED, HE SAW MARVELOUS THINGS, THE SIGHT OF WHICH SEEMED TO FILL HIM WITH CONTENTMENT.
WAS THIS A NEW GIFT? SEEING BEYOND WHAT OTHER MORTALS SAW? HOW TO KNOW, WITHOUT SEEING THROUGH IRVI'S EYES... AND THEREIN LAY THE BOUNDLESS JEALOUSY THAT CONSUMED THE BULL, SO GREAT WAS HIS THIRST FOR POWER OF ANY SORT.
UNTIL ONE DAY, WHEN THE GOODS OF A STRANGE MERCHANT IN THE BAZAAR GAVE THE BULL A MACABRE IDEA, TO WHICH HE GAVE A NAME EVEN MORE TERRIBLE STILL.
YOU WISH ME TO REDUCE A MAN TO "FLUID"?
THAT MAN OVER THERE, TO BE PRECISE. DISTILL HIS ESSENCE TO A LIQUID, SO THAT IF I DRINK OF IT, HE WILL BELONG TO ME.
AND SO IT WAS THAT BARASI, HUMBLE MERCHANT OF LIQUEURS AND FERMENTS, FOUND HIMSELF IMPRISONED FOR LIFE IN THE TYRANT'S PALACE, LOCKED UP IN THE FINEST LABORATORY HE COULD DREAM OF, IN THE SERVICE OF AN AMBITIOUS, IGNORANT, AND COMPLETELY NARCISSISTIC MAN...
...FORCED TO INVENT AN UTTERLY INHUMANE PROCESS OF TRANSMUTING MATTER. WAS IT EVEN POSSIBLE? COULD ONE MAN'S QUALITIES BE CAPTURED AND TRANSFERRED TO ANOTHER?
AND EVEN WERE SUCH A THING CONCEIVABLE, BARASI HAD NO IDEA WHERE TO START.

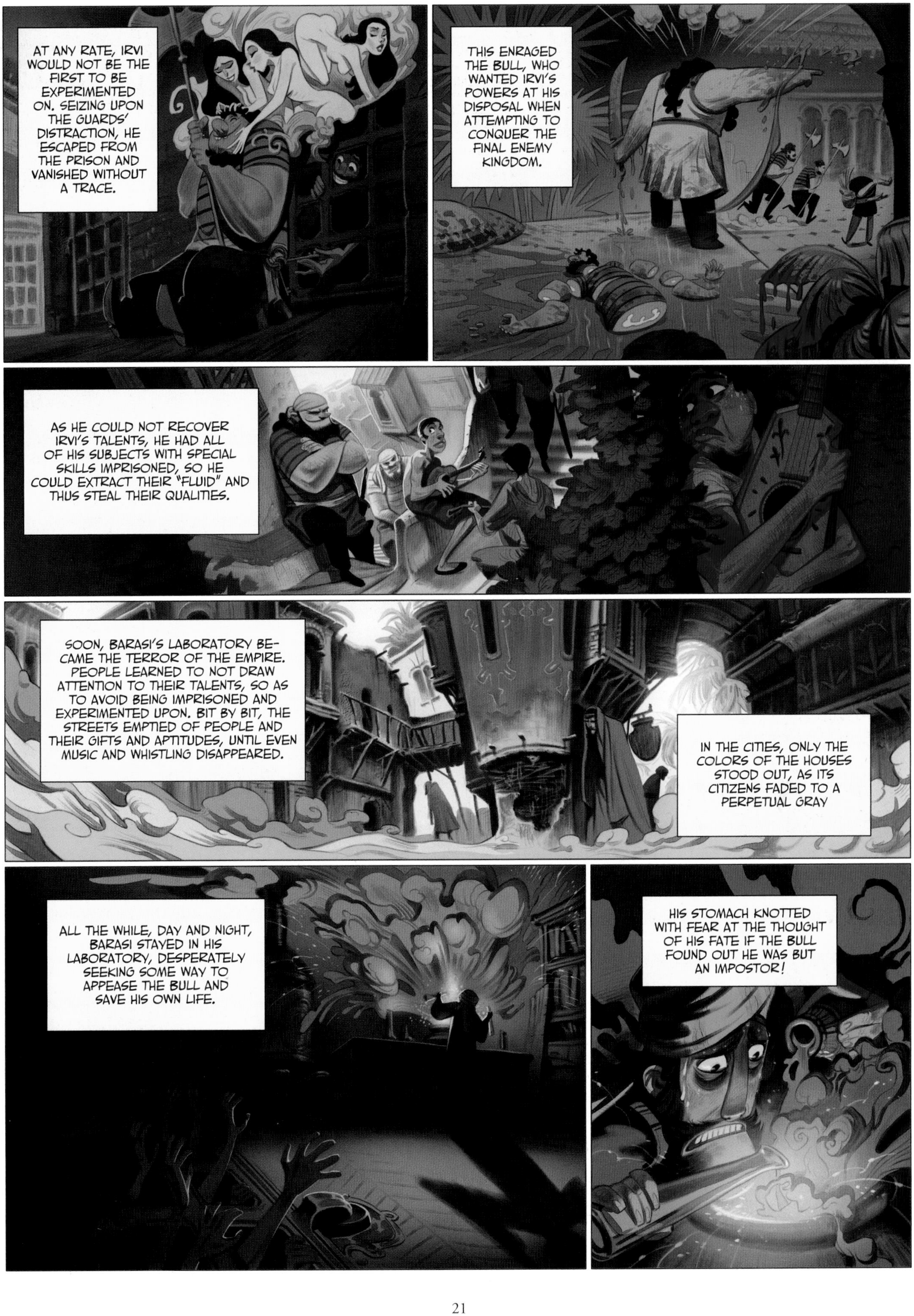
AT ANY RATE, IRVI WOULD NOT BE THE FIRST TO BE EXPERIMENTED ON. SEIZING UPON THE GUARDS' DISTRACTION, HE ESCAPED FROM THE PRISON AND VANISHED WITHOUT A TRACE.
THIS ENRAGED THE BULL, WHO WANTED IRVI'S POWERS AT HIS DISPOSAL WHEN ATTEMPTING TO CONQUER THE FINAL ENEMY KINGDOM.
AS HE COULD NOT RECOVER IRVI'S TALENTS, HE HAD ALL OF HIS SUBJECTS WITH SPECIAL SKILLS IMPRISONED, SO HE COULD EXTRACT THEIR "FLUID" AND THUS STEAL THEIR QUALITIES.
SOON, BARASI'S LABORATORY BE-CAME THE TERROR OF THE EMPIRE. PEOPLE LEARNED TO NOT DRAW ATTENTION TO THEIR TALENTS, SO AS TO AVOID BEING IMPRISONED AND EXPERIMENTED UPON. BIT BY BIT, THE STREETS EMPTIED OF PEOPLE AND THEIR GIFTS AND APTITUDES, UNTIL EVEN MUSIC AND WHISTLING DISAPPEARED.
IN THE CITIES, ONLY THE COLORS OF THE HOUSES STOOD OUT, AS ITS CITIZENS FADED TO A PERPETUAL GRAY
ALL THE WHILE, DAY AND NIGHT, BARASI STAYED IN HIS LABORATORY, DESPERATELY SEEKING SOME WAY TO APPEASE THE BULL AND SAVE HIS OWN LIFE.
HIS STOMACH KNOTTED WITH FEAR AT THE THOUGHT OF HIS FATE IF THE BULL FOUND OUT HE WAS BUT AN IMPOSTOR!

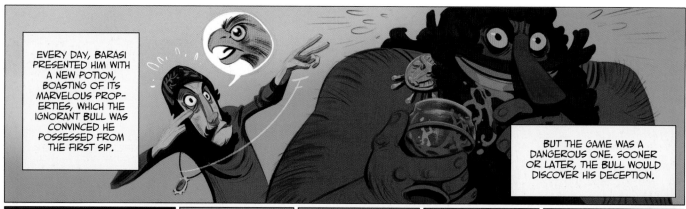

EVERY DAY, BARASI PRESENTED HIM WITH A NEW POTION, BOASTING OF ITS MARVELOUS PROPERTIES, WHICH THE IGNORANT BULL WAS CONVINCED HE POSSESSED FROM THE FIRST SIP.

BUT THE GAME WAS A DANGEROUS ONE. SOONER OR LATER, THE BULL WOULD DISCOVER HIS DECEPTION.

SUMMONING HIS COURAGE, BARASI RESOLVED TO POISON HIS MASTER...

GLOB...
GLOB...
GLOB...

BUOOO

...BUT NEVER MANAGED TO.

HE MADE SEVERAL OTHER ATTEMPTS, TRYING EVERY POISON HE KNEW, BUT IT WAS ALREADY TOO LATE. THE COMBINATION OF ALL THE POTIONS HE'D GIVEN THE BULL HAD CREATED A VERITABLE BARRICADE OF ANTIDOTES INSIDE THE MAN'S BODY.

THIS BECAME CLEAR, TO THE BULL'S GREAT DELIGHT, WHEN A SLAVE TRYING TO POISON HIM WAS CAUGHT RED-HANDED.

KNOWING HIMSELF IMMUNE TO POISON, THE BULL DECIDED TO EXPAND THE BESTIARY OF HIS NAMES, AND PROCLAIMED HIMSELF...

EMPEROR COBRA!

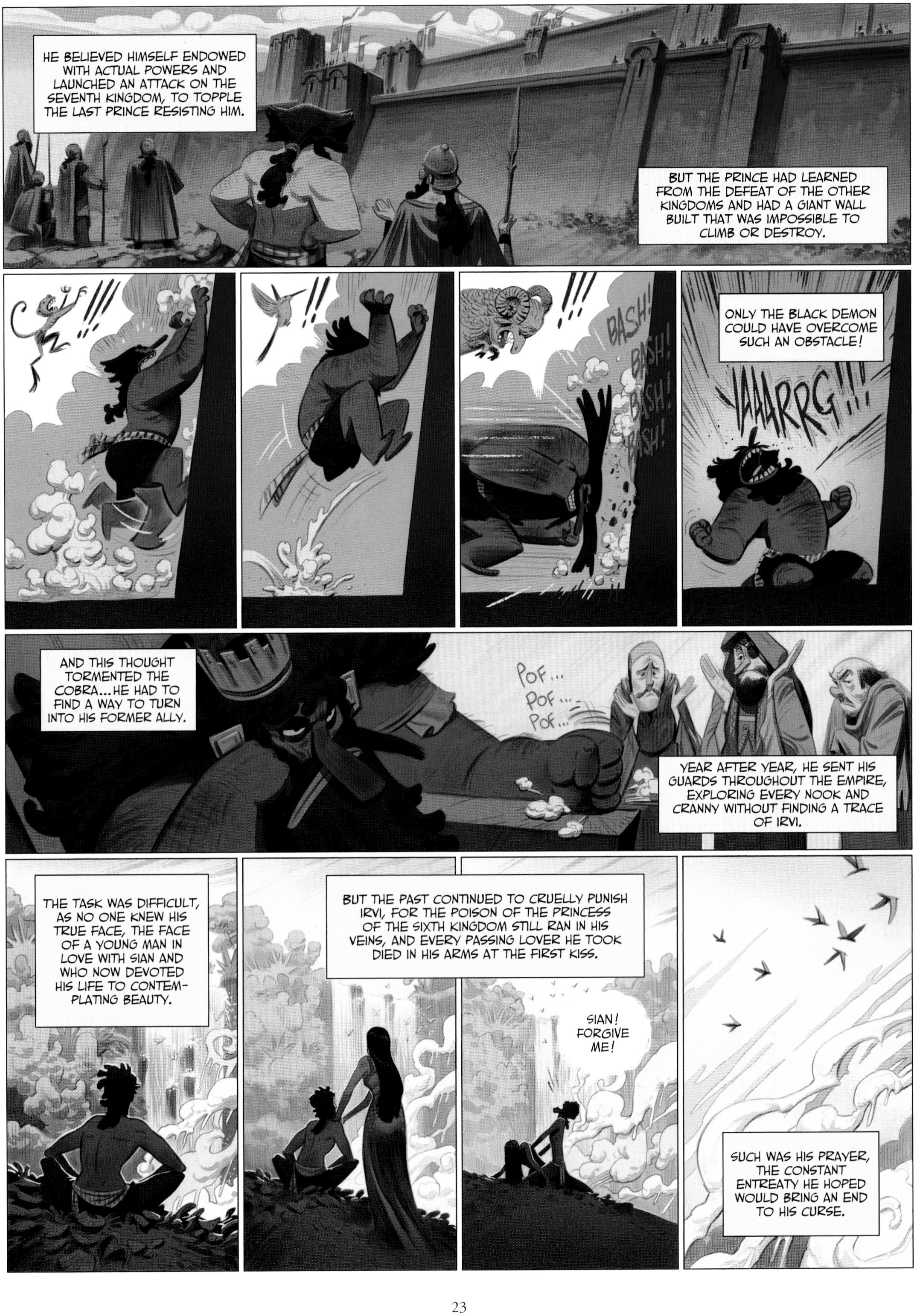
HE BELIEVED HIMSELF ENDOWED WITH ACTUAL POWERS AND LAUNCHED AN ATTACK ON THE SEVENTH KINGDOM, TO TOPPLE THE LAST PRINCE RESISTING HIM.
BUT THE PRINCE HAD LEARNED FROM THE DEFEAT OF THE OTHER KINGDOMS AND HAD A GIANT WALL BUILT THAT WAS IMPOSSIBLE TO CLIMB OR DESTROY.
!!!
!!!
!!!
BASH! BASH! BASH! BASH!
ONLY THE BLACK DEMON COULD HAVE OVERCOME SUCH AN OBSTACLE!
YAAARRG!!!
AND THIS THOUGHT TORMENTED THE COBRA... HE HAD TO FIND A WAY TO TURN INTO HIS FORMER ALLY.
POF... POF... POF...
YEAR AFTER YEAR, HE SENT HIS GUARDS THROUGHOUT THE EMPIRE, EXPLORING EVERY NOOK AND CRANNY WITHOUT FINDING A TRACE OF IRVI.
THE TASK WAS DIFFICULT, AS NO ONE KNEW HIS TRUE FACE, THE FACE OF A YOUNG MAN IN LOVE WITH SIAN AND WHO NOW DEVOTED HIS LIFE TO CONTEM-PLATING BEAUTY.
BUT THE PAST CONTINUED TO CRUELLY PUNISH IRVI, FOR THE POISON OF THE PRINCESS OF THE SIXTH KINGDOM STILL RAN IN HIS VEINS, AND EVERY PASSING LOVER HE TOOK DIED IN HIS ARMS AT THE FIRST KISS.
SIAN! FORGIVE ME!
SUCH WAS HIS PRAYER, THE CONSTANT ENTREATY HE HOPED WOULD BRING AN END TO HIS CURSE.

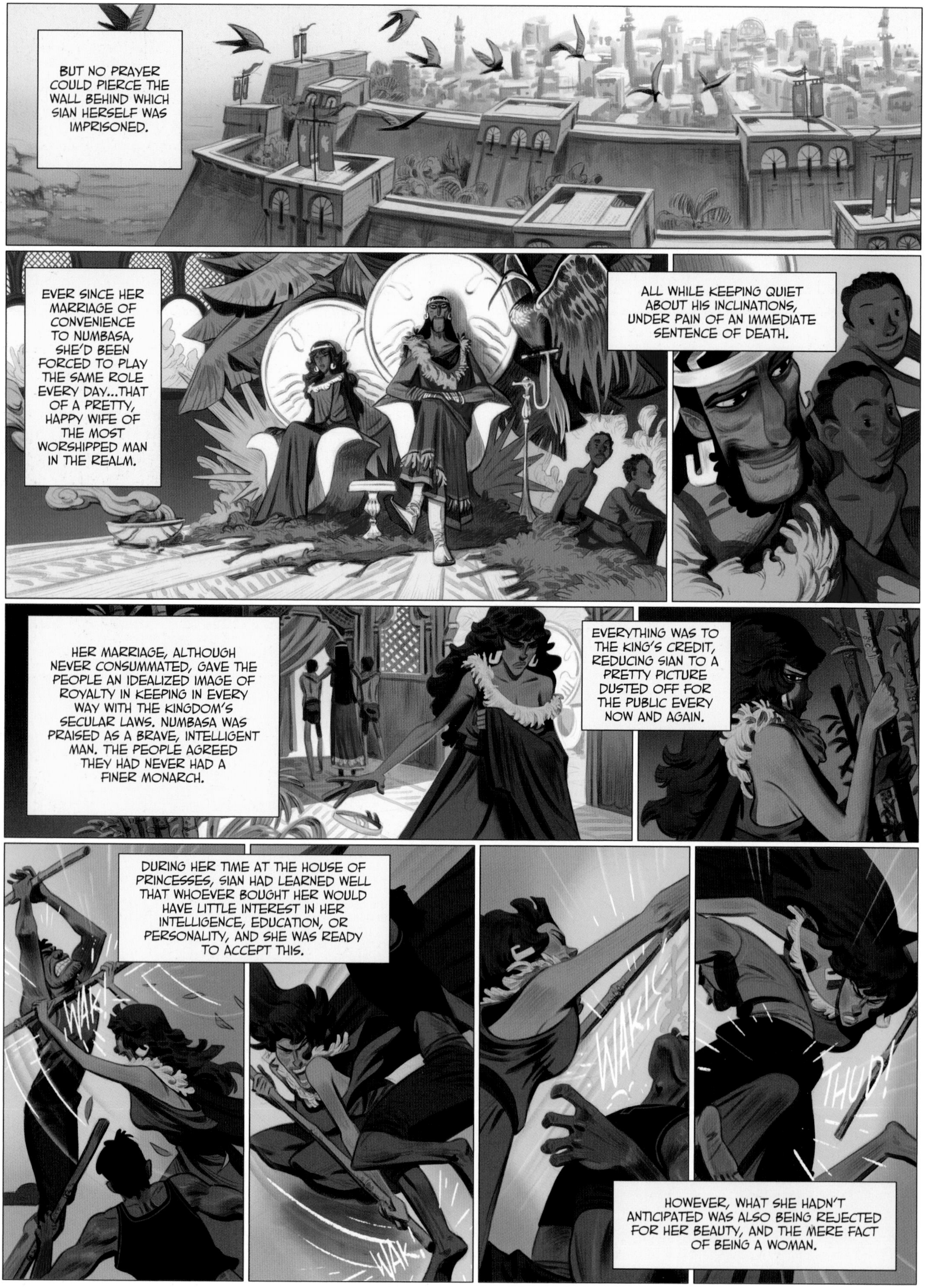
BUT NO PRAYER COULD PIERCE THE WALL BEHIND WHICH SIAN HERSELF WAS IMPRISONED.
EVER SINCE HER MARRIAGE OF CONVENIENCE TO NUMBASA, SHE'D BEEN FORCED TO PLAY THE SAME ROLE EVERY DAY...THAT OF A PRETTY, HAPPY WIFE OF THE MOST WORSHIPPED MAN IN THE REALM.
ALL WHILE KEEPING QUIET ABOUT HIS INCLINATIONS, UNDER PAIN OF AN IMMEDIATE SENTENCE OF DEATH.
HER MARRIAGE, ALTHOUGH NEVER CONSUMMATED, GAVE THE PEOPLE AN IDEALIZED IMAGE OF ROYALTY IN KEEPING IN EVERY WAY WITH THE KINGDOM'S SECULAR LAWS. NUMBASA WAS PRAISED AS A BRAVE, INTELLIGENT MAN. THE PEOPLE AGREED THEY HAD NEVER HAD A FINER MONARCH.
EVERYTHING WAS TO THE KING'S CREDIT, REDUCING SIAN TO A PRETTY PICTURE DUSTED OFF FOR THE PUBLIC EVERY NOW AND AGAIN.
WAK!
DURING HER TIME AT THE HOUSE OF PRINCESSES, SIAN HAD LEARNED WELL THAT WHOEVER BOUGHT HER WOULD HAVE LITTLE INTEREST IN HER INTELLIGENCE, EDUCATION, OR PERSONALITY, AND SHE WAS READY TO ACCEPT THIS.
WAK!
WAK!
THUD!
HOWEVER, WHAT SHE HADN'T ANTICIPATED WAS ALSO BEING REJECTED FOR HER BEAUTY, AND THE MERE FACT OF BEING A WOMAN.

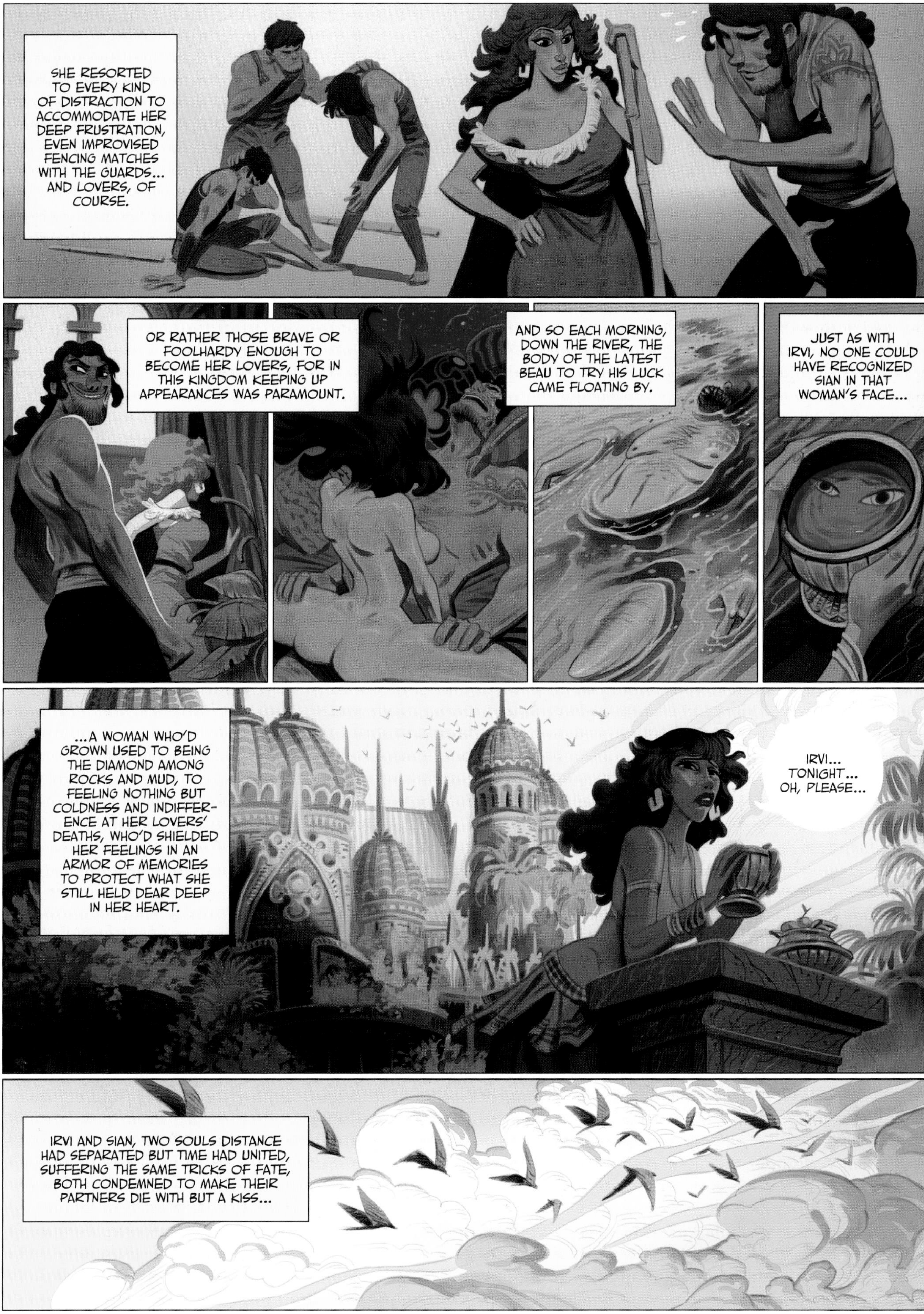
SHE RESORTED TO EVERY KIND OF DISTRACTION TO ACCOMMODATE HER DEEP FRUSTRATION, EVEN IMPROVISED FENCING MATCHES WITH THE GUARDS... AND LOVERS, OF COURSE.
OR RATHER THOSE BRAVE OR FOOLHARDY ENOUGH TO BECOME HER LOVERS, FOR IN THIS KINGDOM KEEPING UP APPEARANCES WAS PARAMOUNT.
AND SO EACH MORNING, DOWN THE RIVER, THE BODY OF THE LATEST BEAU TO TRY HIS LUCK CAME FLOATING BY.
JUST AS WITH IRVI, NO ONE COULD HAVE RECOGNIZED SIAN IN THAT WOMAN'S FACE...
...A WOMAN WHO'D GROWN USED TO BEING THE DIAMOND AMONG ROCKS AND MUD, TO FEELING NOTHING BUT COLDNESS AND INDIFFERENCE AT HER LOVERS' DEATHS, WHO'D SHIELDED HER FEELINGS IN AN ARMOR OF MEMORIES TO PROTECT WHAT SHE STILL HELD DEAR DEEP IN HER HEART.
IRVI... TONIGHT... OH, PLEASE...
IRVI AND SIAN, TWO SOULS DISTANCE HAD SEPARATED BUT TIME HAD UNITED, SUFFERING THE SAME TRICKS OF FATE, BOTH CONDEMNED TO MAKE THEIR PARTNERS DIE WITH BUT A KISS...

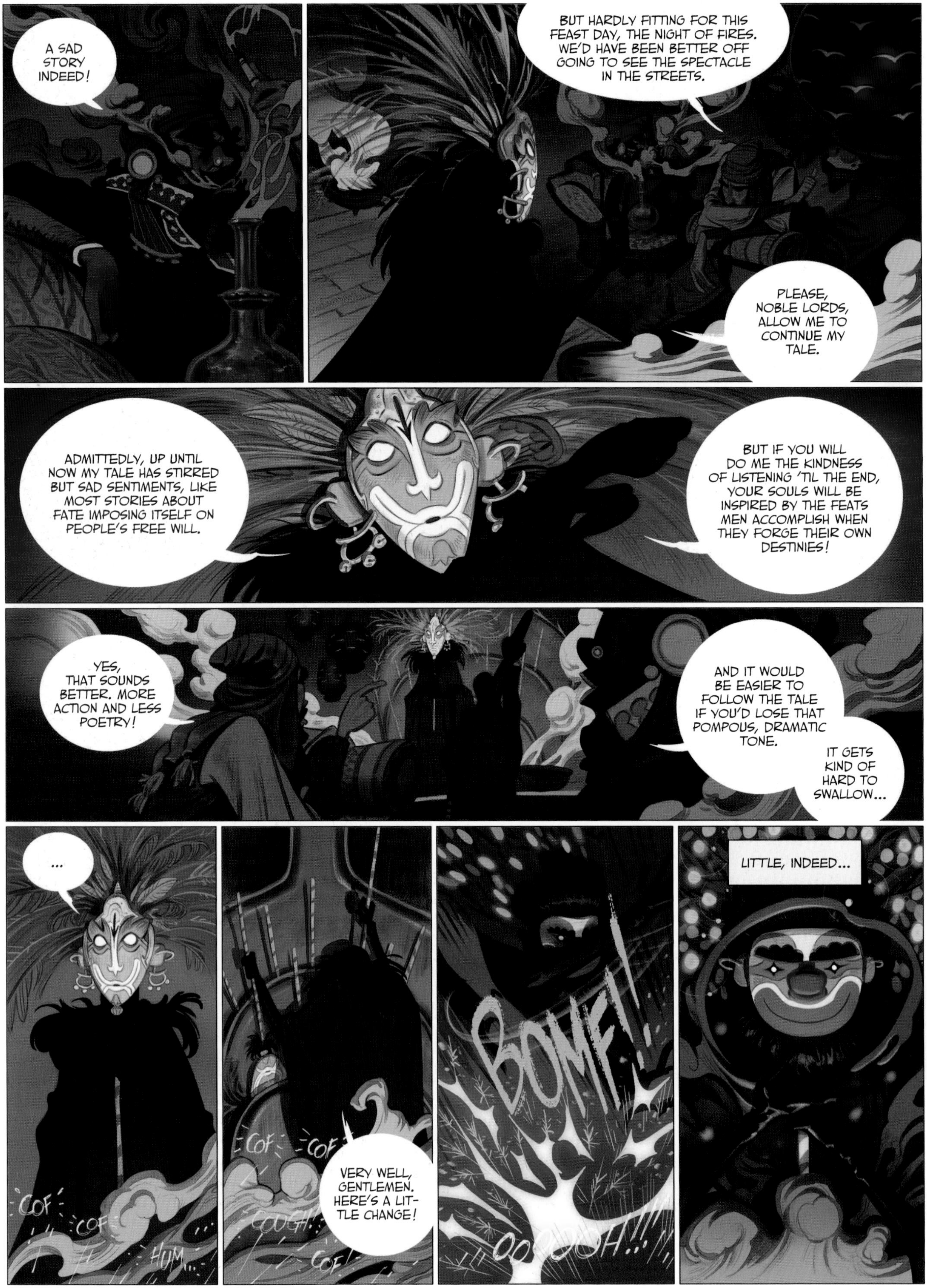

A SAD STORY INDEED!
BUT HARDLY FITTING FOR THIS FEAST DAY, THE NIGHT OF FIRES. WE'D HAVE BEEN BETTER OFF GOING TO SEE THE SPECTACLE IN THE STREETS.
PLEASE, NOBLE LORDS, ALLOW ME TO CONTINUE MY TALE.
ADMITTEDLY, UP UNTIL NOW MY TALE HAS STIRRED BUT SAD SENTIMENTS, LIKE MOST STORIES ABOUT FATE IMPOSING ITSELF ON PEOPLE'S FREE WILL.
BUT IF YOU WILL DO ME THE KINDNESS OF LISTENING 'TIL THE END, YOUR SOULS WILL BE INSPIRED BY THE FEATS MEN ACCOMPLISH WHEN THEY FORGE THEIR OWN DESTINIES!
YES, THAT SOUNDS BETTER. MORE ACTION AND LESS POETRY!
AND IT WOULD BE EASIER TO FOLLOW THE TALE IF YOU'D LOSE THAT POMPOUS, DRAMATIC TONE.
IT GETS KIND OF HARD TO SWALLOW...
...
COF
COF
HUM
COF
COF
COUGH!
COF
VERY WELL, GENTLEMEN. HERE'S A LIT-TLE CHANGE!
BOMF!!
OOOUOH!!!
LITTLE, INDEED...

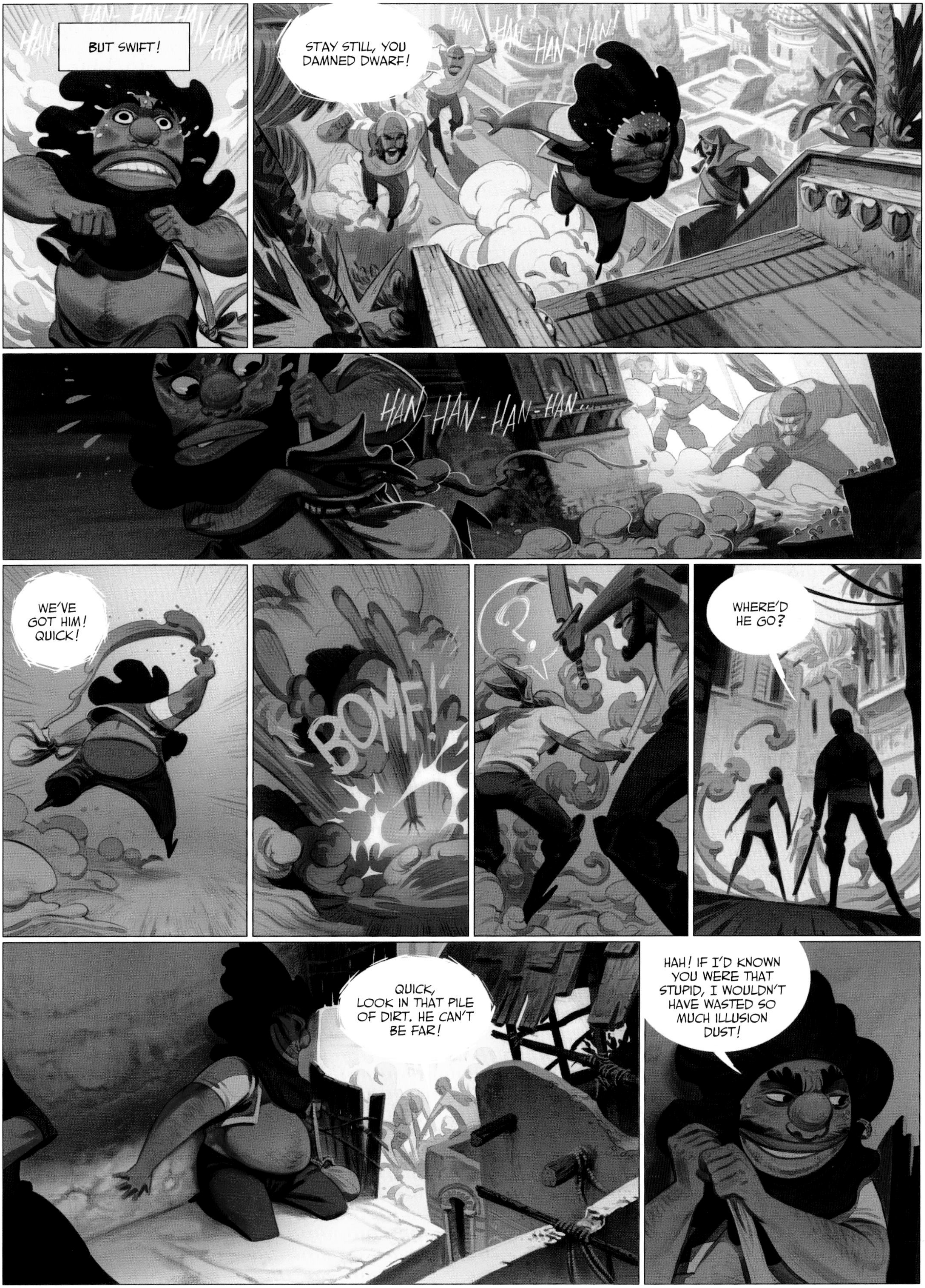
HAN-HAN-HAN-HAN
BUT SWIFT!
STAY STILL, YOU DAMNED DWARF!
HAN-HAN-HAN-HAN!
HAN-HAN-HAN-HAN...
WE'VE GOT HIM! QUICK!
BOMF!
?
WHERE'D HE GO?
QUICK, LOOK IN THAT PILE OF DIRT. HE CAN'T BE FAR!
HAH! IF I'D KNOWN YOU WERE THAT STUPID, I WOULDN'T HAVE WASTED SO MUCH ILLUSION DUST!

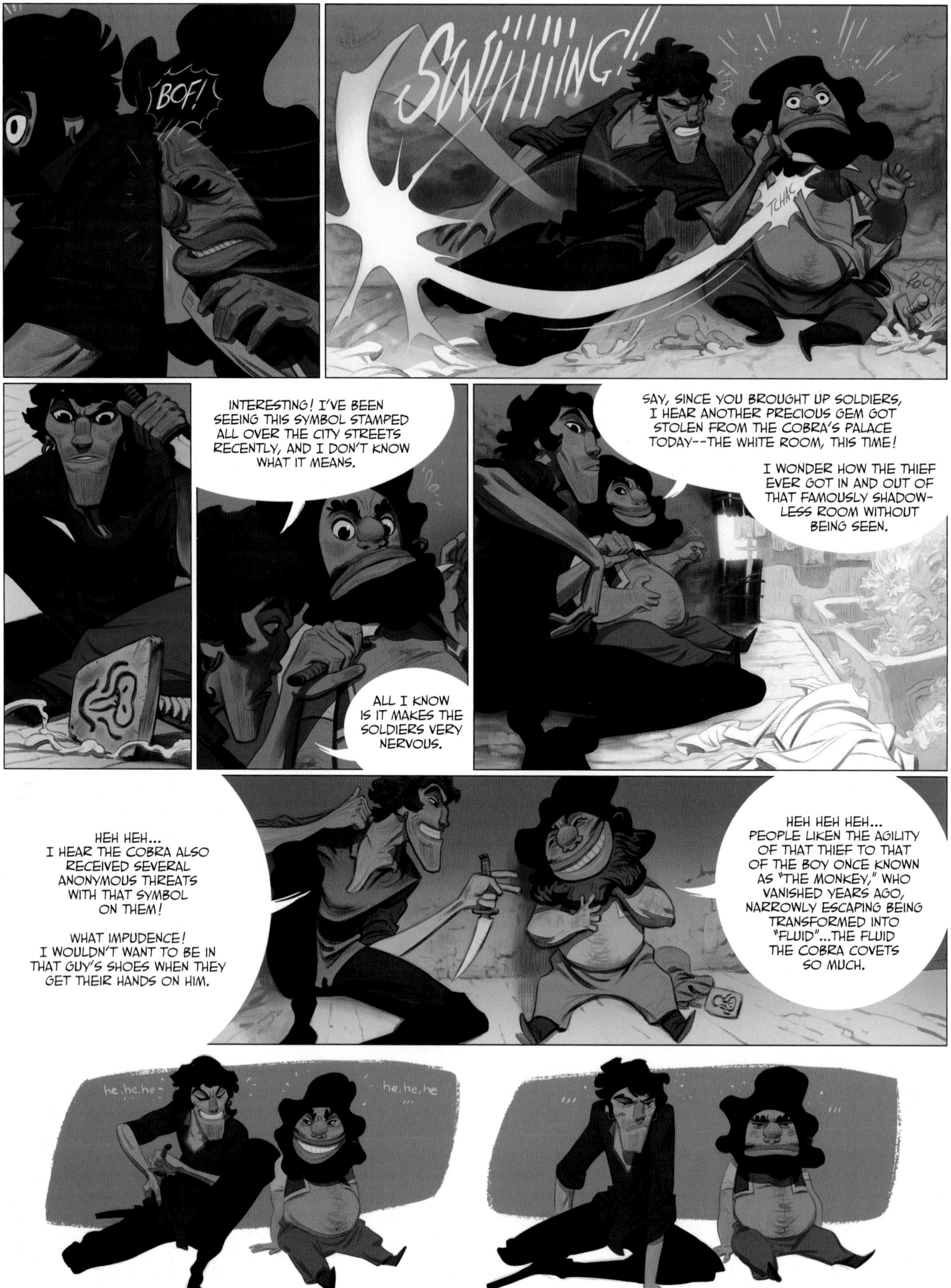
BOF!
SWIIIIIING!!
TCHAC
POC
INTERESTING! I'VE BEEN SEEING THIS SYMBOL STAMPED ALL OVER THE CITY STREETS RECENTLY, AND I DON'T KNOW WHAT IT MEANS.
ALL I KNOW IS IT MAKES THE SOLDIERS VERY NERVOUS.
SAY, SINCE YOU BROUGHT UP SOLDIERS, I HEAR ANOTHER PRECIOUS GEM GOT STOLEN FROM THE COBRA'S PALACE TODAY--THE WHITE ROOM, THIS TIME!
I WONDER HOW THE THIEF EVER GOT IN AND OUT OF THAT FAMOUSLY SHADOW-LESS ROOM WITHOUT BEING SEEN.
HEH HEH... I HEAR THE COBRA ALSO RECEIVED SEVERAL ANONYMOUS THREATS WITH THAT SYMBOL ON THEM!
WHAT IMPUDENCE! I WOULDN'T WANT TO BE IN THAT GUY'S SHOES WHEN THEY GET THEIR HANDS ON HIM.
HEH HEH HEH... PEOPLE LIKEN THE AGILITY OF THAT THIEF TO THAT OF THE BOY ONCE KNOWN AS "THE MONKEY," WHO VANISHED YEARS AGO, NARROWLY ESCAPING BEING TRANSFORMED INTO "FLUID"...THE FLUID THE COBRA COVETS SO MUCH.
he, he, he
he, he, he

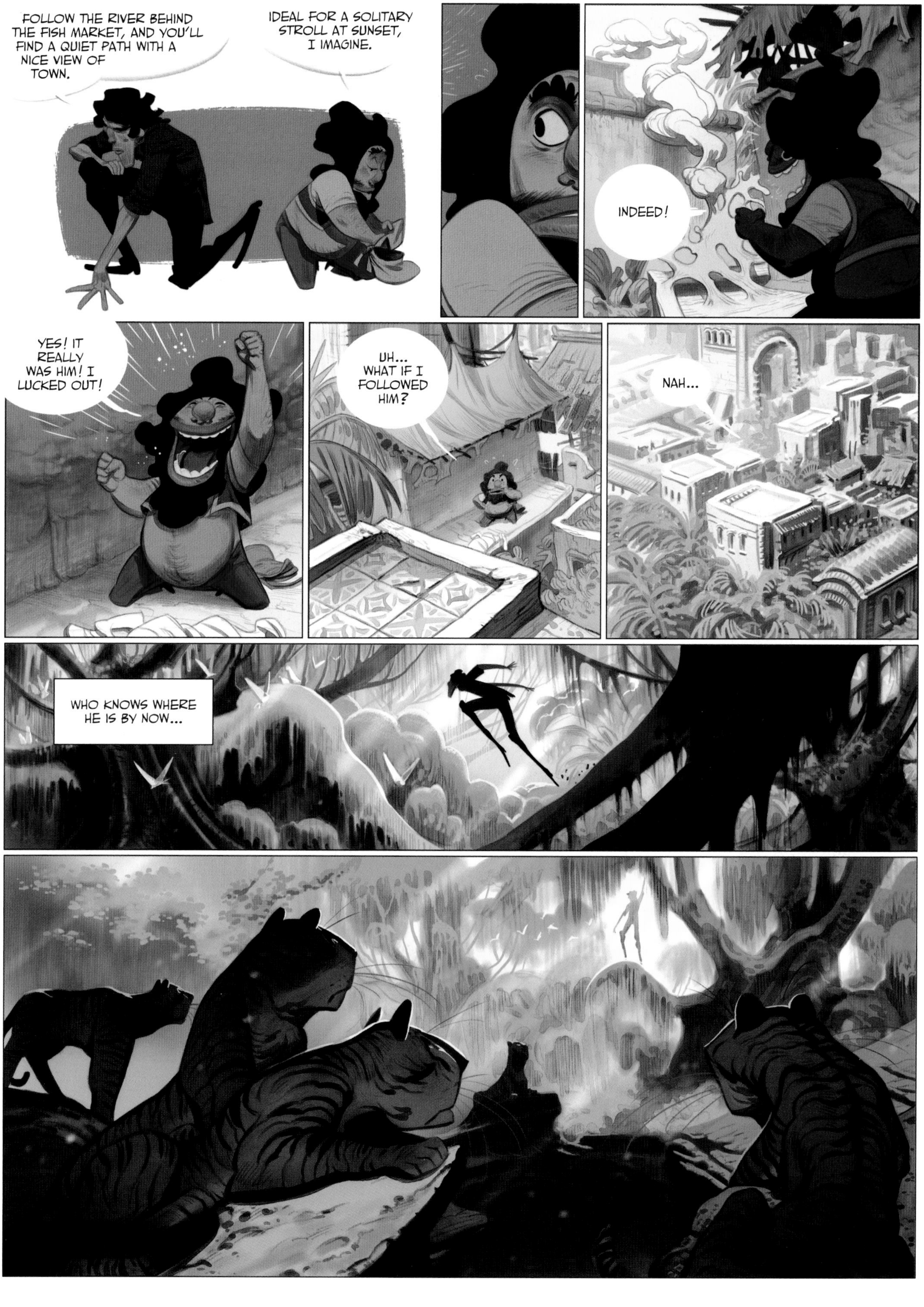
FOLLOW THE RIVER BEHIND THE FISH MARKET, AND YOU'LL FIND A QUIET PATH WITH A NICE VIEW OF TOWN.
IDEAL FOR A SOLITARY STROLL AT SUNSET, I IMAGINE.
INDEED!
YES! IT REALLY WAS HIM! I LUCKED OUT!
UH... WHAT IF I FOLLOWED HIM?
NAH...
WHO KNOWS WHERE HE IS BY NOW...

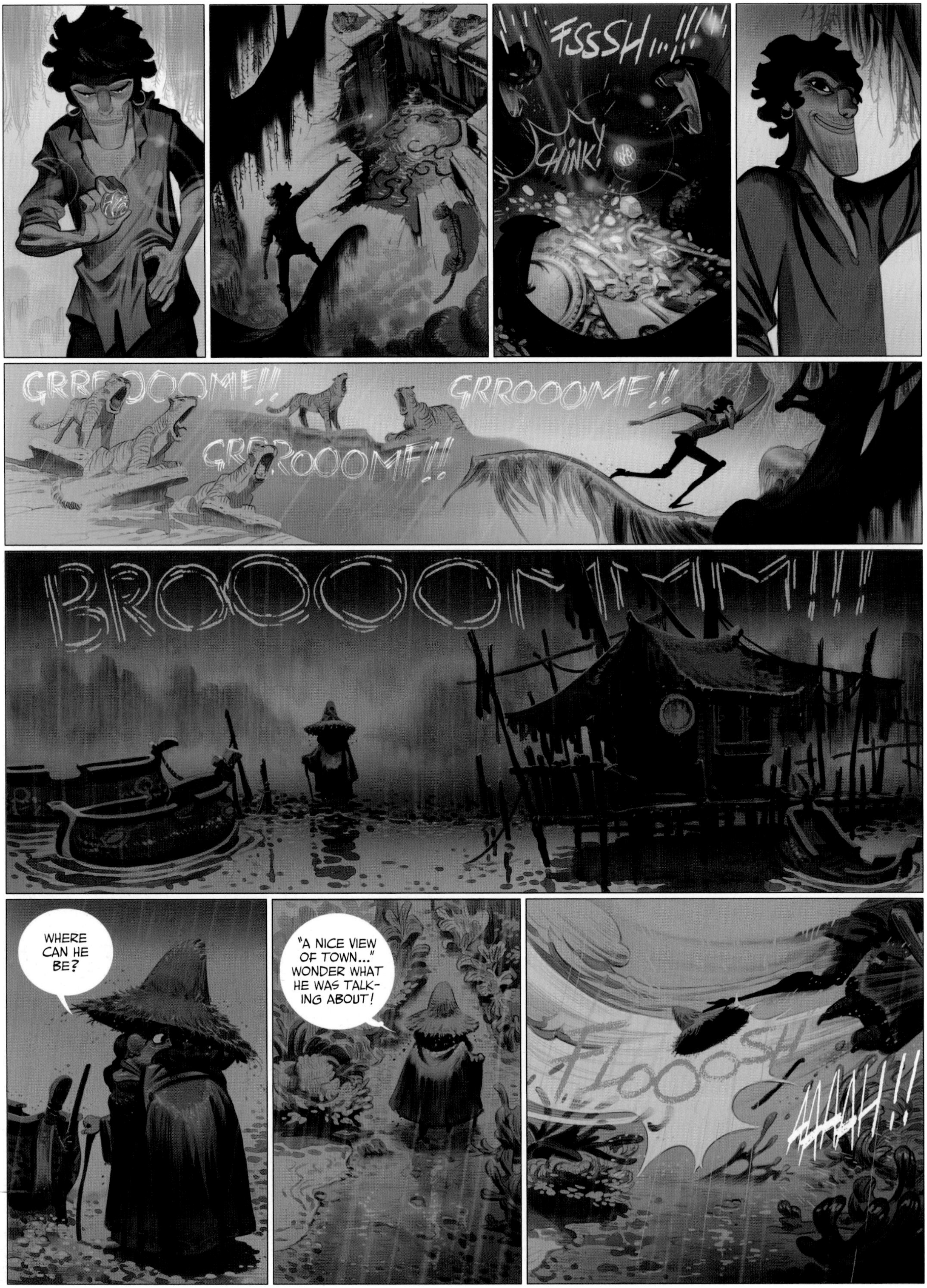
FSSSH...!!
CHINK!
GRRROOOMF!!
GRROOOMF!!
GRRROOOMF!!
BROOOOMMM!!!
WHERE CAN HE BE?
"A NICE VIEW OF TOWN..." WONDER WHAT HE WAS TALKING ABOUT!
FLOOOSH
AAAH!!

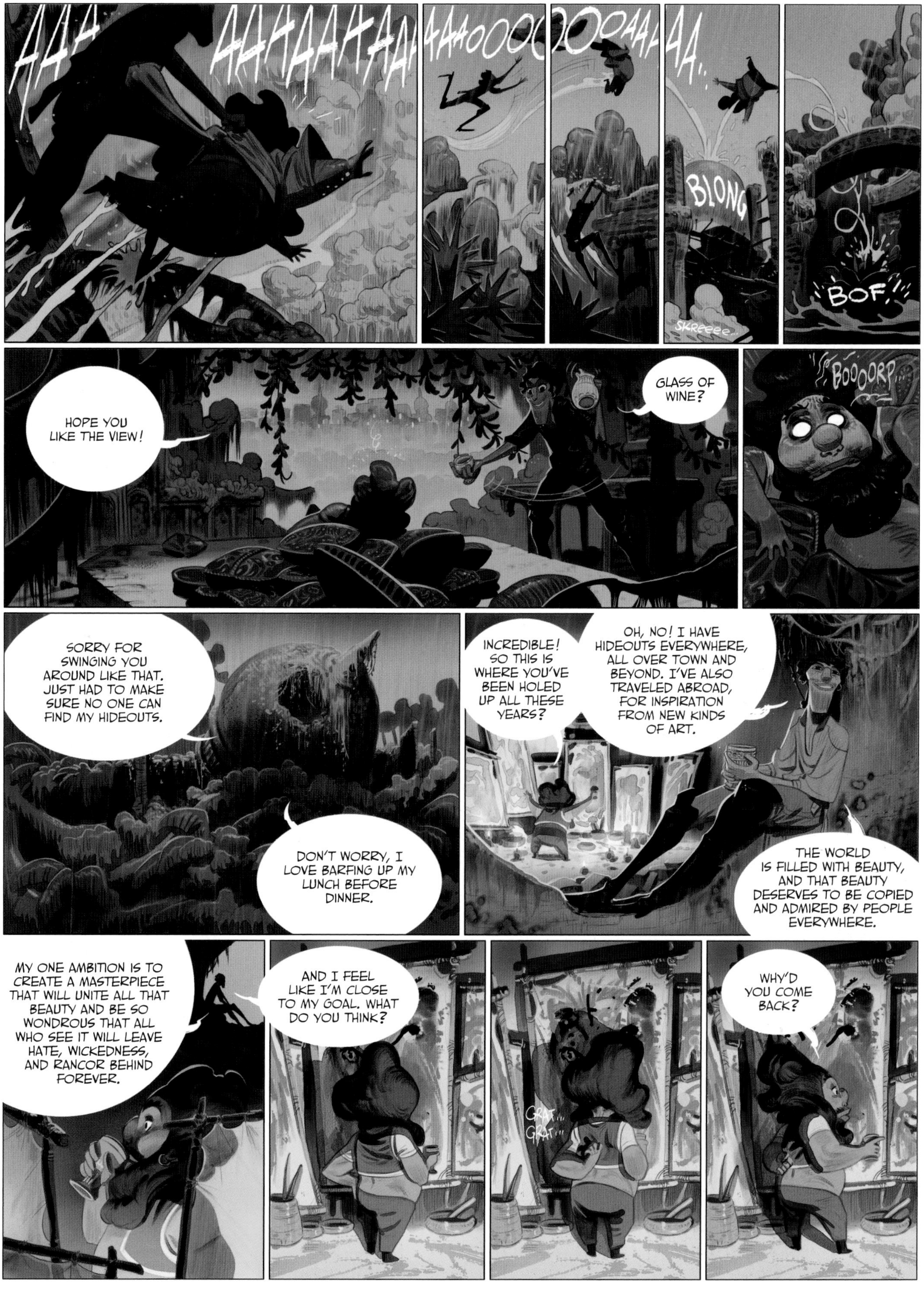

AAAAAAAAAAAAAOOOOOOOOAAAAAA...
BLONG
SKREEEE...
BOF
HOPE YOU LIKE THE VIEW!
GLASS OF WINE?
BOOOORP
SORRY FOR SWINGING YOU AROUND LIKE THAT. JUST HAD TO MAKE SURE NO ONE CAN FIND MY HIDEOUTS.
DON'T WORRY, I LOVE BARFING UP MY LUNCH BEFORE DINNER.
INCREDIBLE! SO THIS IS WHERE YOU'VE BEEN HOLED UP ALL THESE YEARS?
OH, NO! I HAVE HIDEOUTS EVERYWHERE, ALL OVER TOWN AND BEYOND. I'VE ALSO TRAVELED ABROAD, FOR INSPIRATION FROM NEW KINDS OF ART.
THE WORLD IS FILLED WITH BEAUTY, AND THAT BEAUTY DESERVES TO BE COPIED AND ADMIRED BY PEOPLE EVERYWHERE.
MY ONE AMBITION IS TO CREATE A MASTERPIECE THAT WILL UNITE ALL THAT BEAUTY AND BE SO WONDROUS THAT ALL WHO SEE IT WILL LEAVE HATE, WICKEDNESS, AND RANCOR BEHIND FOREVER.
AND I FEEL LIKE I'M CLOSE TO MY GOAL. WHAT DO YOU THINK?
GRAT... GRAT...
WHY'D YOU COME BACK?

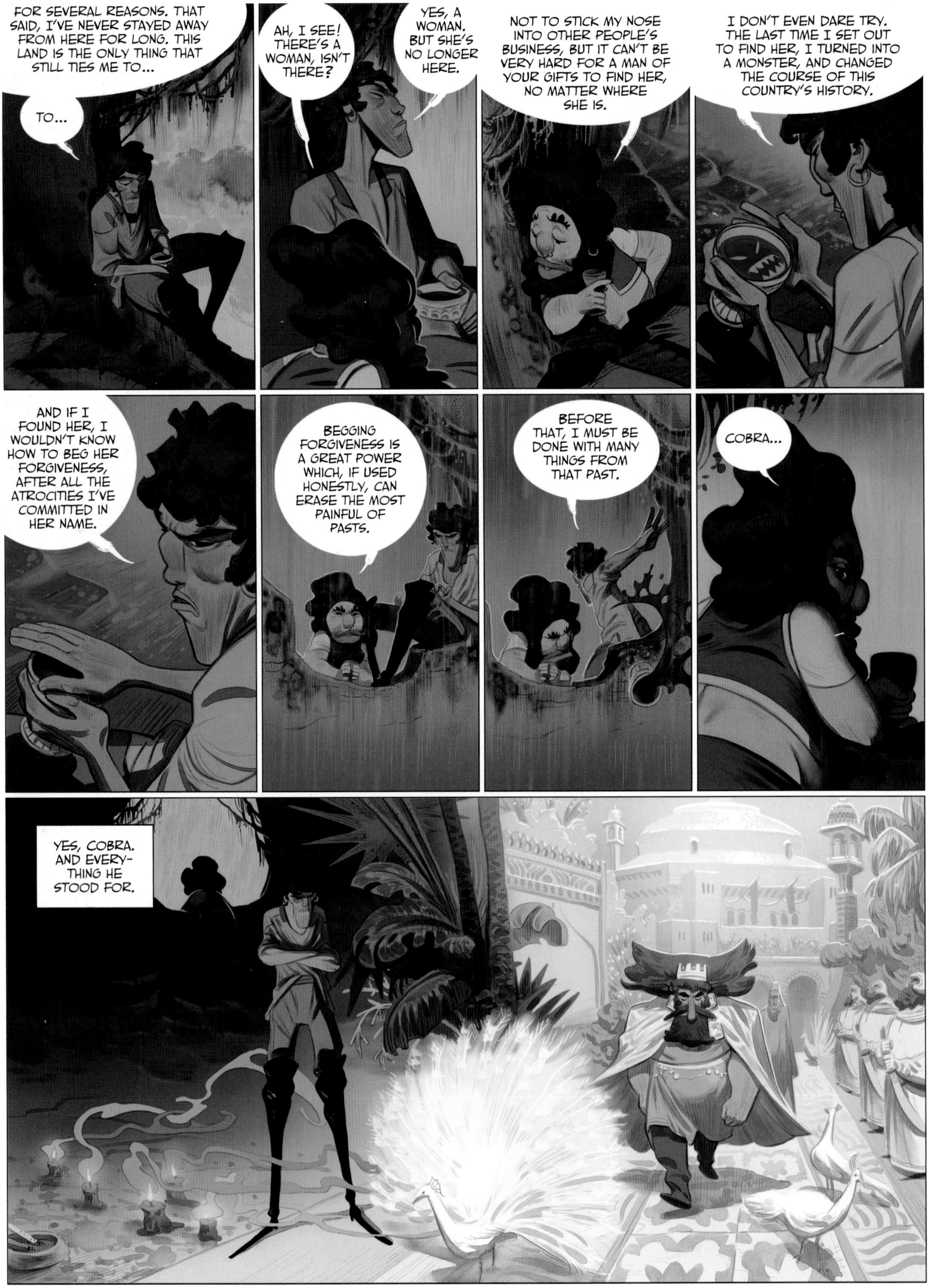
FOR SEVERAL REASONS. THAT SAID, I'VE NEVER STAYED AWAY FROM HERE FOR LONG. THIS LAND IS THE ONLY THING THAT STILL TIES ME TO...
TO...
AH, I SEE! THERE'S A WOMAN, ISN'T THERE?
YES, A WOMAN. BUT SHE'S NO LONGER HERE.
NOT TO STICK MY NOSE INTO OTHER PEOPLE'S BUSINESS, BUT IT CAN'T BE VERY HARD FOR A MAN OF YOUR GIFTS TO FIND HER, NO MATTER WHERE SHE IS.
I DON'T EVEN DARE TRY. THE LAST TIME I SET OUT TO FIND HER, I TURNED INTO A MONSTER, AND CHANGED THE COURSE OF THIS COUNTRY'S HISTORY.
AND IF I FOUND HER, I WOULDN'T KNOW HOW TO BEG HER FORGIVENESS, AFTER ALL THE ATROCITIES I'VE COMMITTED IN HER NAME.
BEGGING FORGIVENESS IS A GREAT POWER WHICH, IF USED HONESTLY, CAN ERASE THE MOST PAINFUL OF PASTS.
BEFORE THAT, I MUST BE DONE WITH MANY THINGS FROM THAT PAST.
COBRA...
YES, COBRA. AND EVERYTHING HE STOOD FOR.

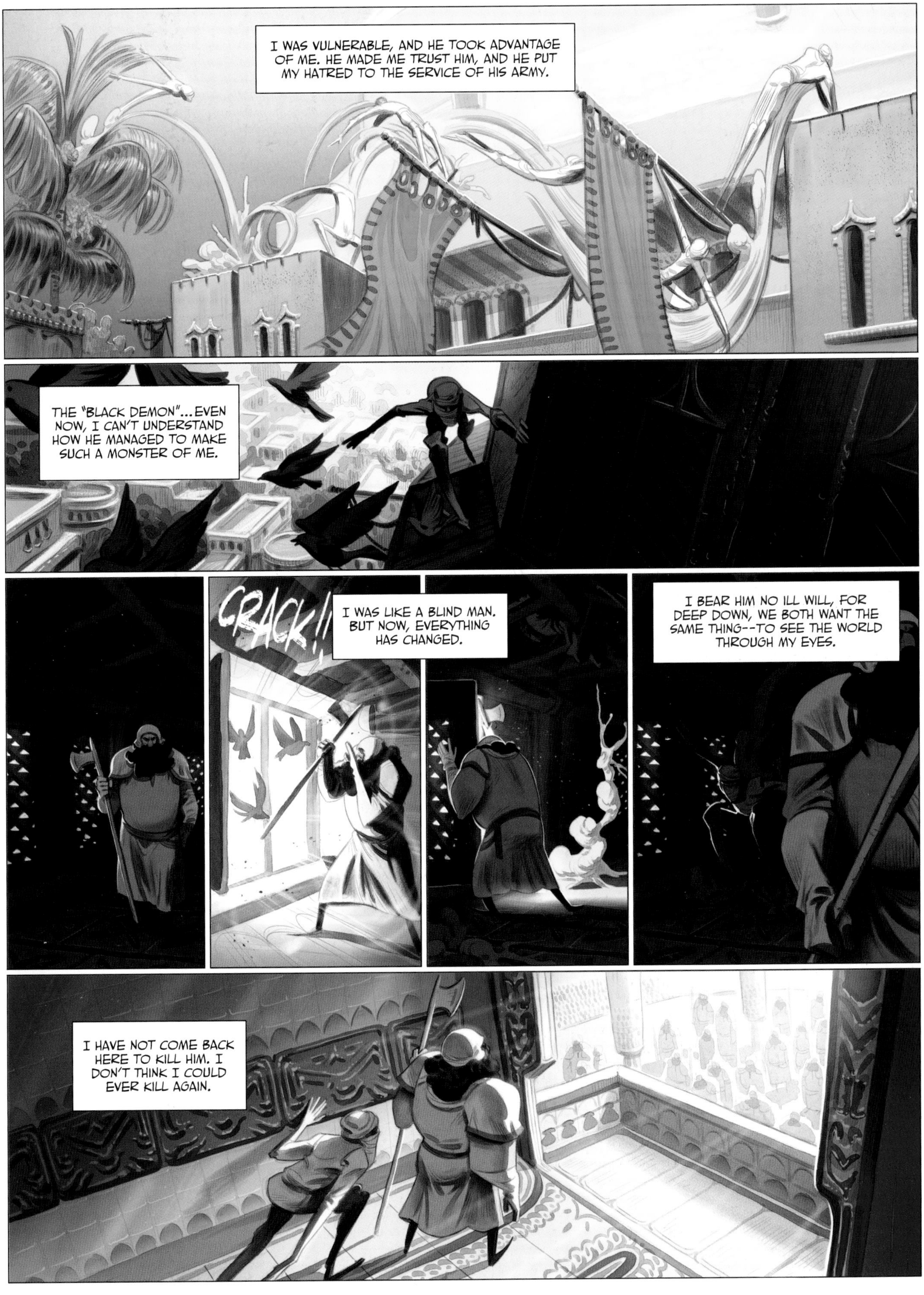
I WAS VULNERABLE, AND HE TOOK ADVANTAGE OF ME. HE MADE ME TRUST HIM, AND HE PUT MY HATRED TO THE SERVICE OF HIS ARMY.
THE "BLACK DEMON"...EVEN NOW, I CAN'T UNDERSTAND HOW HE MANAGED TO MAKE SUCH A MONSTER OF ME.
CRACK!!
I WAS LIKE A BLIND MAN. BUT NOW, EVERYTHING HAS CHANGED.
I BEAR HIM NO ILL WILL, FOR DEEP DOWN, WE BOTH WANT THE SAME THING--TO SEE THE WORLD THROUGH MY EYES.
I HAVE NOT COME BACK HERE TO KILL HIM. I DON'T THINK I COULD EVER KILL AGAIN.

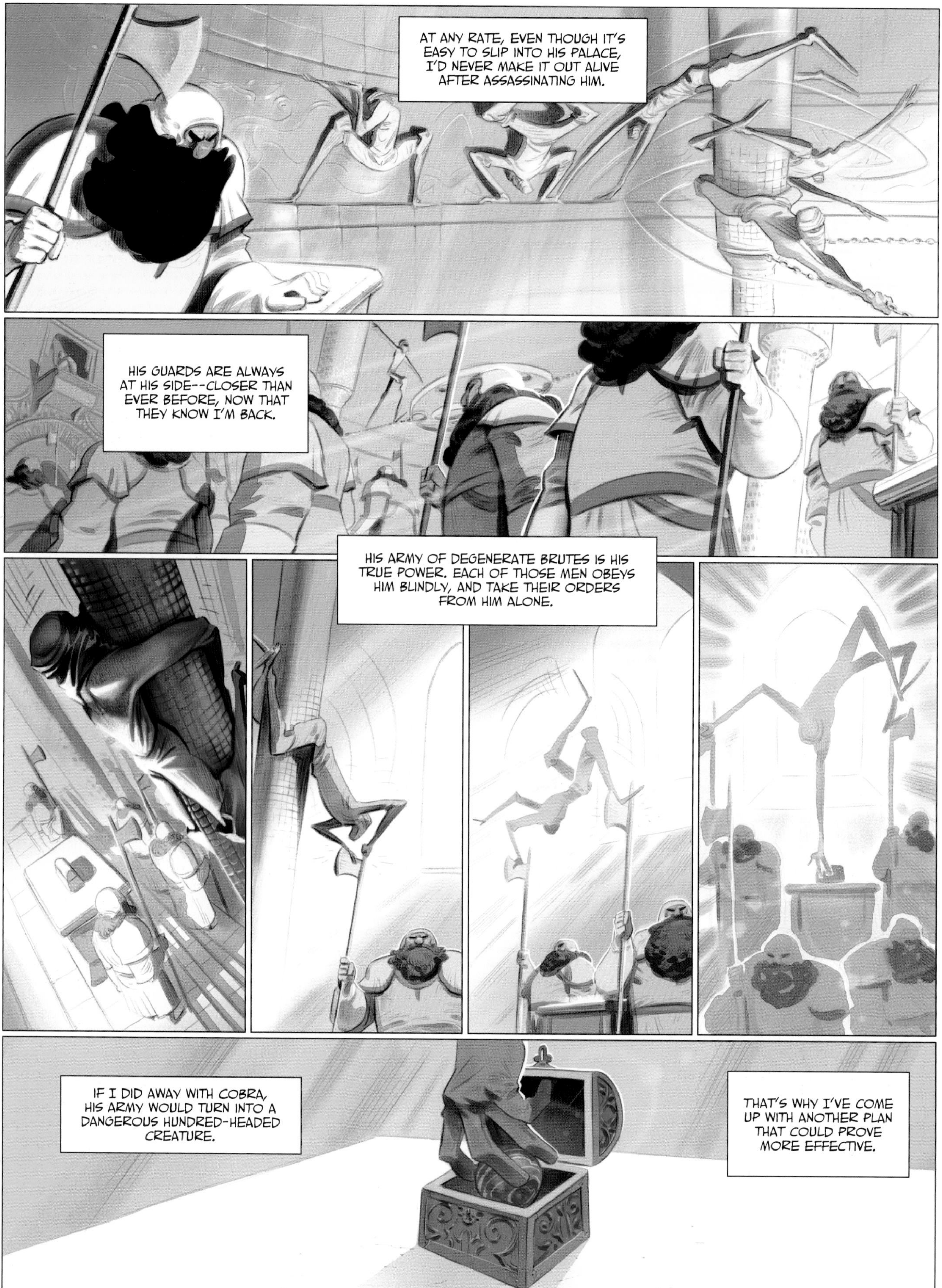
AT ANY RATE, EVEN THOUGH IT'S EASY TO SLIP INTO HIS PALACE, I'D NEVER MAKE IT OUT ALIVE AFTER ASSASSINATING HIM.
HIS GUARDS ARE ALWAYS AT HIS SIDE--CLOSER THAN EVER BEFORE, NOW THAT THEY KNOW I'M BACK.
HIS ARMY OF DEGENERATE BRUTES IS HIS TRUE POWER. EACH OF THOSE MEN OBEYS HIM BLINDLY, AND TAKE THEIR ORDERS FROM HIM ALONE.
IF I DID AWAY WITH COBRA, HIS ARMY WOULD TURN INTO A DANGEROUS HUNDRED-HEADED CREATURE.
THAT'S WHY I'VE COME UP WITH ANOTHER PLAN THAT COULD PROVE MORE EFFECTIVE.

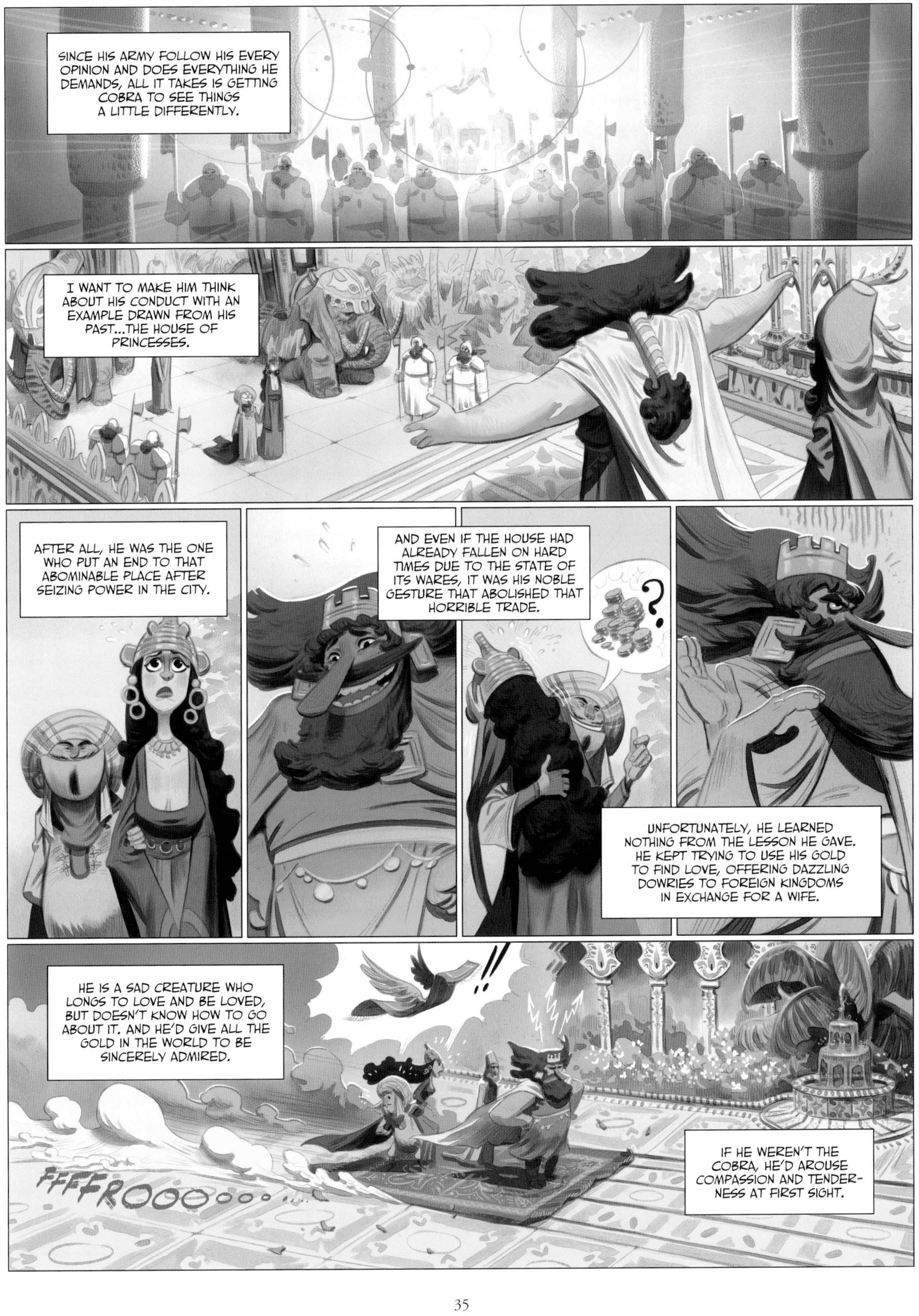
SINCE HIS ARMY FOLLOW HIS EVERY OPINION AND DOES EVERYTHING HE DEMANDS, ALL IT TAKES IS GETTING COBRA TO SEE THINGS A LITTLE DIFFERENTLY.
I WANT TO MAKE HIM THINK ABOUT HIS CONDUCT WITH AN EXAMPLE DRAWN FROM HIS PAST...THE HOUSE OF PRINCESSES.
AFTER ALL, HE WAS THE ONE WHO PUT AN END TO THAT ABOMINABLE PLACE AFTER SEIZING POWER IN THE CITY.
AND EVEN IF THE HOUSE HAD ALREADY FALLEN ON HARD TIMES DUE TO THE STATE OF ITS WARES, IT WAS HIS NOBLE GESTURE THAT ABOLISHED THAT HORRIBLE TRADE.
?
UNFORTUNATELY, HE LEARNED NOTHING FROM THE LESSON HE GAVE. HE KEPT TRYING TO USE HIS GOLD TO FIND LOVE, OFFERING DAZZLING DOWRIES TO FOREIGN KINGDOMS IN EXCHANGE FOR A WIFE.
HE IS A SAD CREATURE WHO LONGS TO LOVE AND BE LOVED, BUT DOESN'T KNOW HOW TO GO ABOUT IT. AND HE'D GIVE ALL THE GOLD IN THE WORLD TO BE SINCERELY ADMIRED.
!!
FFFFROOOooo...
IF HE WEREN'T THE COBRA, HE'D AROUSE COMPASSION AND TENDER-NESS AT FIRST SIGHT.

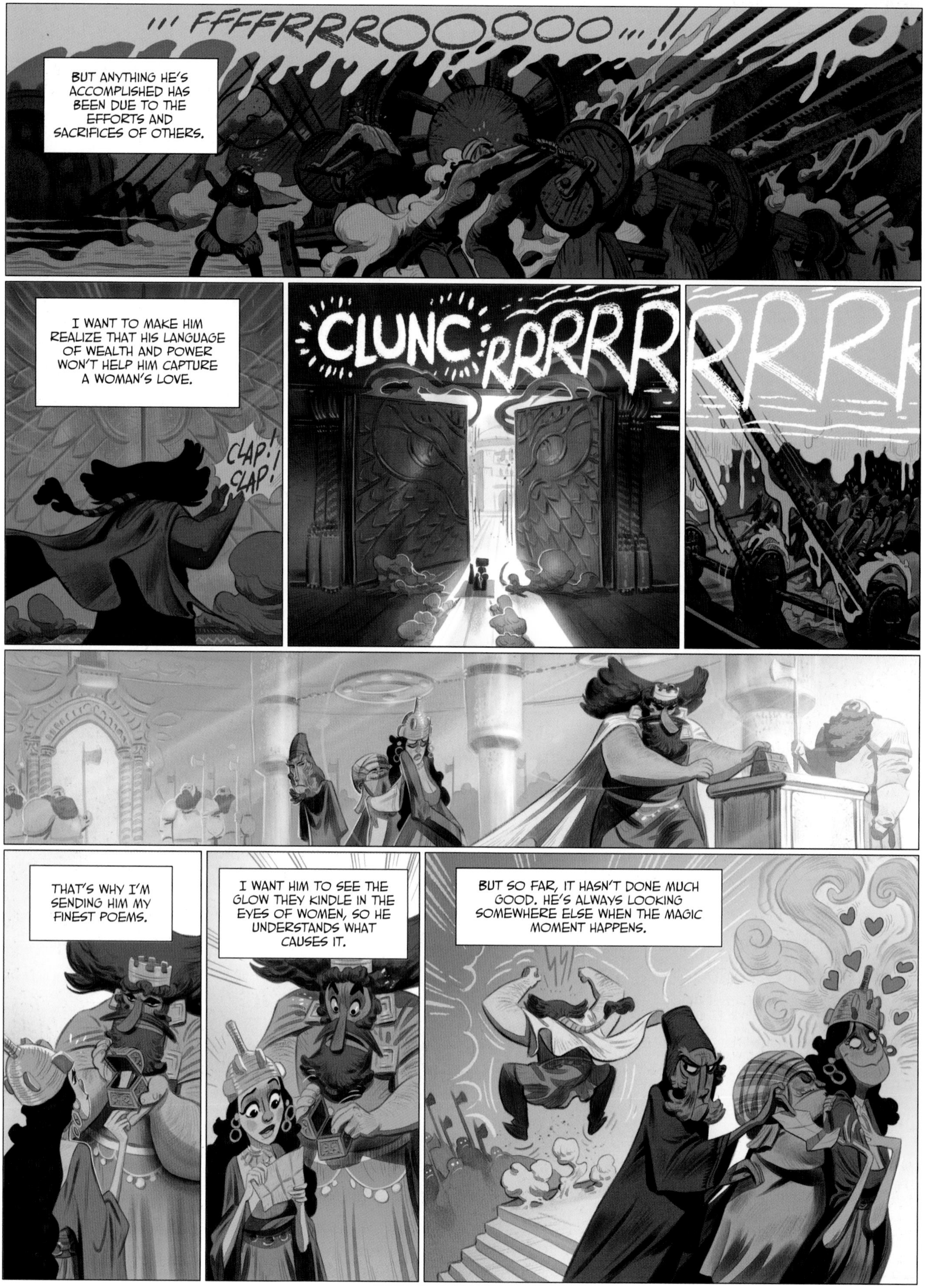

... FFFFRRROOOOOO ... !!
BUT ANYTHING HE'S ACCOMPLISHED HAS BEEN DUE TO THE EFFORTS AND SACRIFICES OF OTHERS.
I WANT TO MAKE HIM REALIZE THAT HIS LANGUAGE OF WEALTH AND POWER WON'T HELP HIM CAPTURE A WOMAN'S LOVE.
CLAP! CLAP!
CLUNC RRRRRRRRRR
THAT'S WHY I'M SENDING HIM MY FINEST POEMS.
I WANT HIM TO SEE THE GLOW THEY KINDLE IN THE EYES OF WOMEN, SO HE UNDERSTANDS WHAT CAUSES IT.
BUT SO FAR, IT HASN'T DONE MUCH GOOD. HE'S ALWAYS LOOKING SOMEWHERE ELSE WHEN THE MAGIC MOMENT HAPPENS.

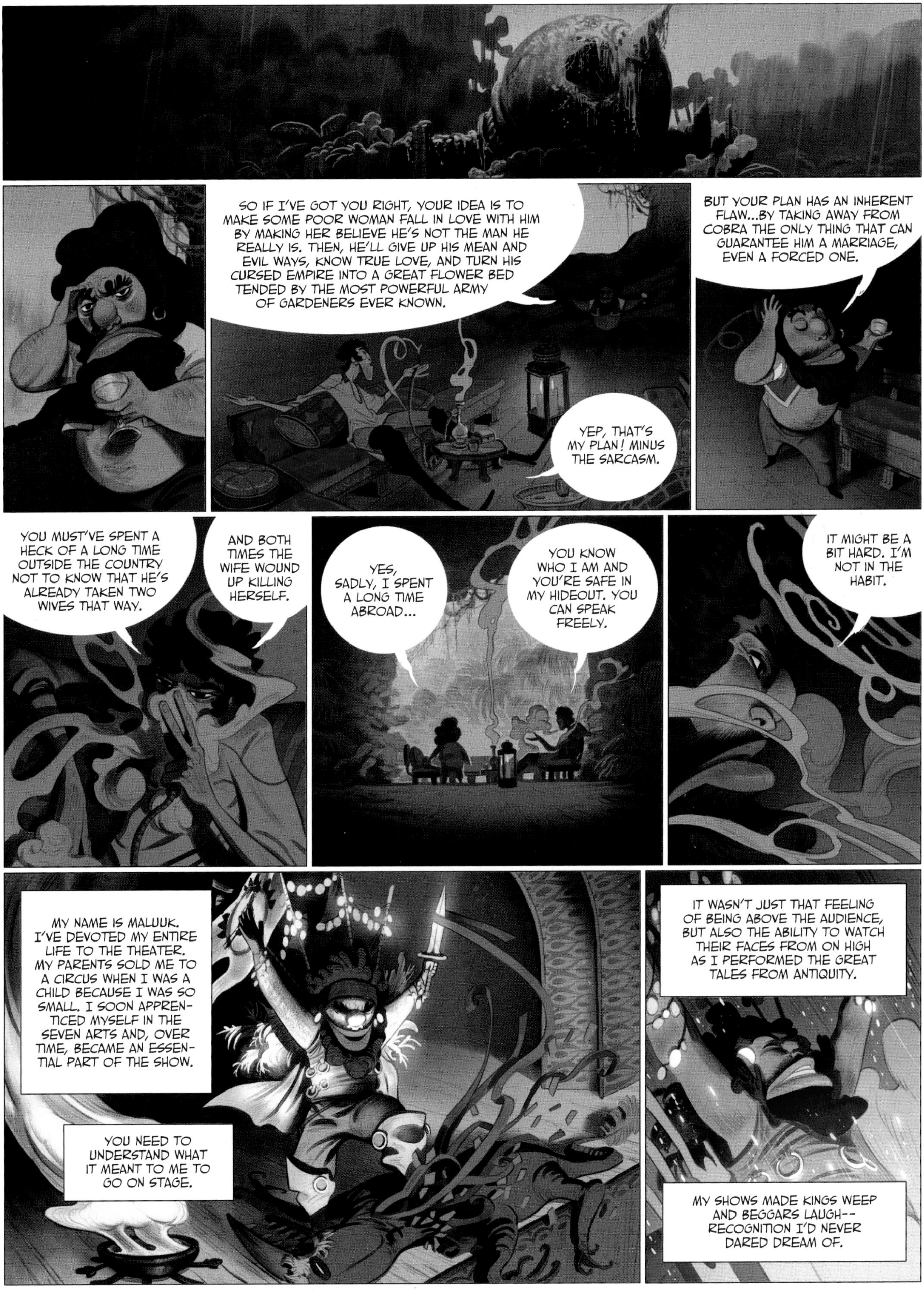
SO IF I'VE GOT YOU RIGHT, YOUR IDEA IS TO MAKE SOME POOR WOMAN FALL IN LOVE WITH HIM BY MAKING HER BELIEVE HE'S NOT THE MAN HE REALLY IS. THEN, HE'LL GIVE UP HIS MEAN AND EVIL WAYS, KNOW TRUE LOVE, AND TURN HIS CURSED EMPIRE INTO A GREAT FLOWER BED TENDED BY THE MOST POWERFUL ARMY OF GARDENERS EVER KNOWN.
YEP, THAT'S MY PLAN! MINUS THE SARCASM.
BUT YOUR PLAN HAS AN INHERENT FLAW...BY TAKING AWAY FROM COBRA THE ONLY THING THAT CAN GUARANTEE HIM A MARRIAGE, EVEN A FORCED ONE.
YOU MUST'VE SPENT A HECK OF A LONG TIME OUTSIDE THE COUNTRY NOT TO KNOW THAT HE'S ALREADY TAKEN TWO WIVES THAT WAY.
AND BOTH TIMES THE WIFE WOUND UP KILLING HERSELF.
YES, SADLY, I SPENT A LONG TIME ABROAD...
YOU KNOW WHO I AM AND YOU'RE SAFE IN MY HIDEOUT. YOU CAN SPEAK FREELY.
IT MIGHT BE A BIT HARD. I'M NOT IN THE HABIT.
MY NAME IS MALUUK. I'VE DEVOTED MY ENTIRE LIFE TO THE THEATER. MY PARENTS SOLD ME TO A CIRCUS WHEN I WAS A CHILD BECAUSE I WAS SO SMALL. I SOON APPRENTICED MYSELF IN THE SEVEN ARTS AND, OVER TIME, BECAME AN ESSENTIAL PART OF THE SHOW.
YOU NEED TO UNDERSTAND WHAT IT MEANT TO ME TO GO ON STAGE.
IT WASN'T JUST THAT FEELING OF BEING ABOVE THE AUDIENCE, BUT ALSO THE ABILITY TO WATCH THEIR FACES FROM ON HIGH AS I PERFORMED THE GREAT TALES FROM ANTIQUITY.
MY SHOWS MADE KINGS WEEP AND BEGGARS LAUGH--RECOGNITION I'D NEVER DARED DREAM OF.

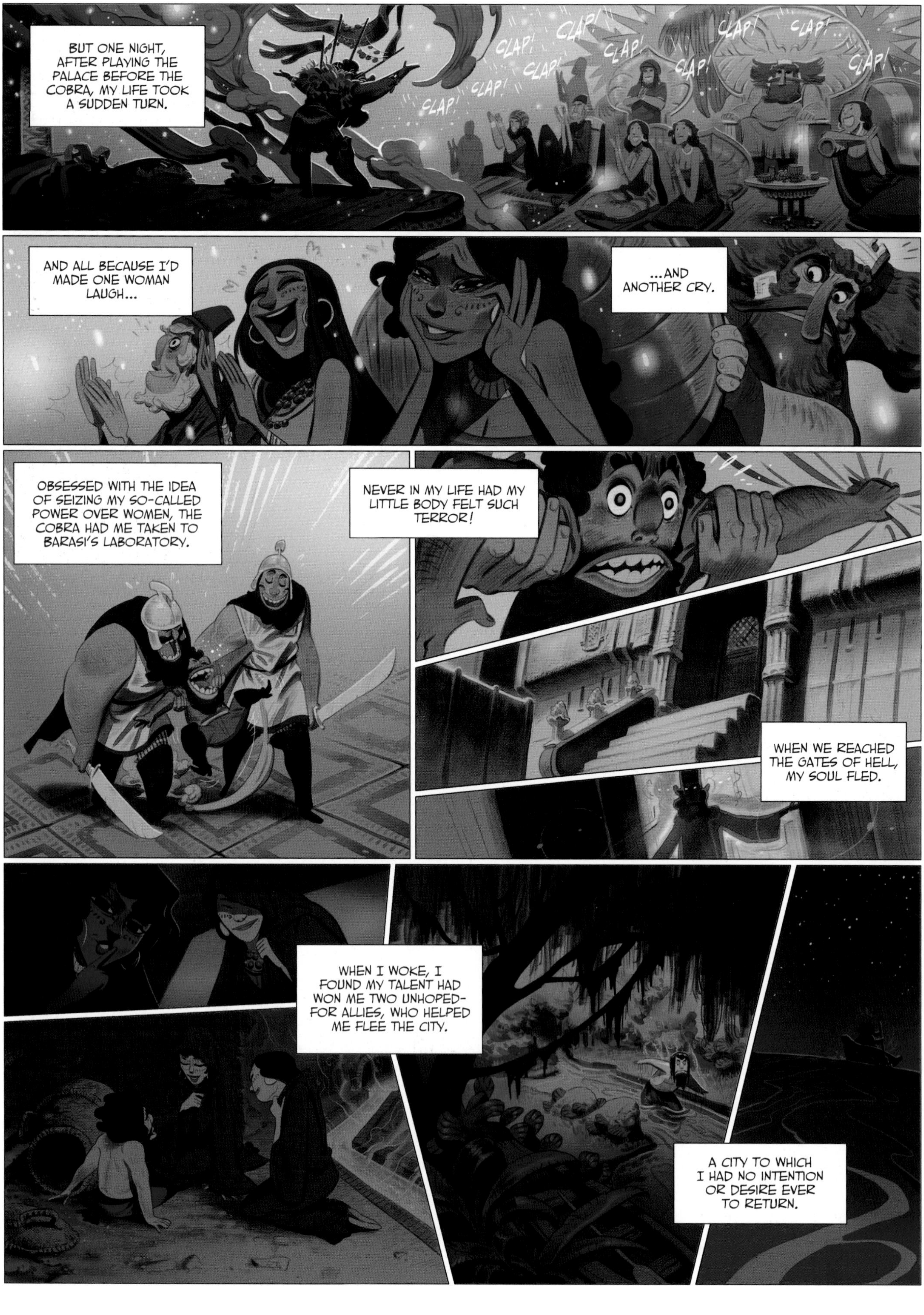
BUT ONE NIGHT, AFTER PLAYING THE PALACE BEFORE THE COBRA, MY LIFE TOOK A SUDDEN TURN.
CLAP! CLAP! CLAP! CLAP! CLAP! CLAP! CLAP! CLAP! CLAP! CLAP!
AND ALL BECAUSE I'D MADE ONE WOMAN LAUGH...
...AND ANOTHER CRY.
OBSESSED WITH THE IDEA OF SEIZING MY SO-CALLED POWER OVER WOMEN, THE COBRA HAD ME TAKEN TO BARASI'S LABORATORY.
NEVER IN MY LIFE HAD MY LITTLE BODY FELT SUCH TERROR!
WHEN WE REACHED THE GATES OF HELL, MY SOUL FLED.
WHEN I WOKE, I FOUND MY TALENT HAD WON ME TWO UNHOPED-FOR ALLIES, WHO HELPED ME FLEE THE CITY.
A CITY TO WHICH I HAD NO INTENTION OR DESIRE EVER TO RETURN.

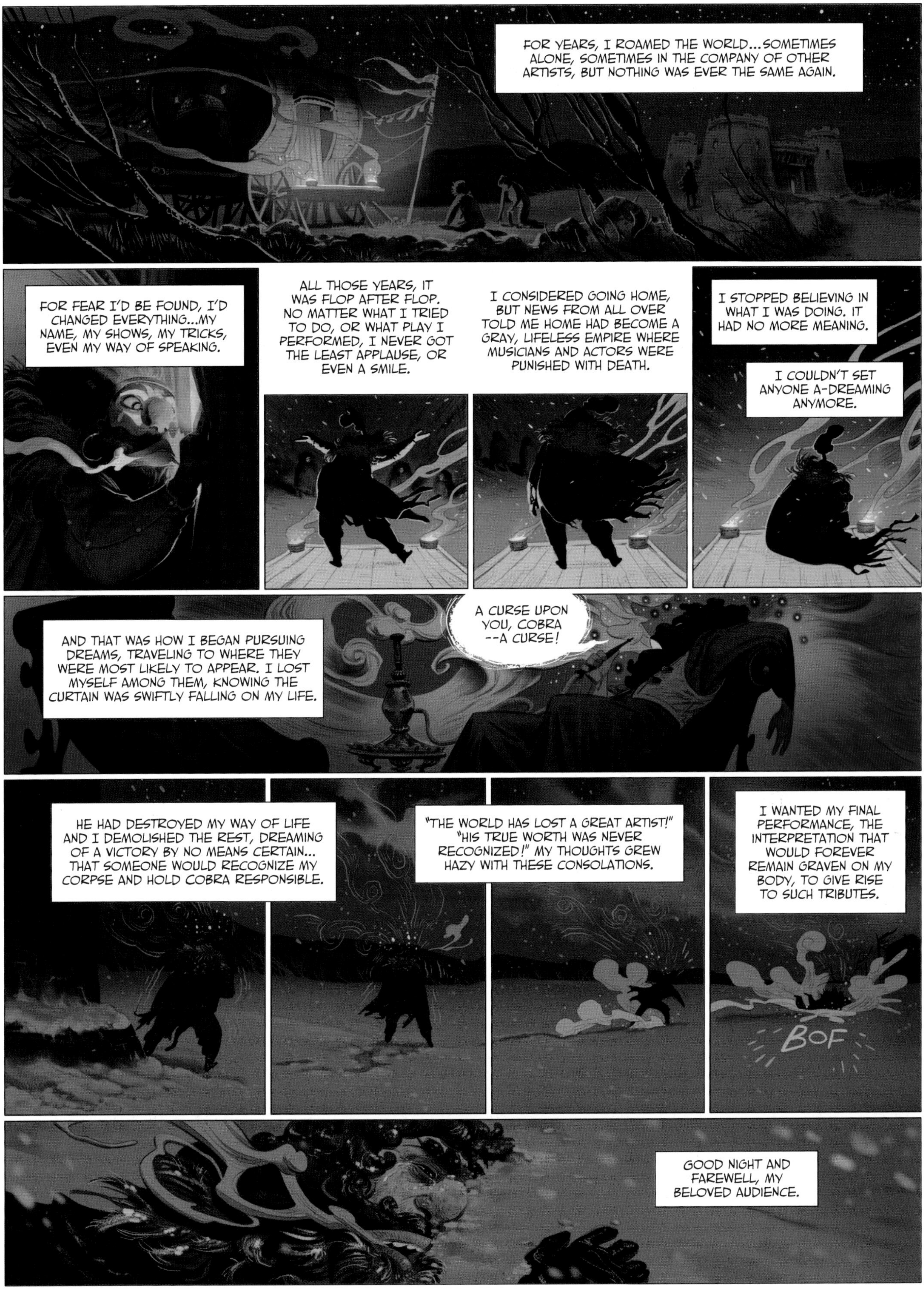
FOR YEARS, I ROAMED THE WORLD...SOMETIMES ALONE, SOMETIMES IN THE COMPANY OF OTHER ARTISTS, BUT NOTHING WAS EVER THE SAME AGAIN.
FOR FEAR I'D BE FOUND, I'D CHANGED EVERYTHING...MY NAME, MY SHOWS, MY TRICKS, EVEN MY WAY OF SPEAKING.
ALL THOSE YEARS, IT WAS FLOP AFTER FLOP. NO MATTER WHAT I TRIED TO DO, OR WHAT PLAY I PERFORMED, I NEVER GOT THE LEAST APPLAUSE, OR EVEN A SMILE.
I CONSIDERED GOING HOME, BUT NEWS FROM ALL OVER TOLD ME HOME HAD BECOME A GRAY, LIFELESS EMPIRE WHERE MUSICIANS AND ACTORS WERE PUNISHED WITH DEATH.
I STOPPED BELIEVING IN WHAT I WAS DOING. IT HAD NO MORE MEANING.
I COULDN'T SET ANYONE A-DREAMING ANYMORE.
AND THAT WAS HOW I BEGAN PURSUING DREAMS, TRAVELING TO WHERE THEY WERE MOST LIKELY TO APPEAR. I LOST MYSELF AMONG THEM, KNOWING THE CURTAIN WAS SWIFTLY FALLING ON MY LIFE.
A CURSE UPON YOU, COBRA --A CURSE!
HE HAD DESTROYED MY WAY OF LIFE AND I DEMOLISHED THE REST, DREAMING OF A VICTORY BY NO MEANS CERTAIN... THAT SOMEONE WOULD RECOGNIZE MY CORPSE AND HOLD COBRA RESPONSIBLE.
"THE WORLD HAS LOST A GREAT ARTIST!" "HIS TRUE WORTH WAS NEVER RECOGNIZED!" MY THOUGHTS GREW HAZY WITH THESE CONSOLATIONS.
I WANTED MY FINAL PERFORMANCE, THE INTERPRETATION THAT WOULD FOREVER REMAIN GRAVEN ON MY BODY, TO GIVE RISE TO SUCH TRIBUTES.
BOF
GOOD NIGHT AND FAREWELL, MY BELOVED AUDIENCE.

AT DAWN ON THE DAY I BELIEVED WOULD BE MY LAST, A MIRACLE OF SORTS HAPPENED. I'D SPENT THE NIGHT WITH OTHER OUTCASTS I DIDN'T EVEN KNOW, AND WHEN I WOKE...

ACTUALLY, I DON'T REMEMBER WHAT I SAID JUST THEN, I JUST BABBLED SOMETHING WITHOUT THINKING, BUT--

AT THAT VERY MOMENT, ONE OF THEM BEGAN TO LAUGH.

WHEN YOU'VE GONE A LONG TIME WITHOUT HEARING LAUGHTER, A LAUGH THAT STRONG AND UNBRIDLED CAN SEEM A BIT INVASIVE AT FIRST-- AGGRESSIVE, LIKE AN ANIMAL'S BELLOW...

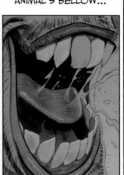

BUT SOON, IT BRINGS YOU BACK TO THAT WELCOMING PLACE YOU NEVER REALLY WANTED TO LEAVE.

HA HA HA! IT'S BEEN A LONG TIME SINCE I'VE LAUGHED SO HARD! CLEARLY THAT'S WHAT WE'RE MISSING AROUND HERE...SOMEONE LIKE YOU!

HEY, WAKE UP, ALL OF YOU! LISTEN TO THIS!

THEY WERE FELLOW COUNTRYMEN WHO'D FLED THE COBRA, OF COURSE.

AND AT THAT MOMENT, EVERYTHING BECAME CLEAR TO ME.

I HAD TO GIVE MY PEOPLE BACK THEIR SMILE, AT ANY PRICE! EVEN IF IT COST ME MY LIFE!

WITH LAUGHTER, I'D BE GIVING THEM BACK THEIR FEELINGS, AND WITH FEELINGS, THEIR DREAMS, AND WITH DREAMS, THEY'D REDISCOVER THE COURAGE TO WIN BACK THEIR FREEDOM.

THE HEROES FROM MY TALES OF ANTIQUITY HAVE ACCOMPANIED ME DURING MY VOYAGE HOME. THEY'VE SUPPORTED ME, GIVEN ME COURAGE. THEY'D EXPERIENCED THE SAME THINGS BEFORE I DID. THEY CRIED... "DEATH TO THE EMPEROR! DEATH TO THE TYRANT!"

IT IS TO THEM THAT I DEDICATE MY FINAL PERFORMANCE... REVOLUTION!

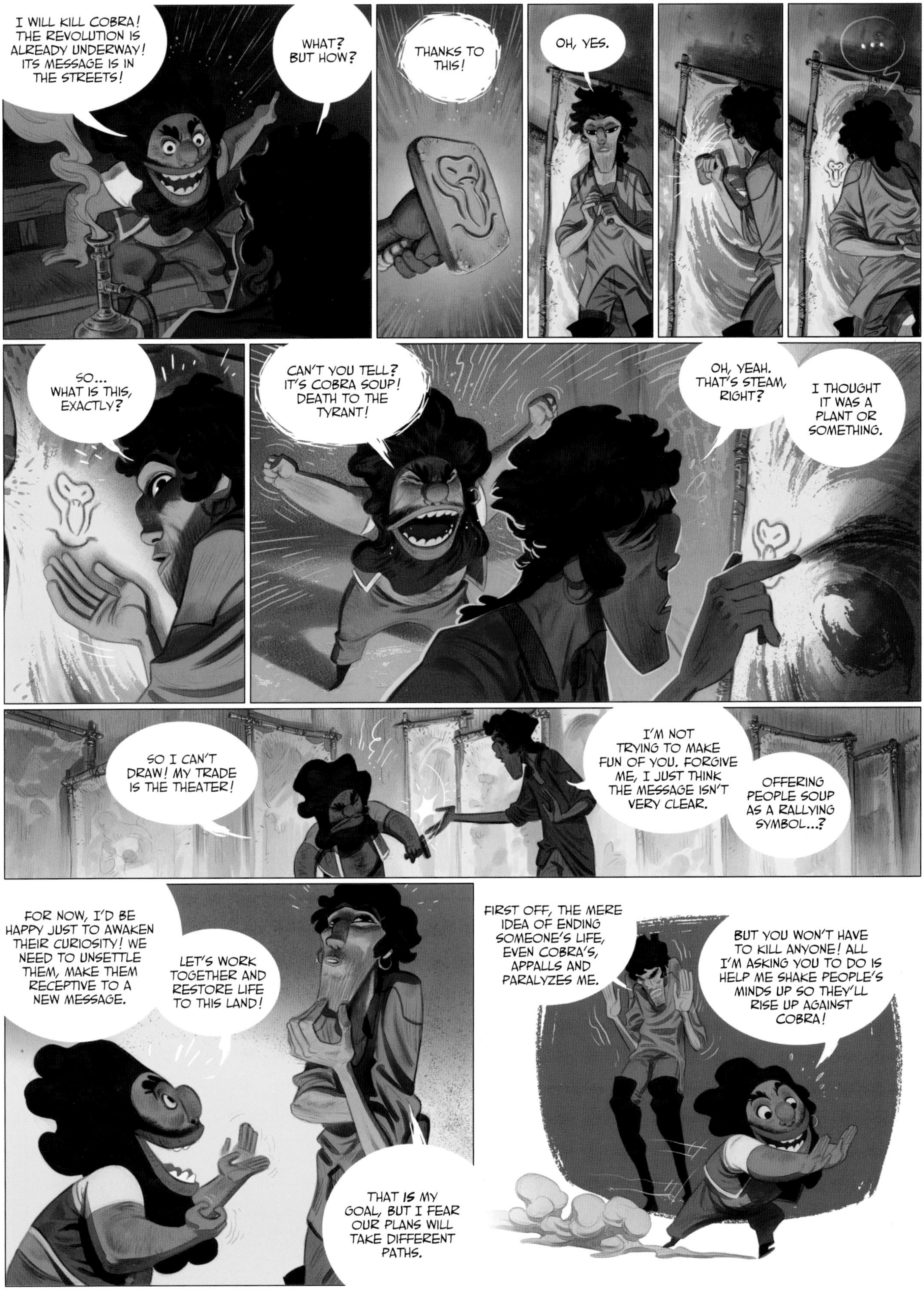

I WILL KILL COBRA! THE REVOLUTION IS ALREADY UNDERWAY! ITS MESSAGE IS IN THE STREETS!
WHAT? BUT HOW?
THANKS TO THIS!
OH, YES.
SO... WHAT IS THIS, EXACTLY?
CAN'T YOU TELL? IT'S COBRA SOUP! DEATH TO THE TYRANT!
OH, YEAH. THAT'S STEAM, RIGHT?
I THOUGHT IT WAS A PLANT OR SOMETHING.
SO I CAN'T DRAW! MY TRADE IS THE THEATER!
I'M NOT TRYING TO MAKE FUN OF YOU. FORGIVE ME, I JUST THINK THE MESSAGE ISN'T VERY CLEAR.
OFFERING PEOPLE SOUP AS A RALLYING SYMBOL...?
FOR NOW, I'D BE HAPPY JUST TO AWAKEN THEIR CURIOSITY! WE NEED TO UNSETTLE THEM, MAKE THEM RECEPTIVE TO A NEW MESSAGE.
LET'S WORK TOGETHER AND RESTORE LIFE TO THIS LAND!
THAT **IS** MY GOAL, BUT I FEAR OUR PLANS WILL TAKE DIFFERENT PATHS.
FIRST OFF, THE MERE IDEA OF ENDING SOMEONE'S LIFE, EVEN COBRA'S, APPALLS AND PARALYZES ME.
BUT YOU WON'T HAVE TO KILL ANYONE! ALL I'M ASKING YOU TO DO IS HELP ME SHAKE PEOPLE'S MINDS UP SO THEY'LL RISE UP AGAINST COBRA!

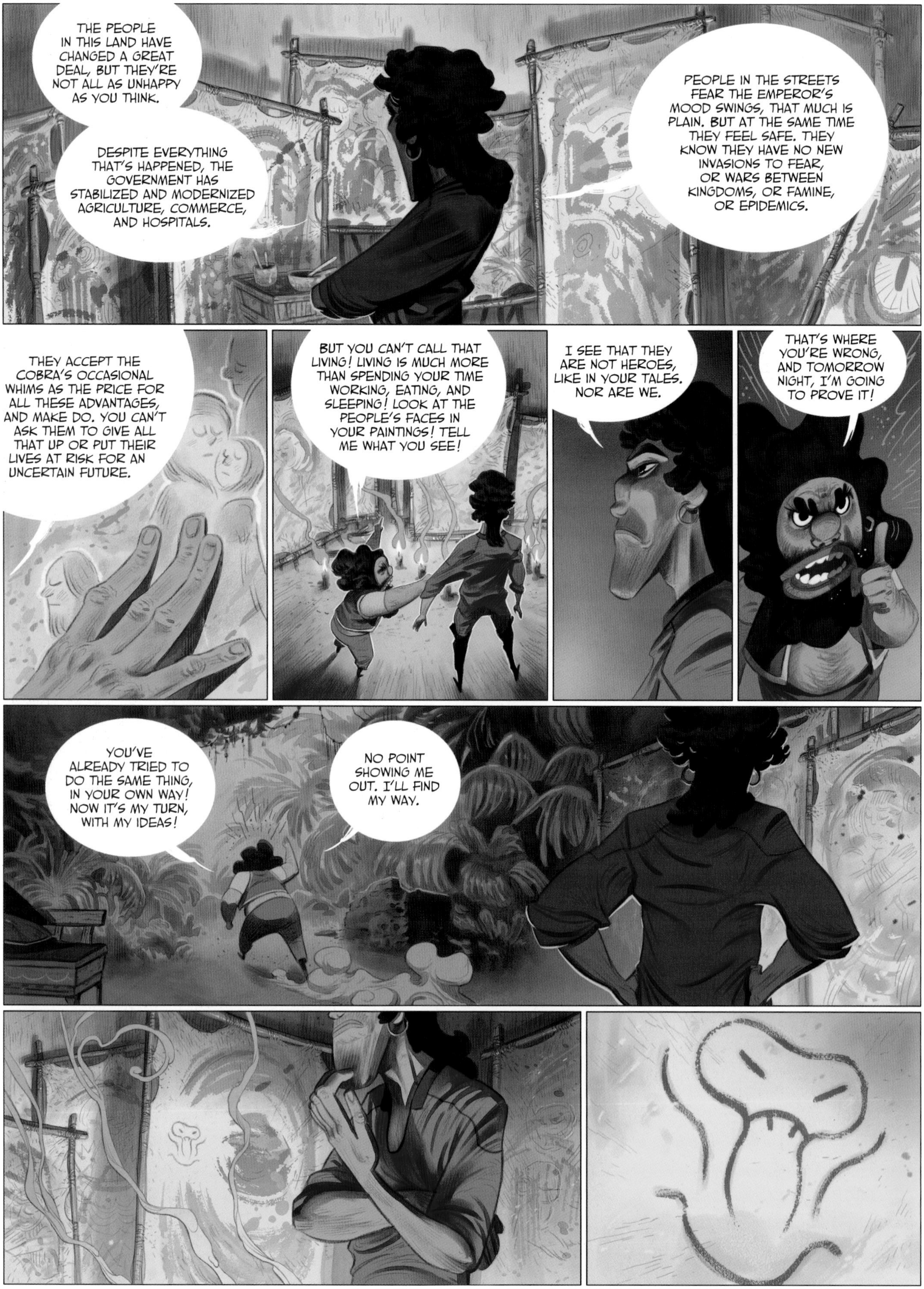

THE PEOPLE IN THIS LAND HAVE CHANGED A GREAT DEAL, BUT THEY'RE NOT ALL AS UNHAPPY AS YOU THINK.
DESPITE EVERYTHING THAT'S HAPPENED, THE GOVERNMENT HAS STABILIZED AND MODERNIZED AGRICULTURE, COMMERCE, AND HOSPITALS.
PEOPLE IN THE STREETS FEAR THE EMPEROR'S MOOD SWINGS, THAT MUCH IS PLAIN. BUT AT THE SAME TIME THEY FEEL SAFE. THEY KNOW THEY HAVE NO NEW INVASIONS TO FEAR, OR WARS BETWEEN KINGDOMS, OR FAMINE, OR EPIDEMICS.
THEY ACCEPT THE COBRA'S OCCASIONAL WHIMS AS THE PRICE FOR ALL THESE ADVANTAGES, AND MAKE DO. YOU CAN'T ASK THEM TO GIVE ALL THAT UP OR PUT THEIR LIVES AT RISK FOR AN UNCERTAIN FUTURE.
BUT YOU CAN'T CALL THAT LIVING! LIVING IS MUCH MORE THAN SPENDING YOUR TIME WORKING, EATING, AND SLEEPING! LOOK AT THE PEOPLE'S FACES IN YOUR PAINTINGS! TELL ME WHAT YOU SEE!
I SEE THAT THEY ARE NOT HEROES, LIKE IN YOUR TALES. NOR ARE WE.
THAT'S WHERE YOU'RE WRONG, AND TOMORROW NIGHT, I'M GOING TO PROVE IT!
YOU'VE ALREADY TRIED TO DO THE SAME THING, IN YOUR OWN WAY! NOW IT'S MY TURN, WITH MY IDEAS!
NO POINT SHOWING ME OUT. I'LL FIND MY WAY.

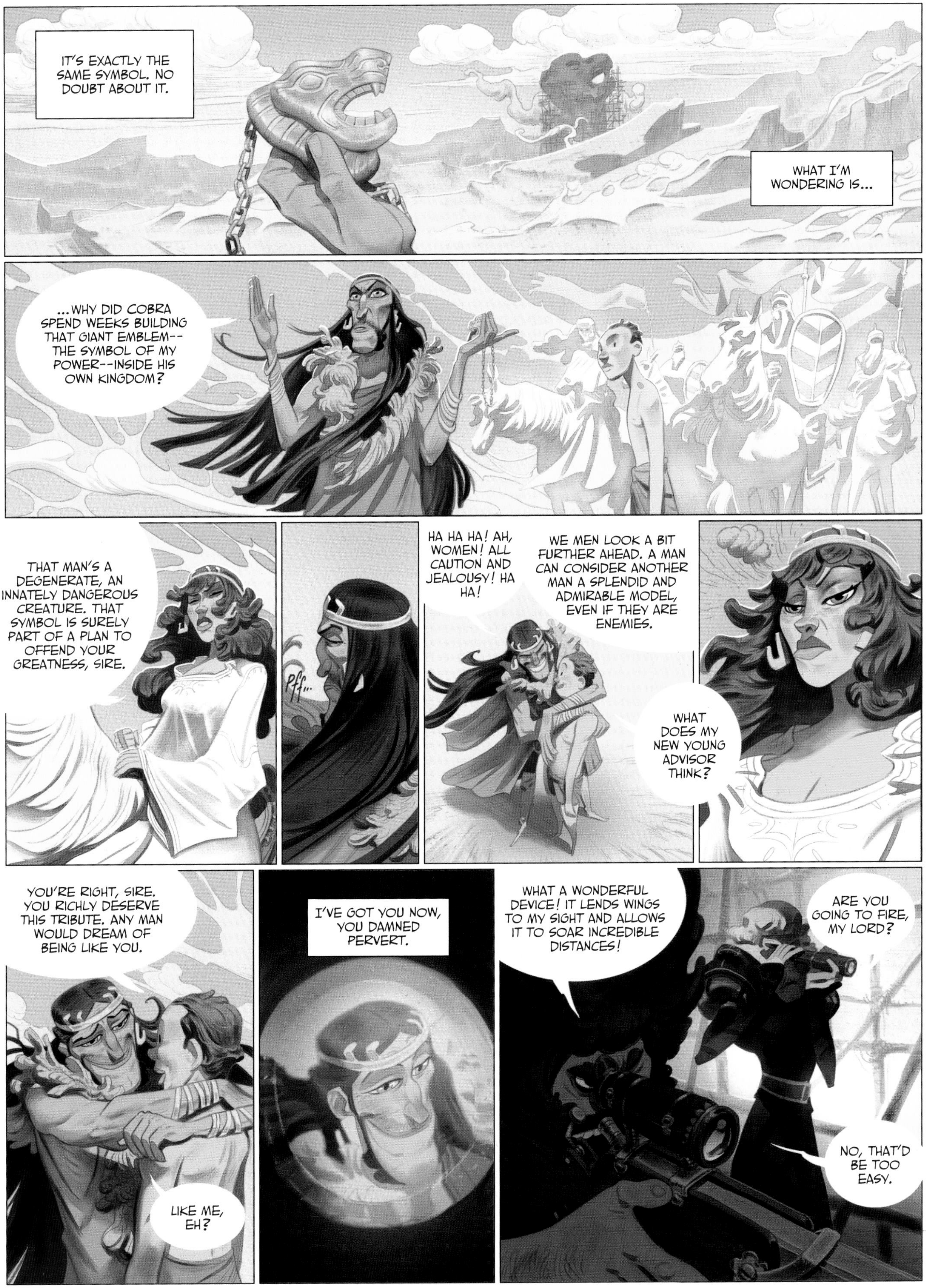
IT'S EXACTLY THE SAME SYMBOL. NO DOUBT ABOUT IT.
WHAT I'M WONDERING IS...
...WHY DID COBRA SPEND WEEKS BUILDING THAT GIANT EMBLEM--THE SYMBOL OF MY POWER--INSIDE HIS OWN KINGDOM?
THAT MAN'S A DEGENERATE, AN INNATELY DANGEROUS CREATURE. THAT SYMBOL IS SURELY PART OF A PLAN TO OFFEND YOUR GREATNESS, SIRE.
Pff...
HA HA HA! AH, WOMEN! ALL CAUTION AND JEALOUSY! HA HA!
WE MEN LOOK A BIT FURTHER AHEAD. A MAN CAN CONSIDER ANOTHER MAN A SPLENDID AND ADMIRABLE MODEL, EVEN IF THEY ARE ENEMIES.
WHAT DOES MY NEW YOUNG ADVISOR THINK?
YOU'RE RIGHT, SIRE. YOU RICHLY DESERVE THIS TRIBUTE. ANY MAN WOULD DREAM OF BEING LIKE YOU.
LIKE ME, EH?
I'VE GOT YOU NOW, YOU DAMNED PERVERT.
WHAT A WONDERFUL DEVICE! IT LENDS WINGS TO MY SIGHT AND ALLOWS IT TO SOAR INCREDIBLE DISTANCES!
ARE YOU GOING TO FIRE, MY LORD?
NO, THAT'D BE TOO EASY.

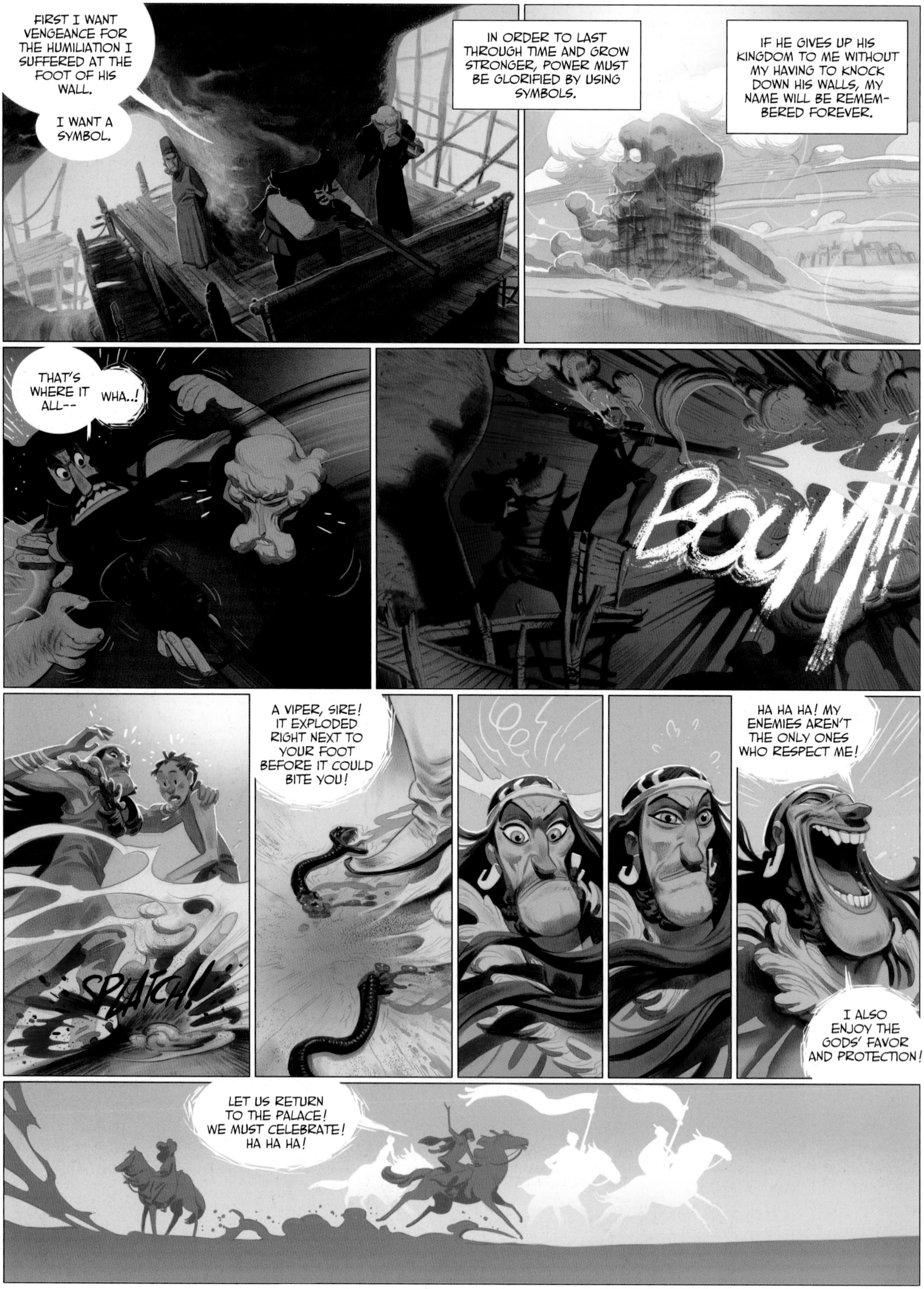

FIRST I WANT VENGEANCE FOR THE HUMILIATION I SUFFERED AT THE FOOT OF HIS WALL.
I WANT A SYMBOL.
IN ORDER TO LAST THROUGH TIME AND GROW STRONGER, POWER MUST BE GLORIFIED BY USING SYMBOLS.
IF HE GIVES UP HIS KINGDOM TO ME WITHOUT MY HAVING TO KNOCK DOWN HIS WALLS, MY NAME WILL BE REMEMBERED FOREVER.
THAT'S WHERE IT ALL--
WHA..!
BOOM!!
SPLATCH!!
A VIPER, SIRE! IT EXPLODED RIGHT NEXT TO YOUR FOOT BEFORE IT COULD BITE YOU!
HA HA HA! MY ENEMIES AREN'T THE ONLY ONES WHO RESPECT ME!
I ALSO ENJOY THE GODS' FAVOR AND PROTECTION!
LET US RETURN TO THE PALACE! WE MUST CELEBRATE! HA HA HA!

I HOPE THE GODS HAVE WORSE AIM NEXT TIME.

HA HA HA! WONDERFUL! WHAT EXTRAORDINARY PRECISION SHOOTING! BOOM! BOOM!

BOOM, AND A VIPER DIES! HA HA HA! BOOM! BOOM! LISTEN UP, BARASI!

YOUR MAJESTY?

WHEN EVERYTHING'S READY, I WANT TO BE KNOWN AS EMPEROR "BOOM." THAT WILL BE THE NAME OF THE SOVEREIGN OF THE SEVEN KINGDOMS. SEE TO IT FOR ME! BOOM! BOOM! HA HA HA!

IT SHALL BE AS YOU COMMAND, MY LORD.

BOOM! BOOOOM! HA HA HA!

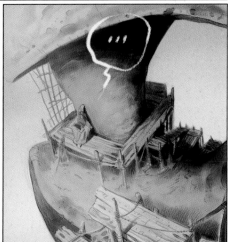

IS THERE NO ONE IN THIS KINGDOM READY TO STAND UP TO THAT IMBECILE?

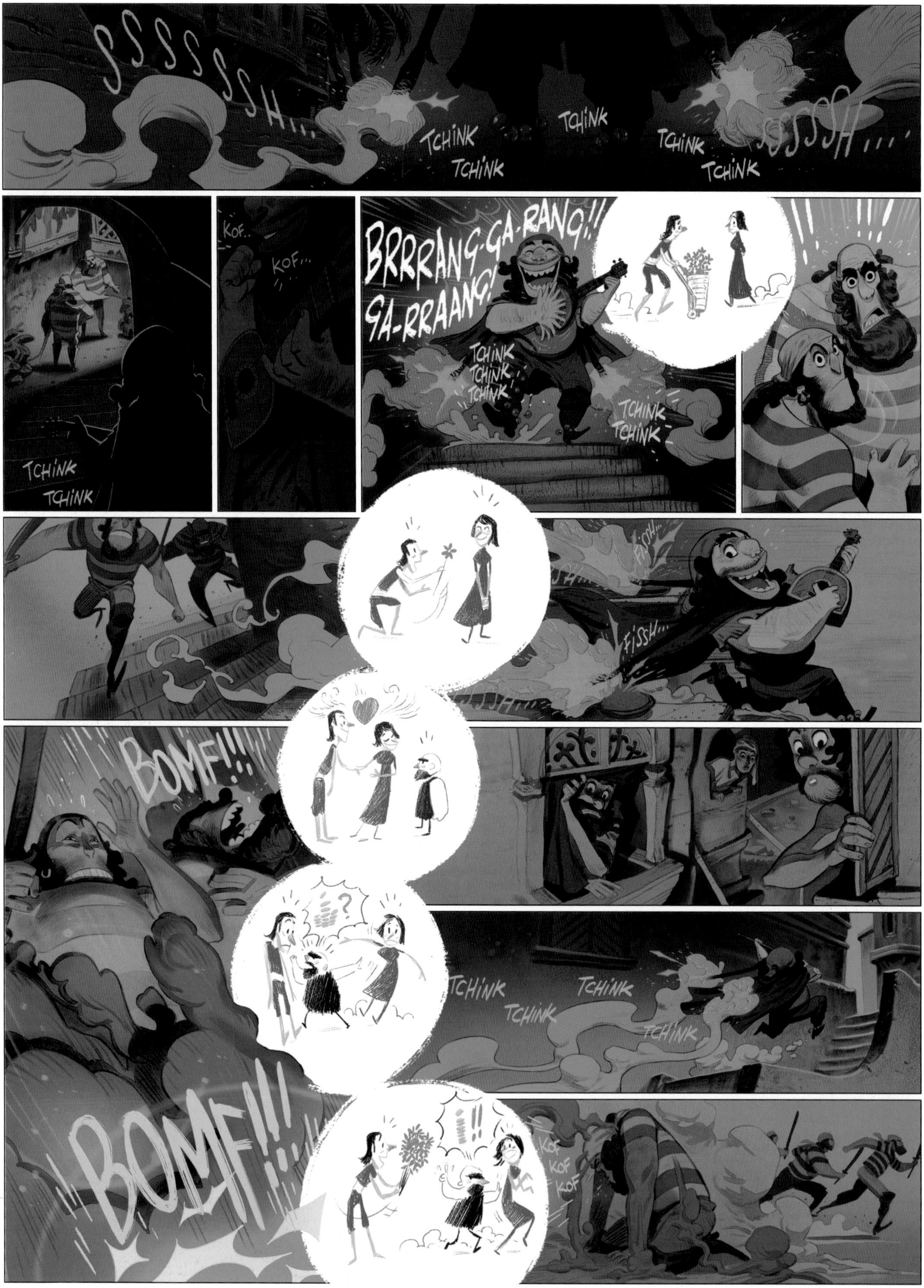
SSSSSSH...
TCHINK
TCHINK
TCHINK
TCHINK
TCHINK
SSSSSH....
TCHINK
TCHINK
KOF..
KOF...
BRRRANG-GA-RANG!!
GA-RRAANG!
TCHINK
TCHINK
TCHINK
TCHINK
TCHINK
FISSH...
FISSH...
BOMF!!!
TCHINK
TCHINK
TCHINK
TCHINK
BOMF!!!
KOF
KOF
KOF

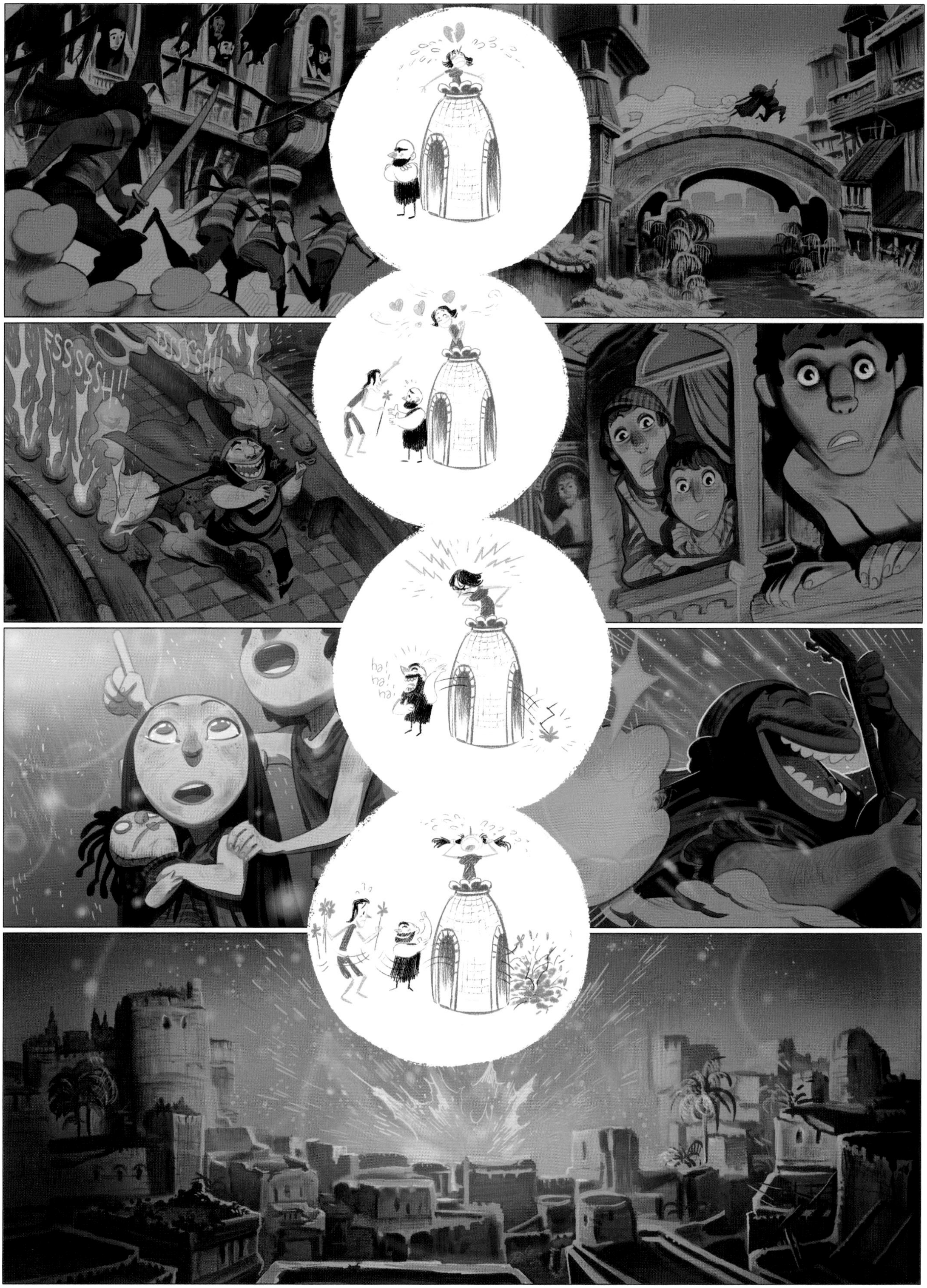
FSSSSSH!!
FSSSSH!!
ha!
ha!
ha!

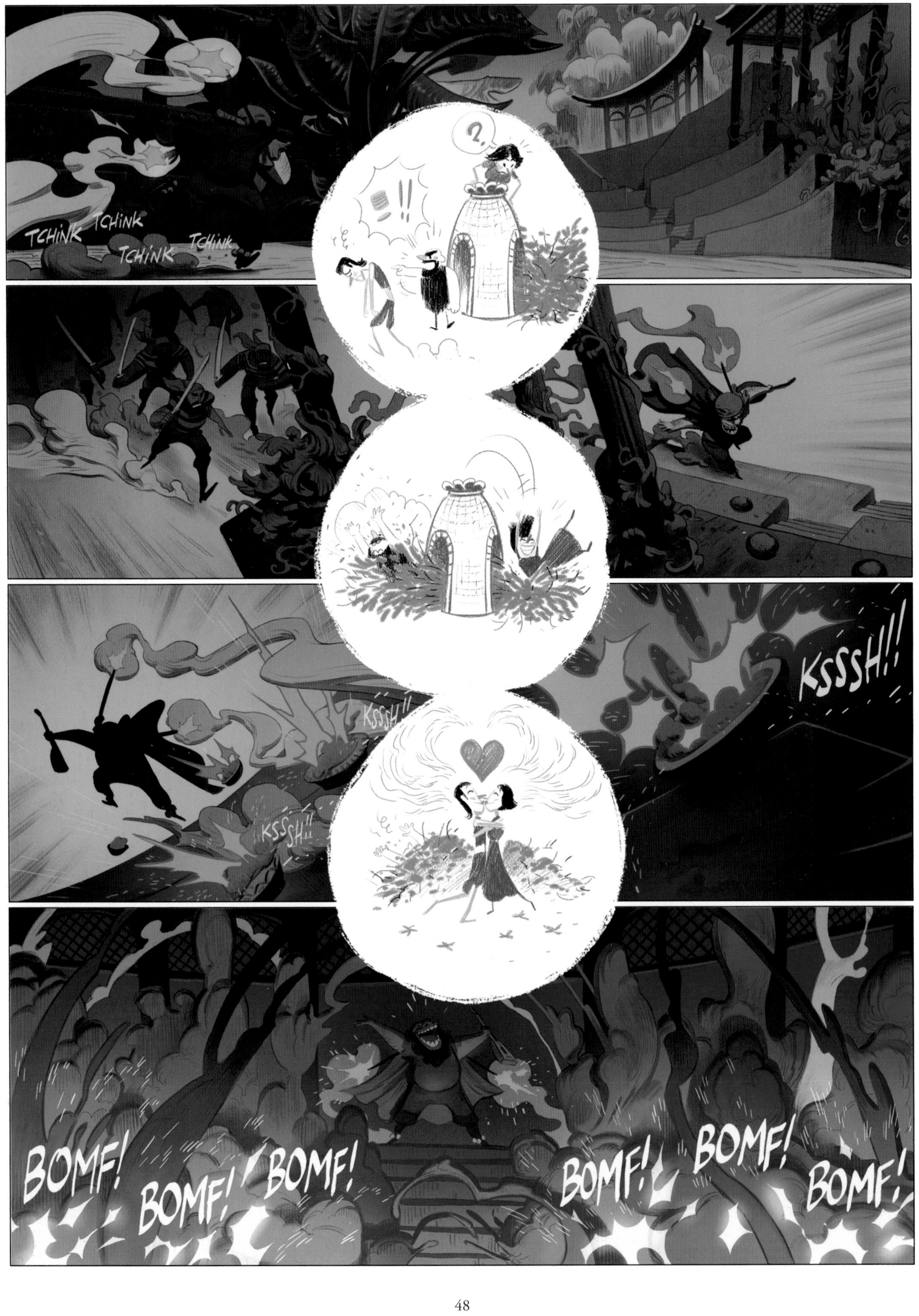
TCHINK
TCHINK
TCHINK
TCHINK
?
!!
KSSSH!!
KSSSH!!
KSSSH!!
BOMF!
BOMF!
BOMF!
BOMF!
BOMF!
BOMF!

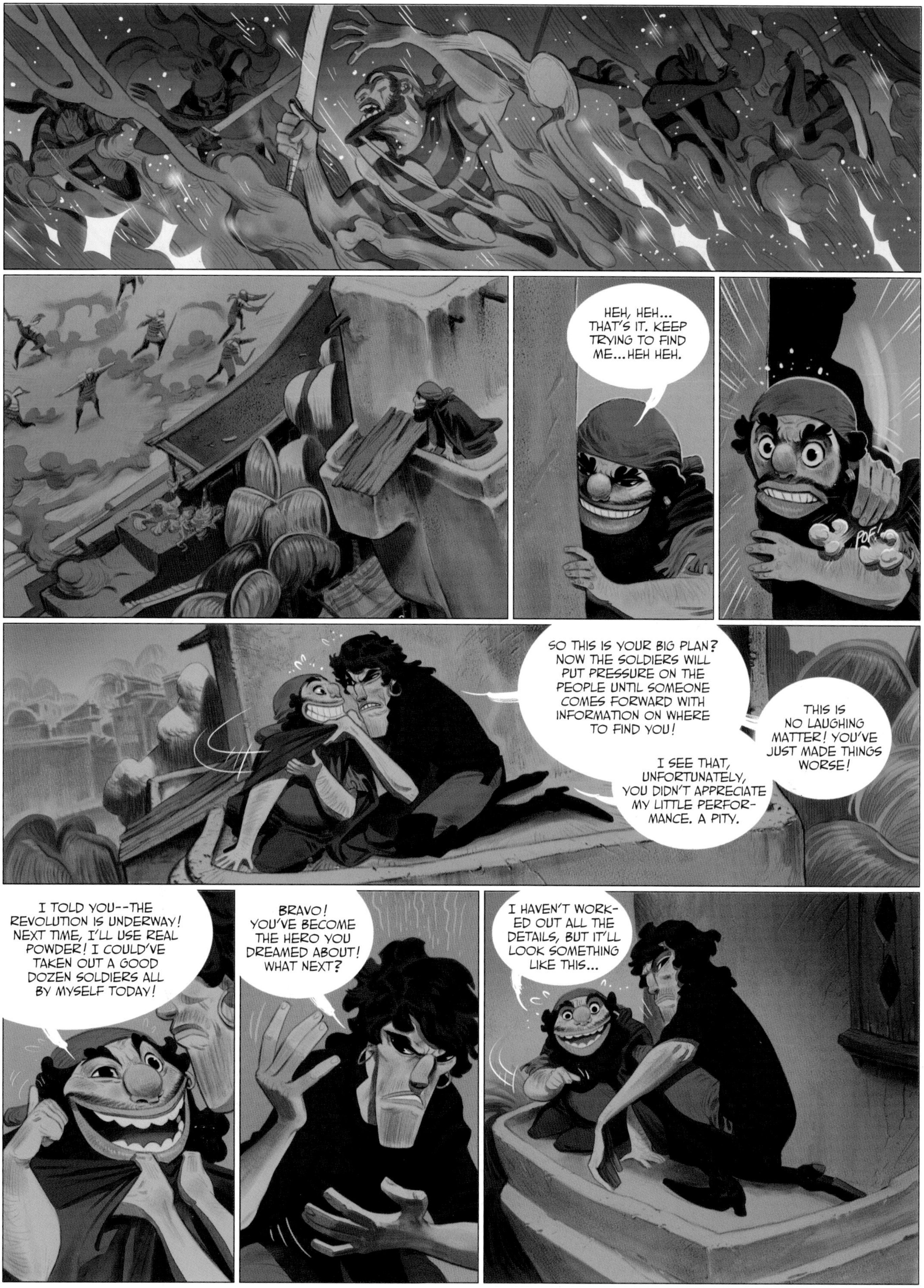
HEH, HEH... THAT'S IT. KEEP TRYING TO FIND ME...HEH HEH.
POF!
SO THIS IS YOUR BIG PLAN? NOW THE SOLDIERS WILL PUT PRESSURE ON THE PEOPLE UNTIL SOMEONE COMES FORWARD WITH INFORMATION ON WHERE TO FIND YOU!
I SEE THAT, UNFORTUNATELY, YOU DIDN'T APPRECIATE MY LITTLE PERFORMANCE. A PITY.
THIS IS NO LAUGHING MATTER! YOU'VE JUST MADE THINGS WORSE!
I TOLD YOU--THE REVOLUTION IS UNDERWAY! NEXT TIME, I'LL USE REAL POWDER! I COULD'VE TAKEN OUT A GOOD DOZEN SOLDIERS ALL BY MYSELF TODAY!
BRAVO! YOU'VE BECOME THE HERO YOU DREAMED ABOUT! WHAT NEXT?
I HAVEN'T WORKED OUT ALL THE DETAILS, BUT IT'LL LOOK SOMETHING LIKE THIS...

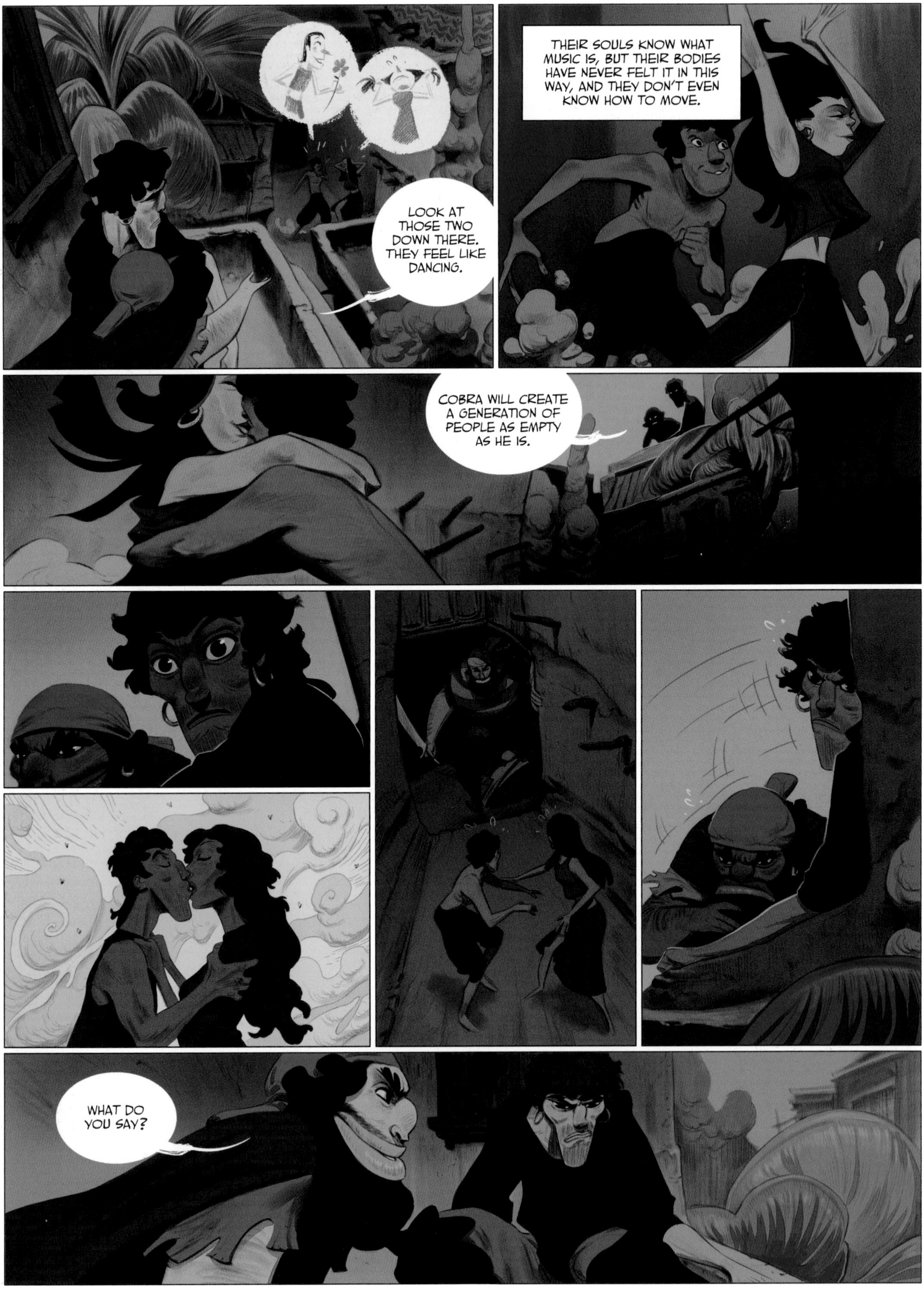
LOOK AT THOSE TWO DOWN THERE. THEY FEEL LIKE DANCING.
THEIR SOULS KNOW WHAT MUSIC IS, BUT THEIR BODIES HAVE NEVER FELT IT IN THIS WAY, AND THEY DON'T EVEN KNOW HOW TO MOVE.
COBRA WILL CREATE A GENERATION OF PEOPLE AS EMPTY AS HE IS.
WHAT DO YOU SAY?

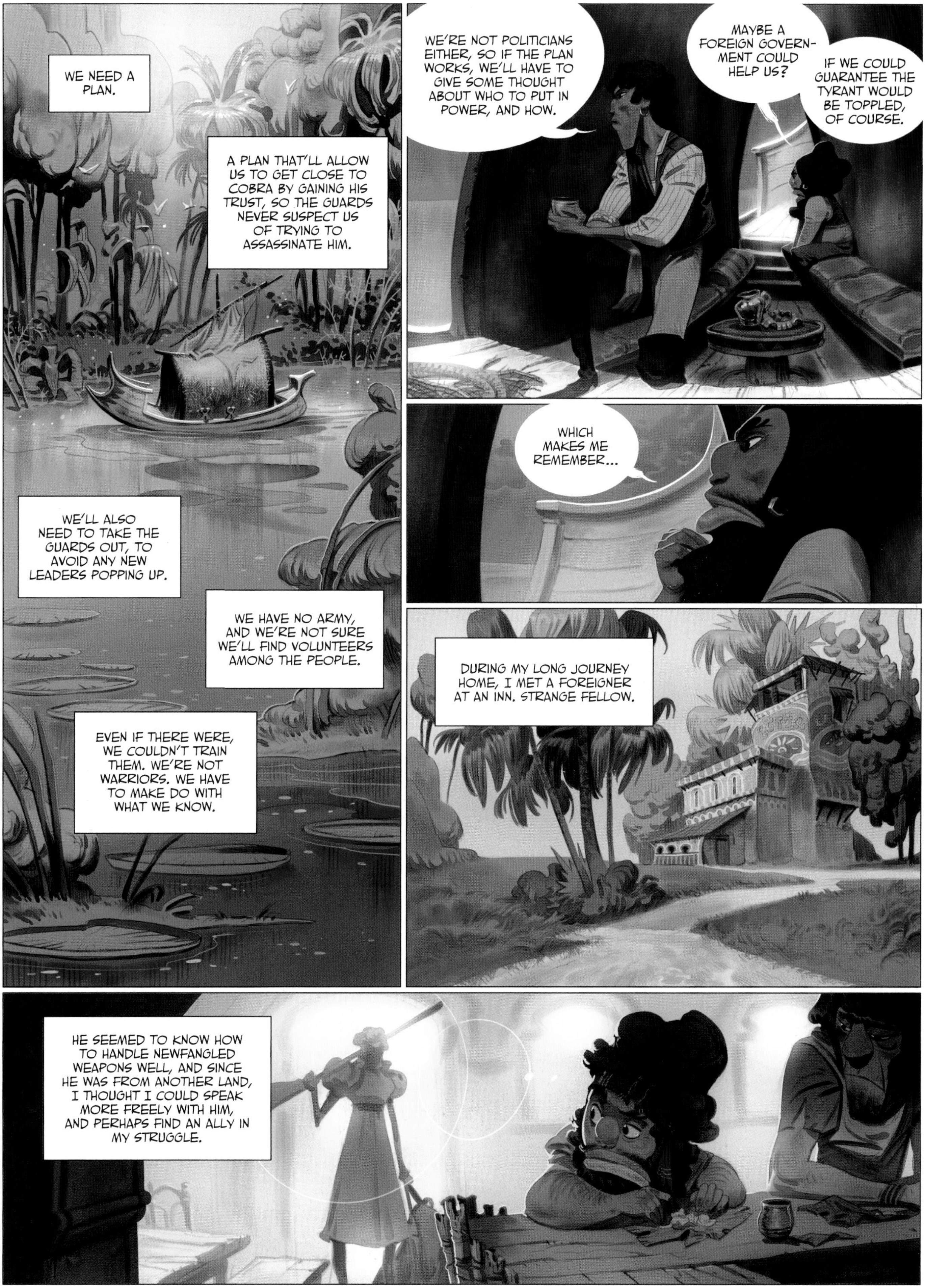
WE NEED A PLAN.
A PLAN THAT'LL ALLOW US TO GET CLOSE TO COBRA BY GAINING HIS TRUST, SO THE GUARDS NEVER SUSPECT US OF TRYING TO ASSASSINATE HIM.
WE'LL ALSO NEED TO TAKE THE GUARDS OUT, TO AVOID ANY NEW LEADERS POPPING UP.
WE HAVE NO ARMY, AND WE'RE NOT SURE WE'LL FIND VOLUNTEERS AMONG THE PEOPLE.
EVEN IF THERE WERE, WE COULDN'T TRAIN THEM. WE'RE NOT WARRIORS. WE HAVE TO MAKE DO WITH WHAT WE KNOW.
WE'RE NOT POLITICIANS EITHER, SO IF THE PLAN WORKS, WE'LL HAVE TO GIVE SOME THOUGHT ABOUT WHO TO PUT IN POWER, AND HOW.
MAYBE A FOREIGN GOVERNMENT COULD HELP US?
IF WE COULD GUARANTEE THE TYRANT WOULD BE TOPPLED, OF COURSE.
WHICH MAKES ME REMEMBER...
DURING MY LONG JOURNEY HOME, I MET A FOREIGNER AT AN INN. STRANGE FELLOW.
HE SEEMED TO KNOW HOW TO HANDLE NEWFANGLED WEAPONS WELL, AND SINCE HE WAS FROM ANOTHER LAND, I THOUGHT I COULD SPEAK MORE FREELY WITH HIM, AND PERHAPS FIND AN ALLY IN MY STRUGGLE.

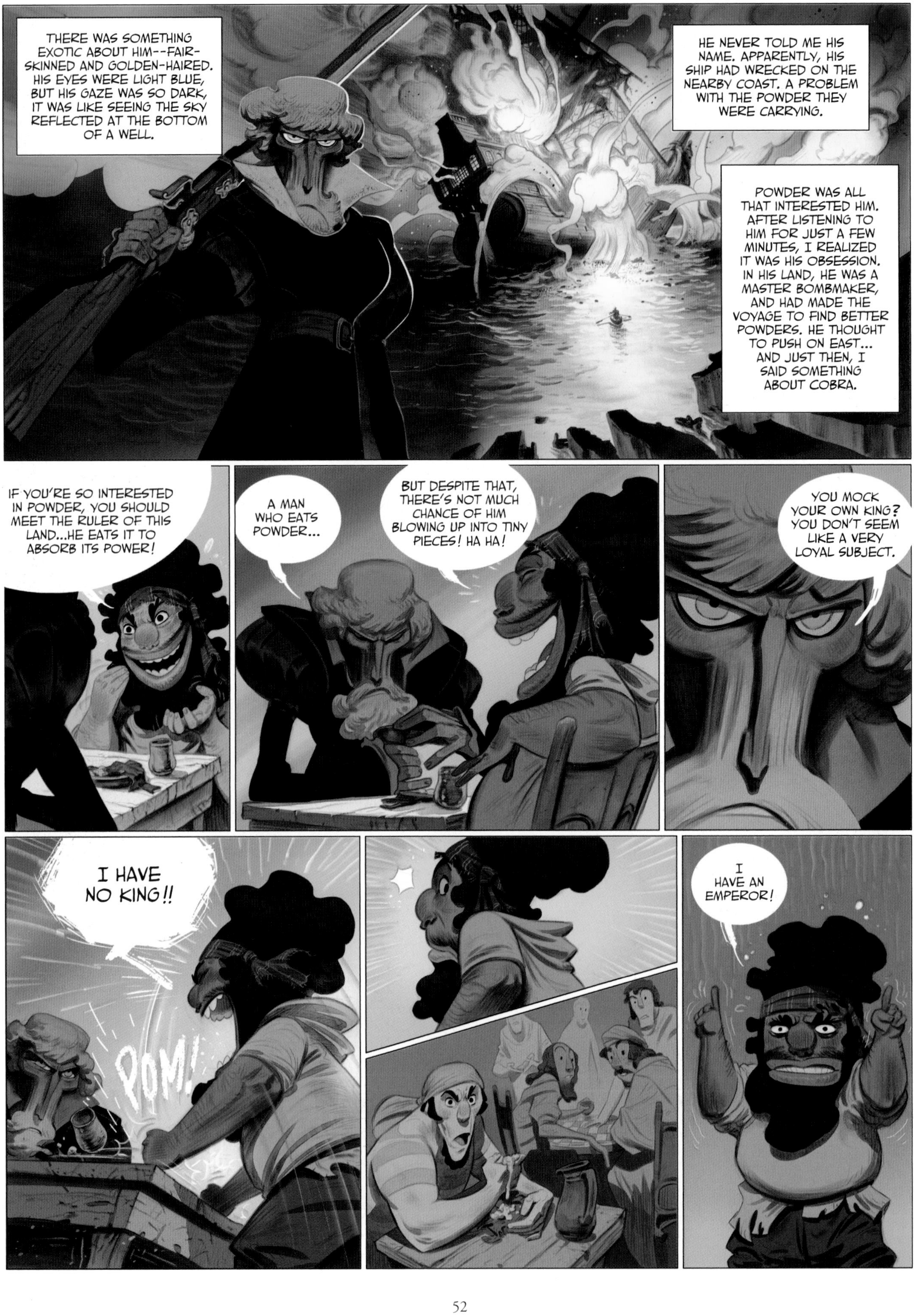
THERE WAS SOMETHING EXOTIC ABOUT HIM--FAIR-SKINNED AND GOLDEN-HAIRED. HIS EYES WERE LIGHT BLUE, BUT HIS GAZE WAS SO DARK, IT WAS LIKE SEEING THE SKY REFLECTED AT THE BOTTOM OF A WELL.
HE NEVER TOLD ME HIS NAME. APPARENTLY, HIS SHIP HAD WRECKED ON THE NEARBY COAST. A PROBLEM WITH THE POWDER THEY WERE CARRYING.
POWDER WAS ALL THAT INTERESTED HIM. AFTER LISTENING TO HIM FOR JUST A FEW MINUTES, I REALIZED IT WAS HIS OBSESSION. IN HIS LAND, HE WAS A MASTER BOMBMAKER, AND HAD MADE THE VOYAGE TO FIND BETTER POWDERS. HE THOUGHT TO PUSH ON EAST... AND JUST THEN, I SAID SOMETHING ABOUT COBRA.
IF YOU'RE SO INTERESTED IN POWDER, YOU SHOULD MEET THE RULER OF THIS LAND...HE EATS IT TO ABSORB ITS POWER!
A MAN WHO EATS POWDER...
BUT DESPITE THAT, THERE'S NOT MUCH CHANCE OF HIM BLOWING UP INTO TINY PIECES! HA HA!
YOU MOCK YOUR OWN KING? YOU DON'T SEEM LIKE A VERY LOYAL SUBJECT.
I HAVE NO KING!!
POM!
I HAVE AN EMPEROR!

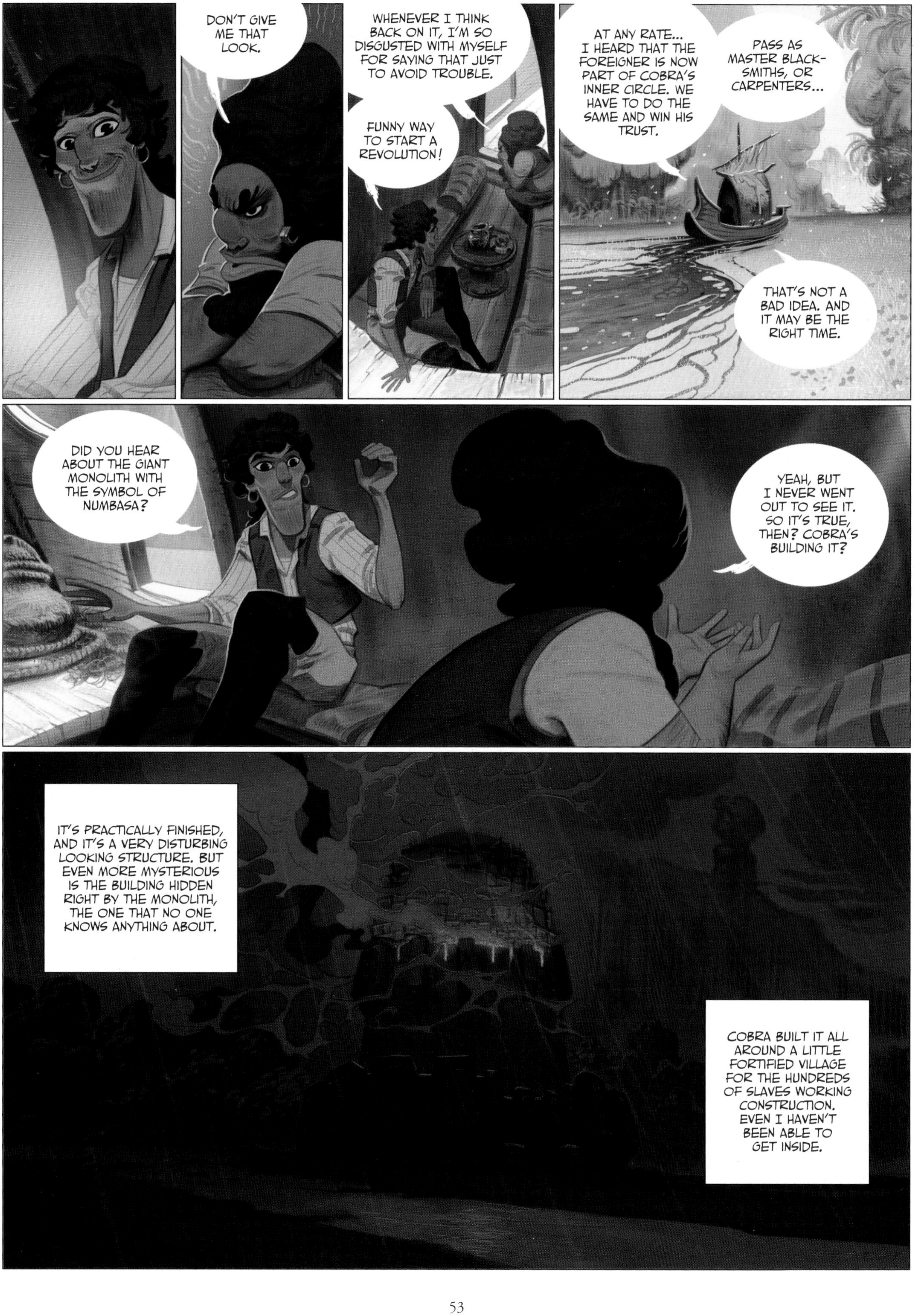
DON'T GIVE ME THAT LOOK.
WHENEVER I THINK BACK ON IT, I'M SO DISGUSTED WITH MYSELF FOR SAYING THAT JUST TO AVOID TROUBLE.
FUNNY WAY TO START A REVOLUTION!
AT ANY RATE... I HEARD THAT THE FOREIGNER IS NOW PART OF COBRA'S INNER CIRCLE. WE HAVE TO DO THE SAME AND WIN HIS TRUST.
PASS AS MASTER BLACK-SMITHS, OR CARPENTERS...
THAT'S NOT A BAD IDEA. AND IT MAY BE THE RIGHT TIME.
DID YOU HEAR ABOUT THE GIANT MONOLITH WITH THE SYMBOL OF NUMBASA?
YEAH, BUT I NEVER WENT OUT TO SEE IT. SO IT'S TRUE, THEN? COBRA'S BUILDING IT?
IT'S PRACTICALLY FINISHED, AND IT'S A VERY DISTURBING LOOKING STRUCTURE. BUT EVEN MORE MYSTERIOUS IS THE BUILDING HIDDEN RIGHT BY THE MONOLITH, THE ONE THAT NO ONE KNOWS ANYTHING ABOUT.
COBRA BUILT IT ALL AROUND A LITTLE FORTIFIED VILLAGE FOR THE HUNDREDS OF SLAVES WORKING CONSTRUCTION. EVEN I HAVEN'T BEEN ABLE TO GET INSIDE.

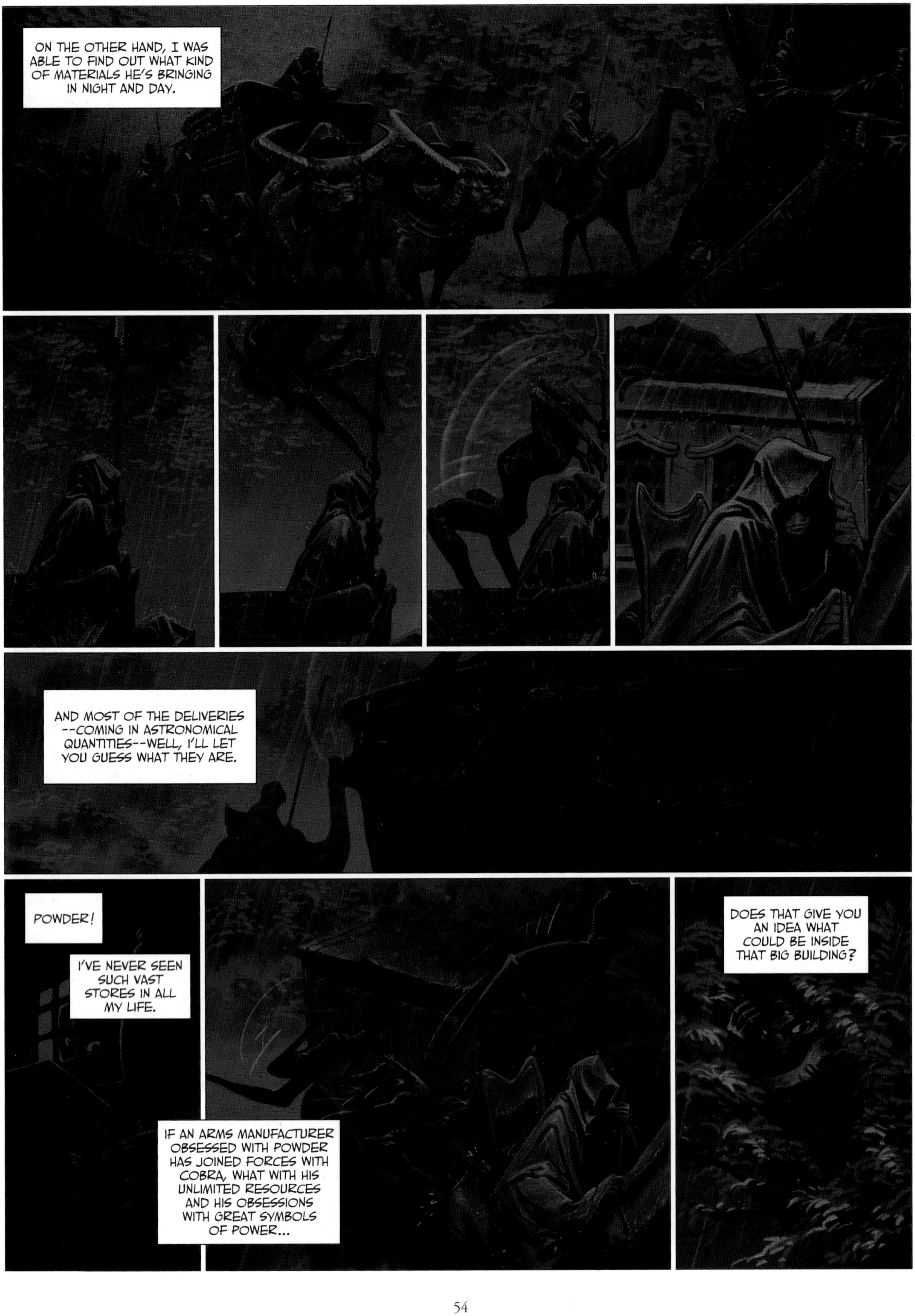
ON THE OTHER HAND, I WAS ABLE TO FIND OUT WHAT KIND OF MATERIALS HE'S BRINGING IN NIGHT AND DAY.
AND MOST OF THE DELIVERIES --COMING IN ASTRONOMICAL QUANTITIES--WELL, I'LL LET YOU GUESS WHAT THEY ARE.
POWDER!
I'VE NEVER SEEN SUCH VAST STORES IN ALL MY LIFE.
IF AN ARMS MANUFACTURER OBSESSED WITH POWDER HAS JOINED FORCES WITH COBRA, WHAT WITH HIS UNLIMITED RESOURCES AND HIS OBSESSIONS WITH GREAT SYMBOLS OF POWER...
DOES THAT GIVE YOU AN IDEA WHAT COULD BE INSIDE THAT BIG BUILDING?

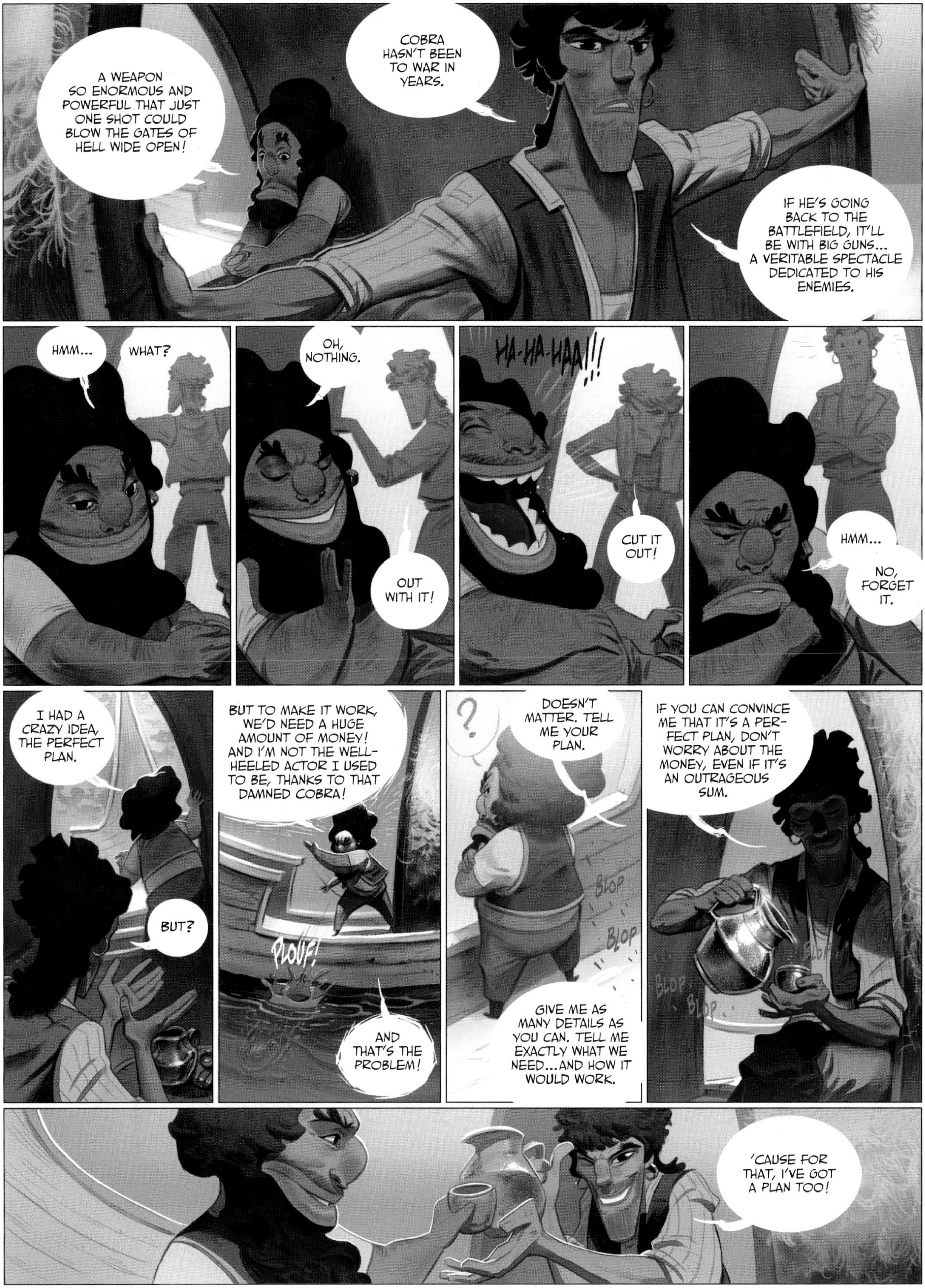
A WEAPON SO ENORMOUS AND POWERFUL THAT JUST ONE SHOT COULD BLOW THE GATES OF HELL WIDE OPEN!
COBRA HASN'T BEEN TO WAR IN YEARS.
IF HE'S GOING BACK TO THE BATTLEFIELD, IT'LL BE WITH BIG GUNS... A VERITABLE SPECTACLE DEDICATED TO HIS ENEMIES.
HMM...
WHAT?
OH, NOTHING.
OUT WITH IT!
HA-HA-HAA!!!
CUT IT OUT!
HMM...
NO, FORGET IT.
I HAD A CRAZY IDEA, THE PERFECT PLAN.
BUT?
BUT TO MAKE IT WORK, WE'D NEED A HUGE AMOUNT OF MONEY! AND I'M NOT THE WELL-HEELED ACTOR I USED TO BE, THANKS TO THAT DAMNED COBRA!
PLOUF!
AND THAT'S THE PROBLEM!
?
DOESN'T MATTER. TELL ME YOUR PLAN.
BLOP
BLOP
GIVE ME AS MANY DETAILS AS YOU CAN. TELL ME EXACTLY WHAT WE NEED...AND HOW IT WOULD WORK.
IF YOU CAN CONVINCE ME THAT IT'S A PERFECT PLAN, DON'T WORRY ABOUT THE MONEY, EVEN IF IT'S AN OUTRAGEOUS SUM.
BLOP
BLOP
BLOP
'CAUSE FOR THAT, I'VE GOT A PLAN TOO!

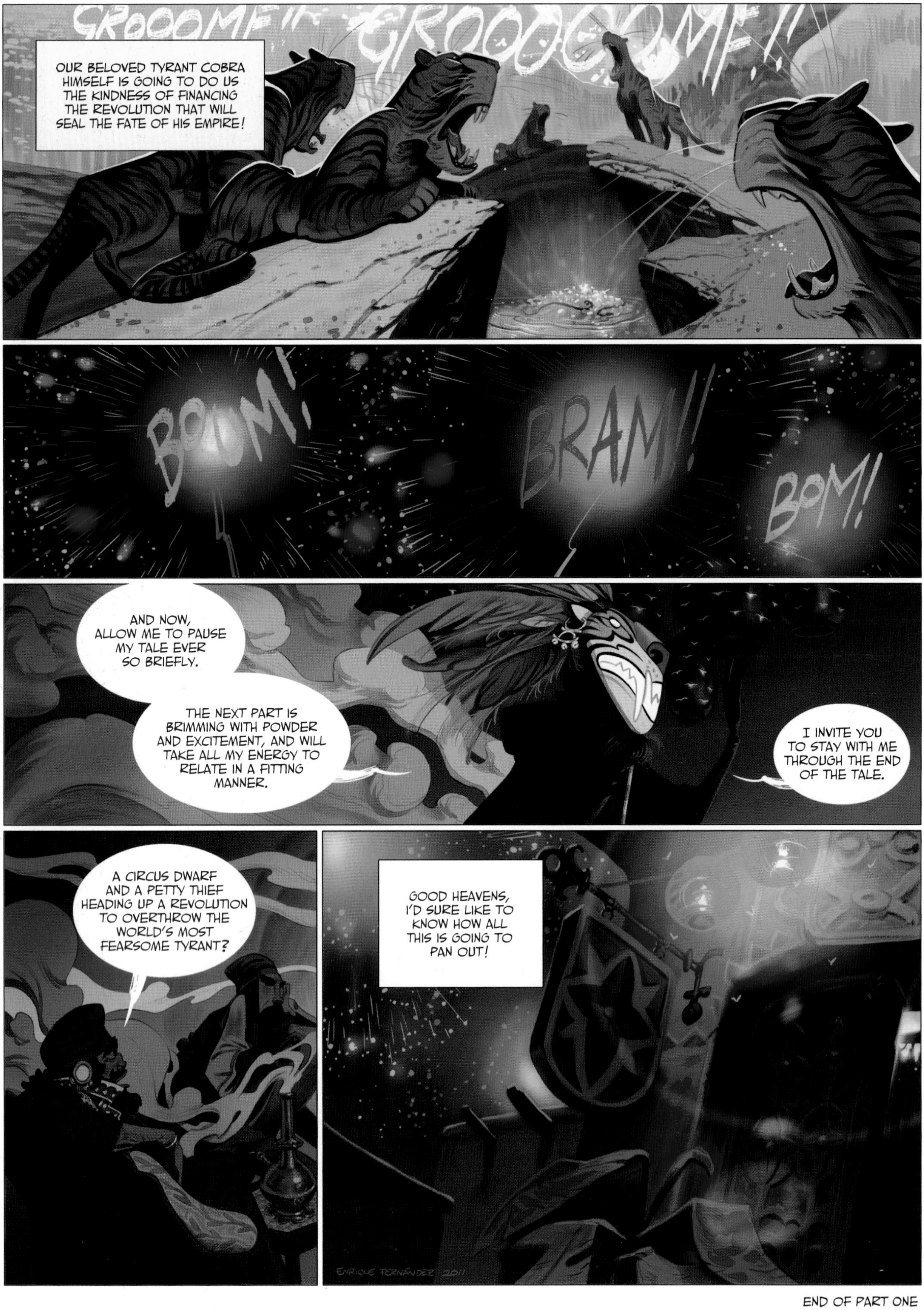
GROOOMF!!
GROOOOOMF!!
OUR BELOVED TYRANT COBRA HIMSELF IS GOING TO DO US THE KINDNESS OF FINANCING THE REVOLUTION THAT WILL SEAL THE FATE OF HIS EMPIRE!
BOOM!
BRAM!
BOM!
AND NOW, ALLOW ME TO PAUSE MY TALE EVER SO BRIEFLY.
THE NEXT PART IS BRIMMING WITH POWDER AND EXCITEMENT, AND WILL TAKE ALL MY ENERGY TO RELATE IN A FITTING MANNER.
I INVITE YOU TO STAY WITH ME THROUGH THE END OF THE TALE.
A CIRCUS DWARF AND A PETTY THIEF HEADING UP A REVOLUTION TO OVERTHROW THE WORLD'S MOST FEARSOME TYRANT?
GOOD HEAVENS, I'D SURE LIKE TO KNOW HOW ALL THIS IS GOING TO PAN OUT!
ENRIQUE FERNÁNDEZ 2011

END OF PART ONE

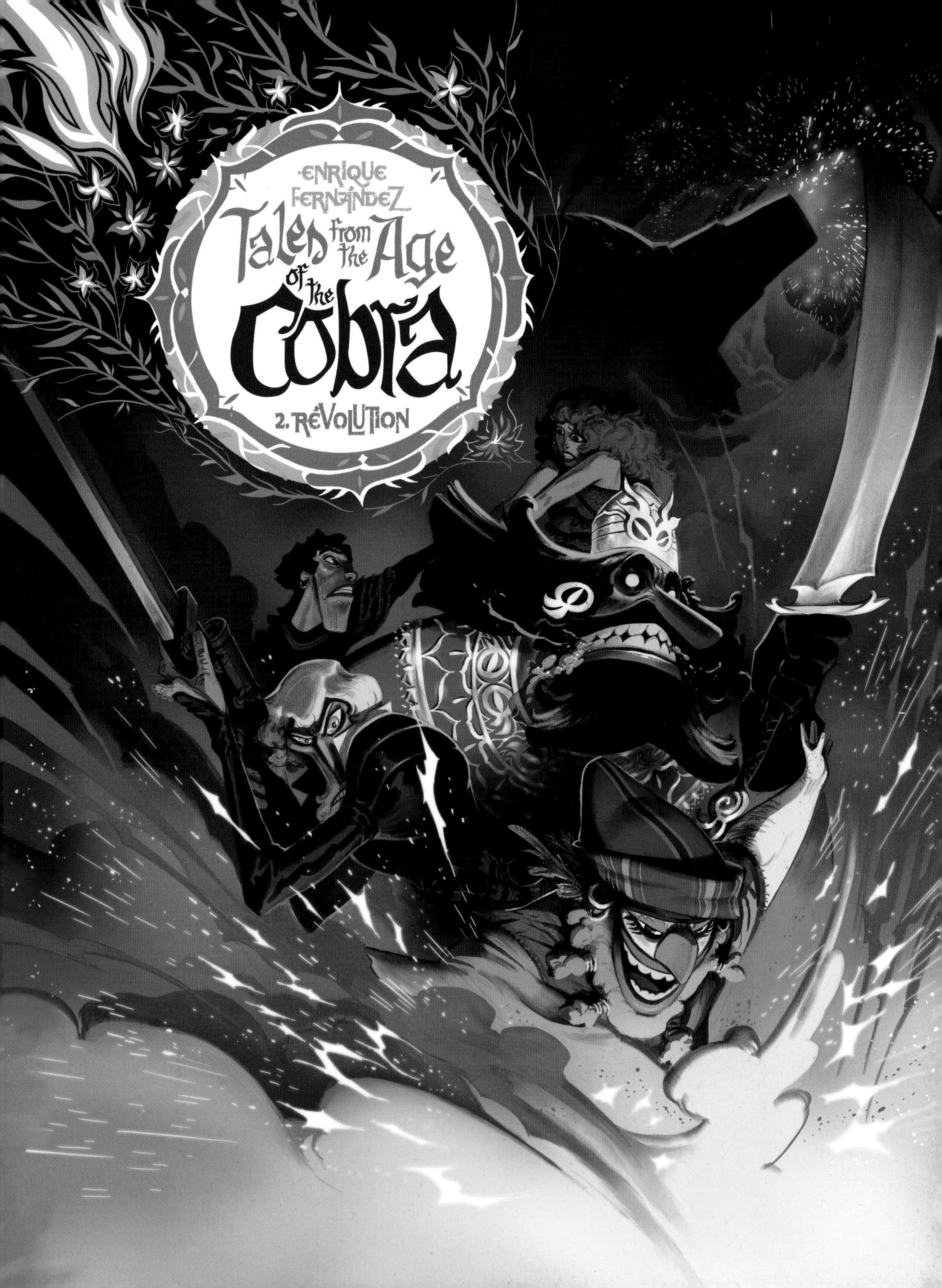
ENRIQUE
FERNÁNDEZ
Tales from the Age of the Cobra
2. RÉVOLUTION

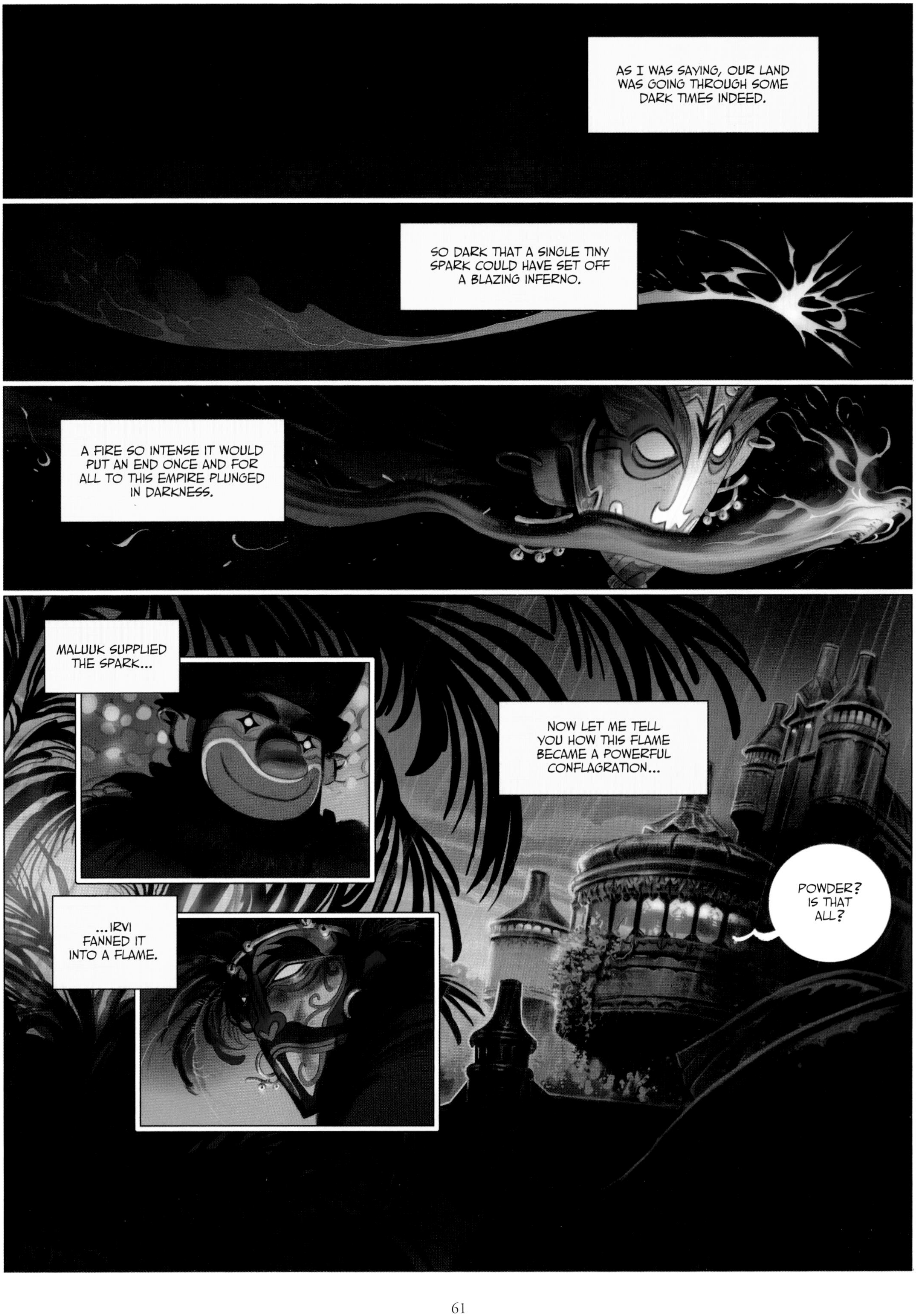
AS I WAS SAYING, OUR LAND WAS GOING THROUGH SOME DARK TIMES INDEED.
SO DARK THAT A SINGLE TINY SPARK COULD HAVE SET OFF A BLAZING INFERNO.
A FIRE SO INTENSE IT WOULD PUT AN END ONCE AND FOR ALL TO THIS EMPIRE PLUNGED IN DARKNESS.
MALUUK SUPPLIED THE SPARK...
...IRVI FANNED IT INTO A FLAME.
NOW LET ME TELL YOU HOW THIS FLAME BECAME A POWERFUL CONFLAGRATION...
POWDER? IS THAT ALL?

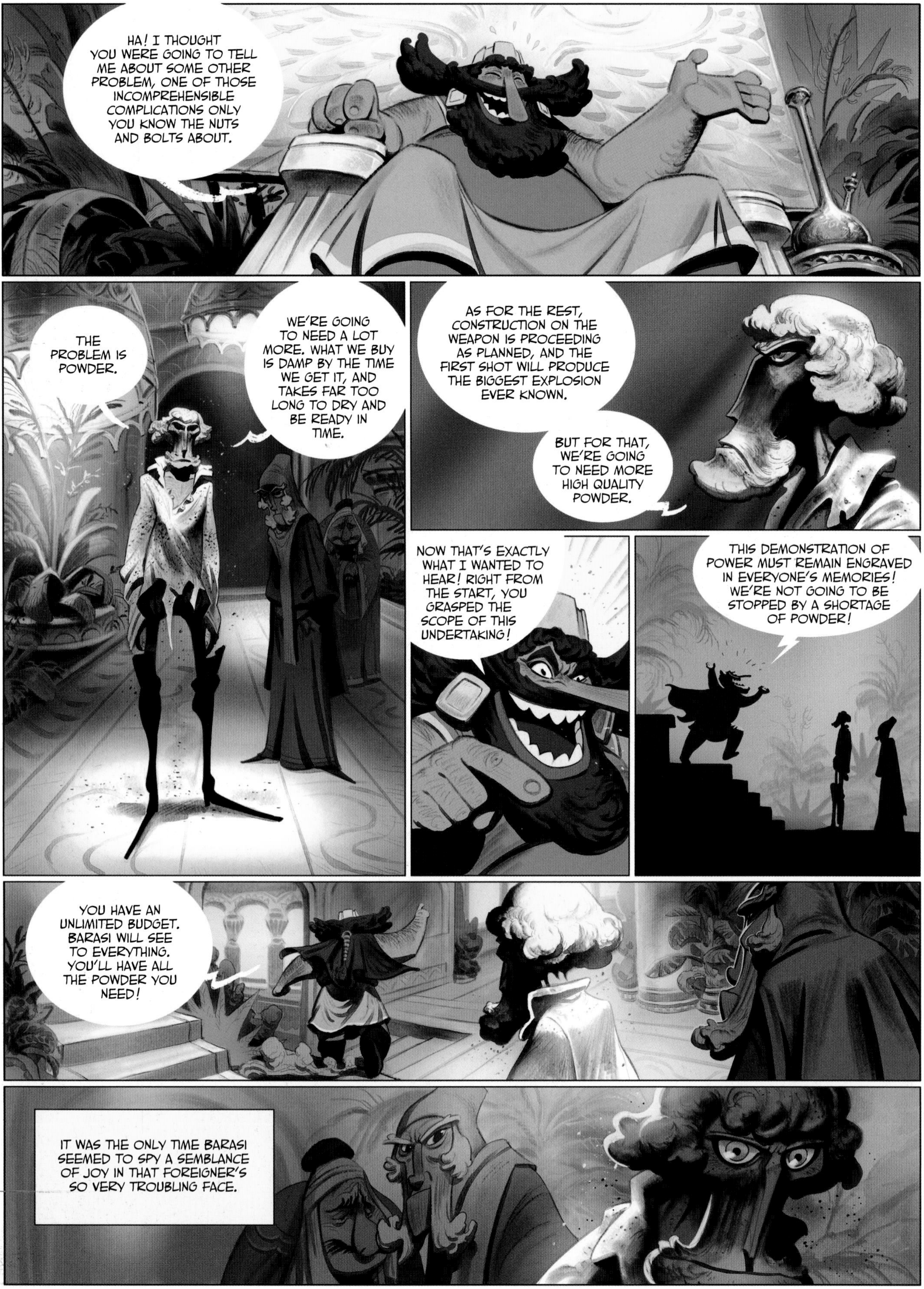
HA! I THOUGHT YOU WERE GOING TO TELL ME ABOUT SOME OTHER PROBLEM, ONE OF THOSE INCOMPREHENSIBLE COMPLICATIONS ONLY YOU KNOW THE NUTS AND BOLTS ABOUT.
THE PROBLEM IS POWDER.
WE'RE GOING TO NEED A LOT MORE. WHAT WE BUY IS DAMP BY THE TIME WE GET IT, AND TAKES FAR TOO LONG TO DRY AND BE READY IN TIME.
AS FOR THE REST, CONSTRUCTION ON THE WEAPON IS PROCEEDING AS PLANNED, AND THE FIRST SHOT WILL PRODUCE THE BIGGEST EXPLOSION EVER KNOWN.
BUT FOR THAT, WE'RE GOING TO NEED MORE HIGH QUALITY POWDER.
NOW THAT'S EXACTLY WHAT I WANTED TO HEAR! RIGHT FROM THE START, YOU GRASPED THE SCOPE OF THIS UNDERTAKING!
THIS DEMONSTRATION OF POWER MUST REMAIN ENGRAVED IN EVERYONE'S MEMORIES! WE'RE NOT GOING TO BE STOPPED BY A SHORTAGE OF POWDER!
YOU HAVE AN UNLIMITED BUDGET. BARASI WILL SEE TO EVERYTHING. YOU'LL HAVE ALL THE POWDER YOU NEED!
IT WAS THE ONLY TIME BARASI SEEMED TO SPY A SEMBLANCE OF JOY IN THAT FOREIGNER'S SO VERY TROUBLING FACE.

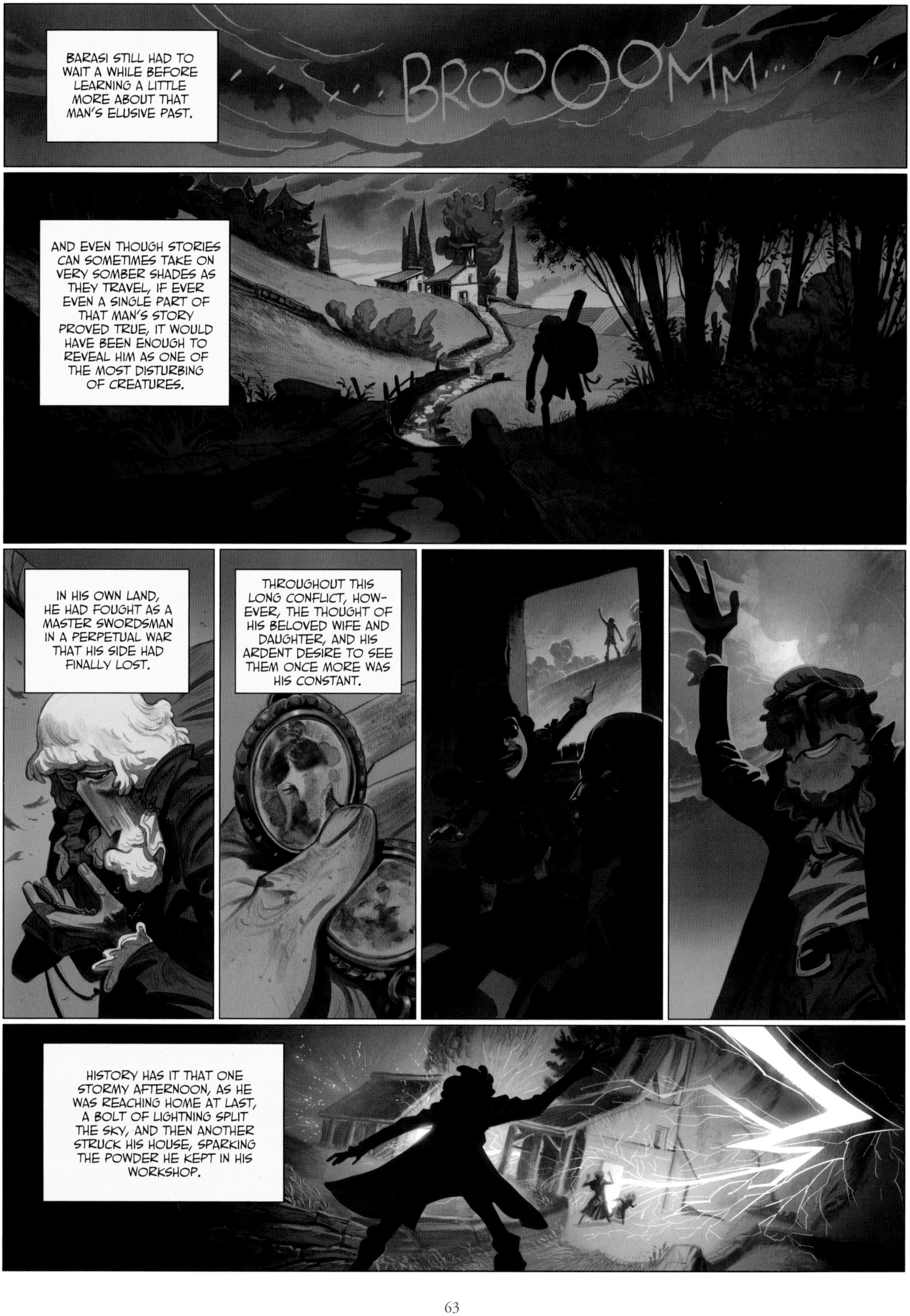

BARASI STILL HAD TO WAIT A WHILE BEFORE LEARNING A LITTLE MORE ABOUT THAT MAN'S ELUSIVE PAST.
BROOOOMM...
AND EVEN THOUGH STORIES CAN SOMETIMES TAKE ON VERY SOMBER SHADES AS THEY TRAVEL, IF EVER EVEN A SINGLE PART OF THAT MAN'S STORY PROVED TRUE, IT WOULD HAVE BEEN ENOUGH TO REVEAL HIM AS ONE OF THE MOST DISTURBING OF CREATURES.
IN HIS OWN LAND, HE HAD FOUGHT AS A MASTER SWORDSMAN IN A PERPETUAL WAR THAT HIS SIDE HAD FINALLY LOST.
THROUGHOUT THIS LONG CONFLICT, HOW-EVER, THE THOUGHT OF HIS BELOVED WIFE AND DAUGHTER, AND HIS ARDENT DESIRE TO SEE THEM ONCE MORE WAS HIS CONSTANT.
HISTORY HAS IT THAT ONE STORMY AFTERNOON, AS HE WAS REACHING HOME AT LAST, A BOLT OF LIGHTNING SPLIT THE SKY, AND THEN ANOTHER STRUCK HIS HOUSE, SPARKING THE POWDER HE KEPT IN HIS WORKSHOP.

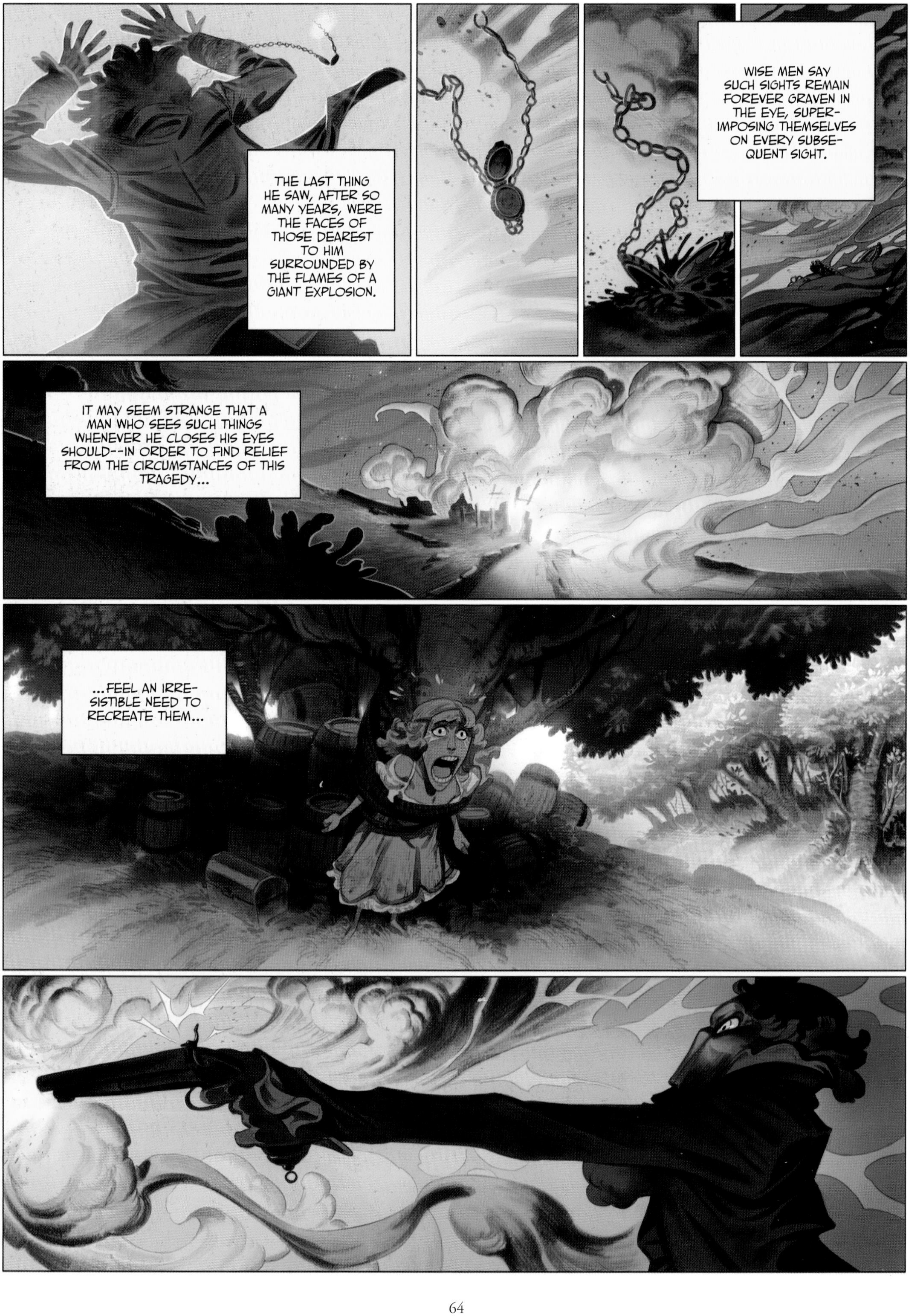
THE LAST THING HE SAW, AFTER SO MANY YEARS, WERE THE FACES OF THOSE DEAREST TO HIM SURROUNDED BY THE FLAMES OF A GIANT EXPLOSION.
WISE MEN SAY SUCH SIGHTS REMAIN FOREVER GRAVEN IN THE EYE, SUPER-IMPOSING THEMSELVES ON EVERY SUBSE-QUENT SIGHT.
IT MAY SEEM STRANGE THAT A MAN WHO SEES SUCH THINGS WHENEVER HE CLOSES HIS EYES SHOULD--IN ORDER TO FIND RELIEF FROM THE CIRCUMSTANCES OF THIS TRAGEDY...
...FEEL AN IRRE-SISTIBLE NEED TO RECREATE THEM...

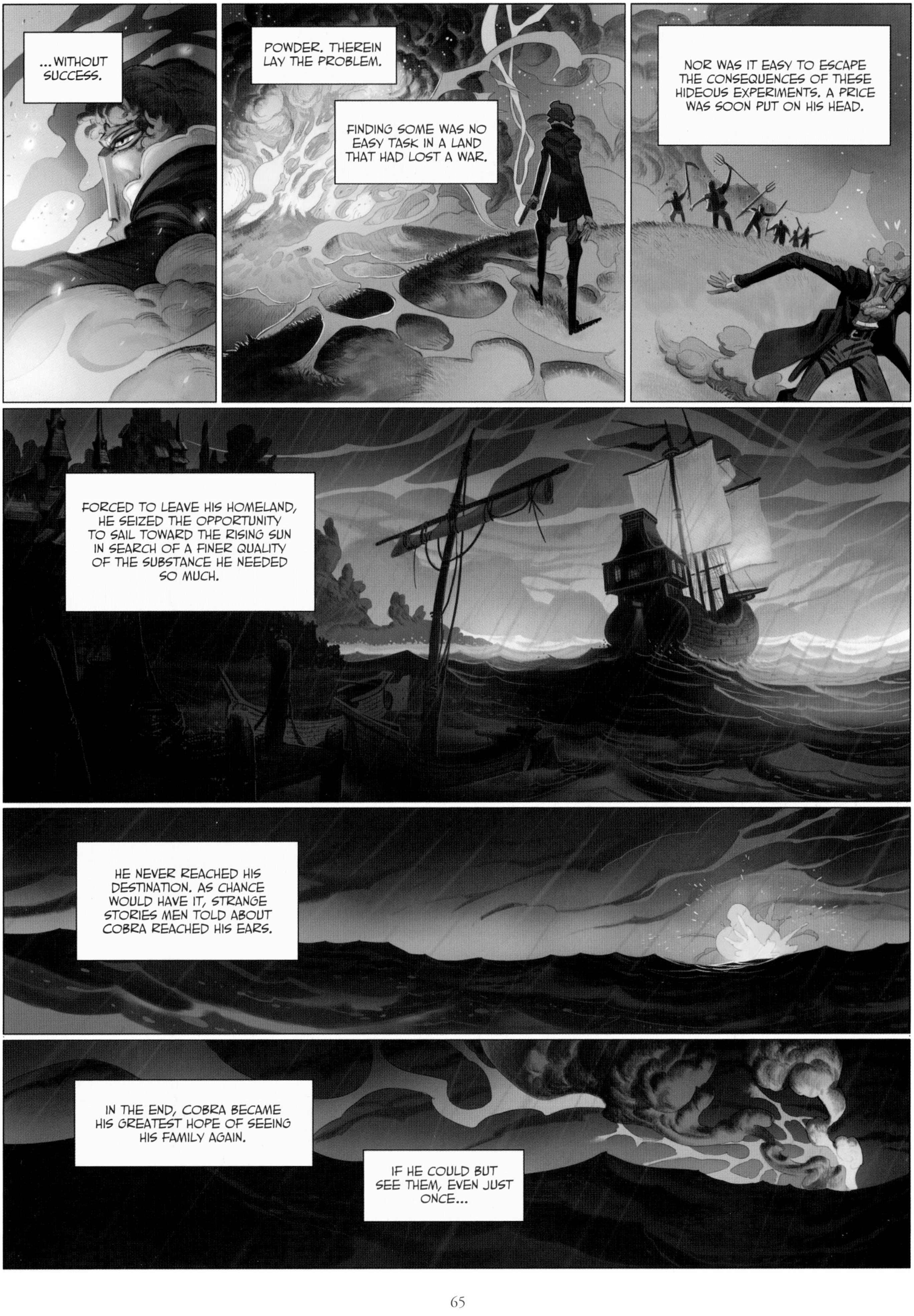

...WITHOUT SUCCESS.
POWDER. THEREIN LAY THE PROBLEM.
FINDING SOME WAS NO EASY TASK IN A LAND THAT HAD LOST A WAR.
NOR WAS IT EASY TO ESCAPE THE CONSEQUENCES OF THESE HIDEOUS EXPERIMENTS. A PRICE WAS SOON PUT ON HIS HEAD.
FORCED TO LEAVE HIS HOMELAND, HE SEIZED THE OPPORTUNITY TO SAIL TOWARD THE RISING SUN IN SEARCH OF A FINER QUALITY OF THE SUBSTANCE HE NEEDED SO MUCH.
HE NEVER REACHED HIS DESTINATION. AS CHANCE WOULD HAVE IT, STRANGE STORIES MEN TOLD ABOUT COBRA REACHED HIS EARS.
IN THE END, COBRA BECAME HIS GREATEST HOPE OF SEEING HIS FAMILY AGAIN.
IF HE COULD BUT SEE THEM, EVEN JUST ONCE...

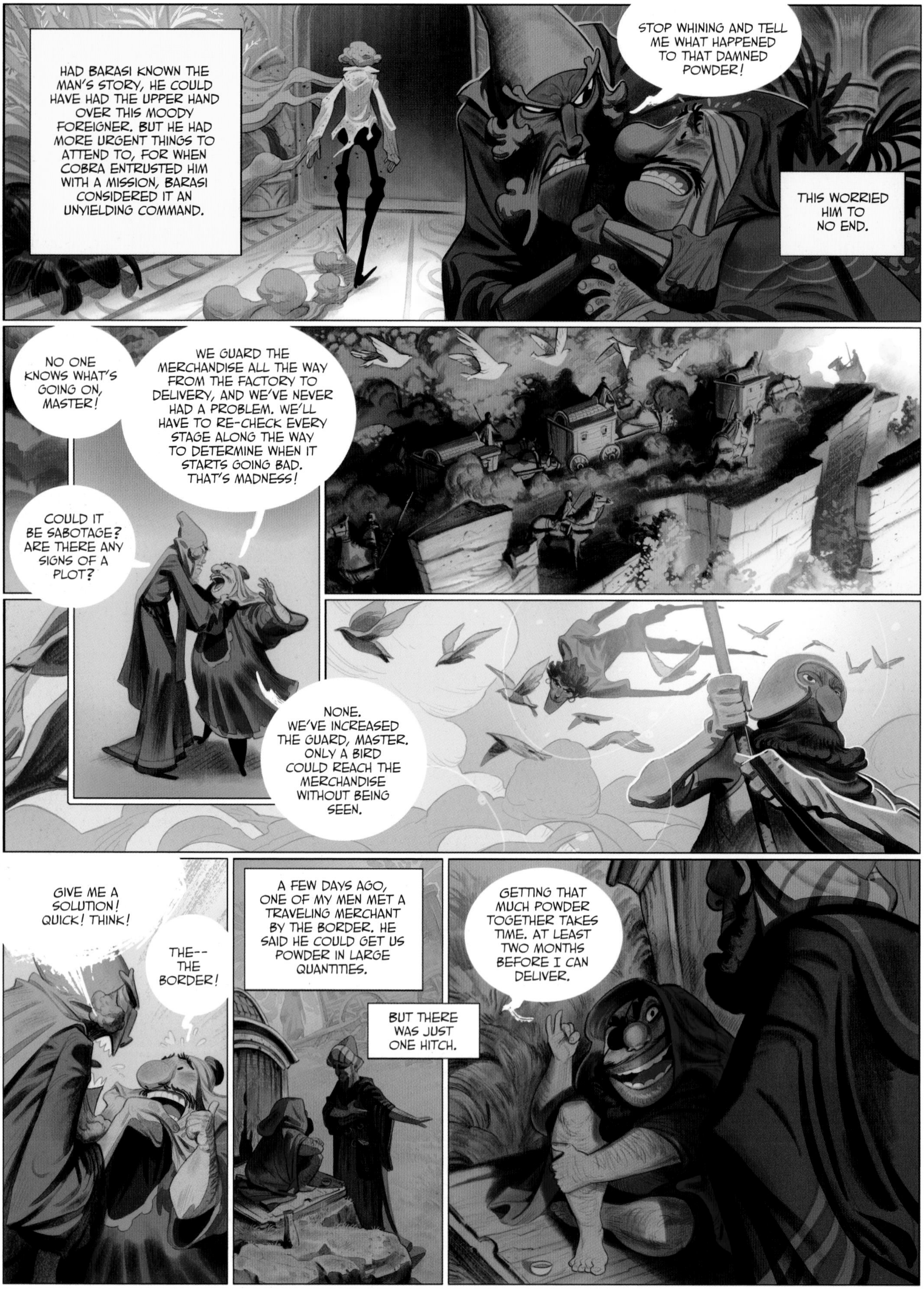
HAD BARASI KNOWN THE MAN'S STORY, HE COULD HAVE HAD THE UPPER HAND OVER THIS MOODY FOREIGNER. BUT HE HAD MORE URGENT THINGS TO ATTEND TO, FOR WHEN COBRA ENTRUSTED HIM WITH A MISSION, BARASI CONSIDERED IT AN UNYIELDING COMMAND.
STOP WHINING AND TELL ME WHAT HAPPENED TO THAT DAMNED POWDER!
THIS WORRIED HIM TO NO END.
NO ONE KNOWS WHAT'S GOING ON, MASTER!
WE GUARD THE MERCHANDISE ALL THE WAY FROM THE FACTORY TO DELIVERY, AND WE'VE NEVER HAD A PROBLEM. WE'LL HAVE TO RE-CHECK EVERY STAGE ALONG THE WAY TO DETERMINE WHEN IT STARTS GOING BAD. THAT'S MADNESS!
COULD IT BE SABOTAGE? ARE THERE ANY SIGNS OF A PLOT?
NONE. WE'VE INCREASED THE GUARD, MASTER. ONLY A BIRD COULD REACH THE MERCHANDISE WITHOUT BEING SEEN.
GIVE ME A SOLUTION! QUICK! THINK!
THE-- THE BORDER!
A FEW DAYS AGO, ONE OF MY MEN MET A TRAVELING MERCHANT BY THE BORDER. HE SAID HE COULD GET US POWDER IN LARGE QUANTITIES.
BUT THERE WAS JUST ONE HITCH.
GETTING THAT MUCH POWDER TOGETHER TAKES TIME. AT LEAST TWO MONTHS BEFORE I CAN DELIVER.

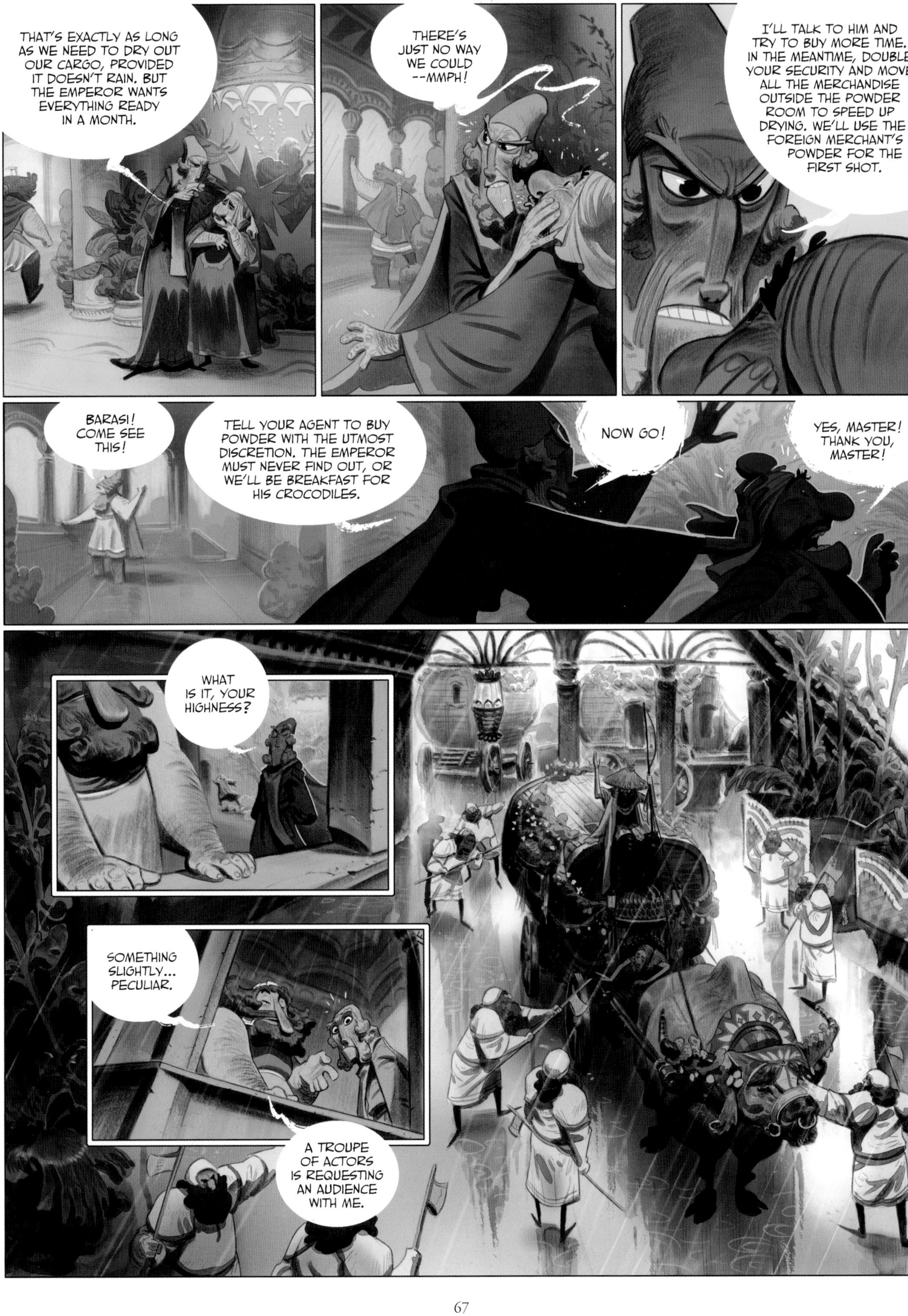

THAT'S EXACTLY AS LONG AS WE NEED TO DRY OUT OUR CARGO, PROVIDED IT DOESN'T RAIN. BUT THE EMPEROR WANTS EVERYTHING READY IN A MONTH.
THERE'S JUST NO WAY WE COULD --MMPH!
I'LL TALK TO HIM AND TRY TO BUY MORE TIME. IN THE MEANTIME, DOUBLE YOUR SECURITY AND MOVE ALL THE MERCHANDISE OUTSIDE THE POWDER ROOM TO SPEED UP DRYING. WE'LL USE THE FOREIGN MERCHANT'S POWDER FOR THE FIRST SHOT.
BARASI! COME SEE THIS!
TELL YOUR AGENT TO BUY POWDER WITH THE UTMOST DISCRETION. THE EMPEROR MUST NEVER FIND OUT, OR WE'LL BE BREAKFAST FOR HIS CROCODILES.
NOW GO!
YES, MASTER! THANK YOU, MASTER!
WHAT IS IT, YOUR HIGHNESS?
SOMETHING SLIGHTLY... PECULIAR.
A TROUPE OF ACTORS IS REQUESTING AN AUDIENCE WITH ME.

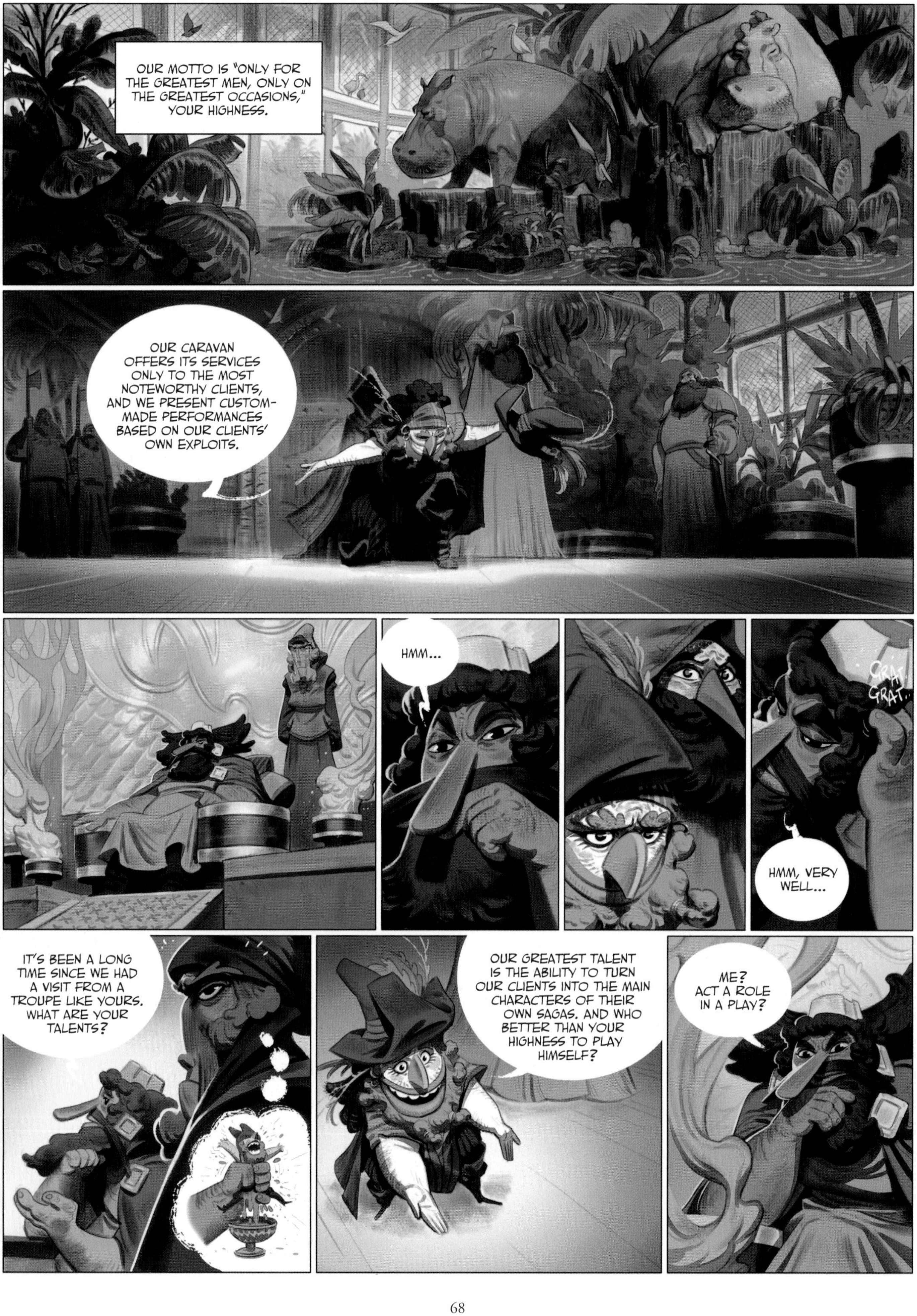
OUR MOTTO IS "ONLY FOR THE GREATEST MEN, ONLY ON THE GREATEST OCCASIONS," YOUR HIGHNESS.
OUR CARAVAN OFFERS ITS SERVICES ONLY TO THE MOST NOTEWORTHY CLIENTS, AND WE PRESENT CUSTOM-MADE PERFORMANCES BASED ON OUR CLIENTS' OWN EXPLOITS.
HMM...
GRAT GRAT...
HMM, VERY WELL...
IT'S BEEN A LONG TIME SINCE WE HAD A VISIT FROM A TROUPE LIKE YOURS. WHAT ARE YOUR TALENTS?
OUR GREATEST TALENT IS THE ABILITY TO TURN OUR CLIENTS INTO THE MAIN CHARACTERS OF THEIR OWN SAGAS. AND WHO BETTER THAN YOUR HIGHNESS TO PLAY HIMSELF?
ME? ACT A ROLE IN A PLAY?

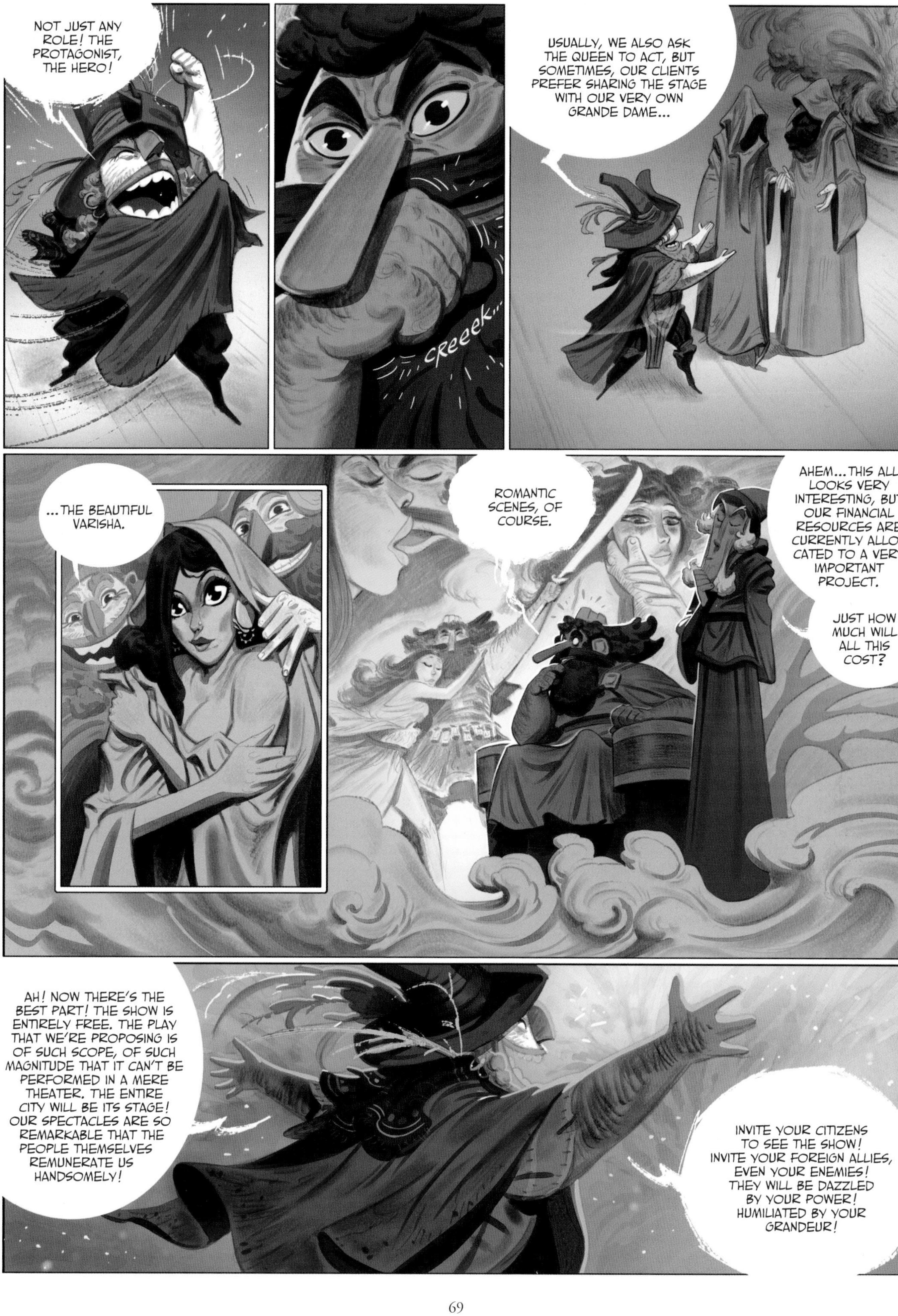
NOT JUST ANY ROLE! THE PROTAGONIST, THE HERO!
CREEEK...
USUALLY, WE ALSO ASK THE QUEEN TO ACT, BUT SOMETIMES, OUR CLIENTS PREFER SHARING THE STAGE WITH OUR VERY OWN GRANDE DAME...
...THE BEAUTIFUL VARISHA.
ROMANTIC SCENES, OF COURSE.
AHEM...THIS ALL LOOKS VERY INTERESTING, BUT OUR FINANCIAL RESOURCES ARE CURRENTLY ALLOCATED TO A VERY IMPORTANT PROJECT.
JUST HOW MUCH WILL ALL THIS COST?
AH! NOW THERE'S THE BEST PART! THE SHOW IS ENTIRELY FREE. THE PLAY THAT WE'RE PROPOSING IS OF SUCH SCOPE, OF SUCH MAGNITUDE THAT IT CAN'T BE PERFORMED IN A MERE THEATER. THE ENTIRE CITY WILL BE ITS STAGE! OUR SPECTACLES ARE SO REMARKABLE THAT THE PEOPLE THEMSELVES REMUNERATE US HANDSOMELY!
INVITE YOUR CITIZENS TO SEE THE SHOW! INVITE YOUR FOREIGN ALLIES, EVEN YOUR ENEMIES! THEY WILL BE DAZZLED BY YOUR POWER! HUMILIATED BY YOUR GRANDEUR!

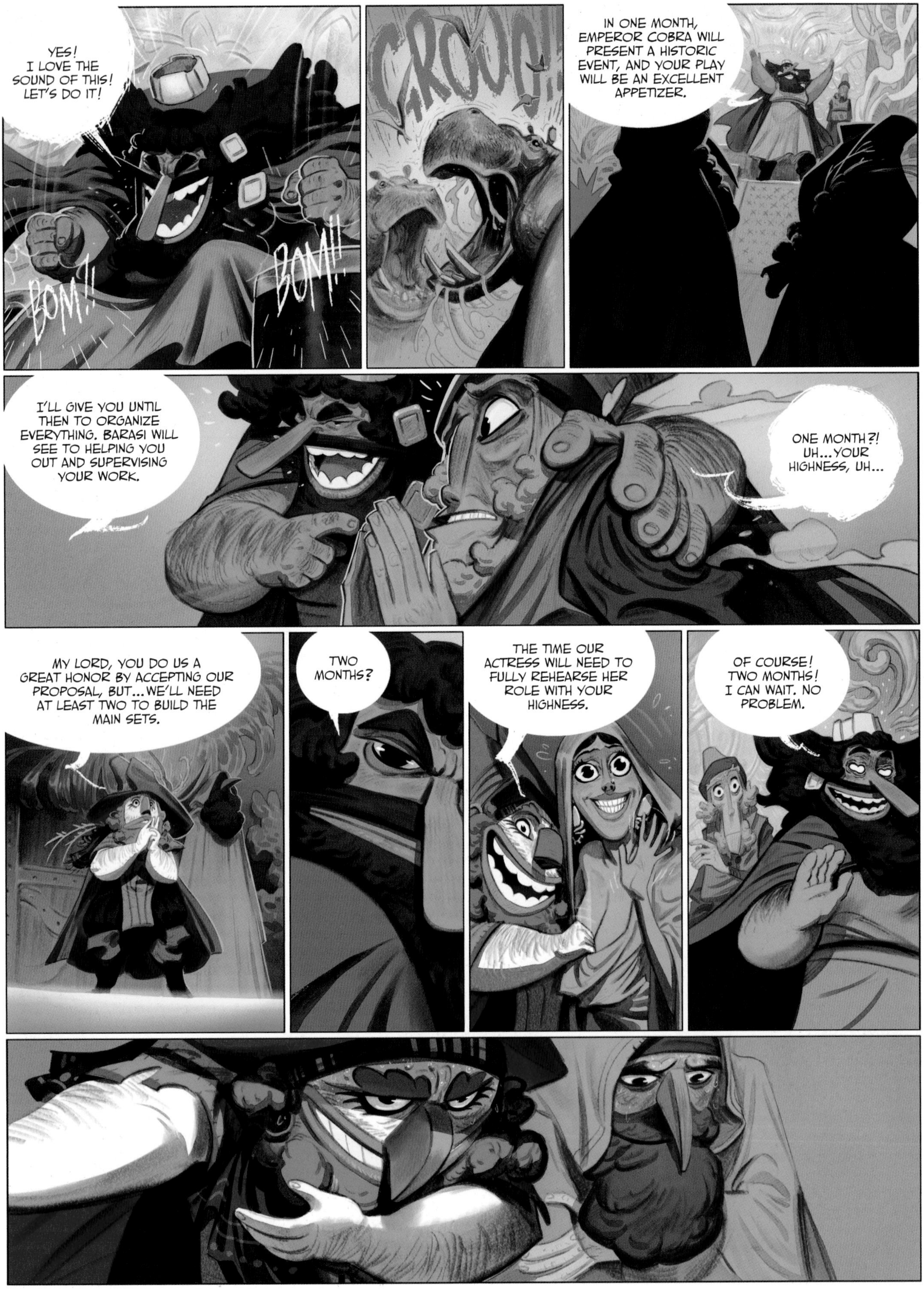
YES! I LOVE THE SOUND OF THIS! LET'S DO IT!
BOM!!
BOM!!
CROOO!!
IN ONE MONTH, EMPEROR COBRA WILL PRESENT A HISTORIC EVENT, AND YOUR PLAY WILL BE AN EXCELLENT APPETIZER.
I'LL GIVE YOU UNTIL THEN TO ORGANIZE EVERYTHING. BARASI WILL SEE TO HELPING YOU OUT AND SUPERVISING YOUR WORK.
ONE MONTH?! UH...YOUR HIGHNESS, UH...
MY LORD, YOU DO US A GREAT HONOR BY ACCEPTING OUR PROPOSAL, BUT...WE'LL NEED AT LEAST TWO TO BUILD THE MAIN SETS.
TWO MONTHS?
THE TIME OUR ACTRESS WILL NEED TO FULLY REHEARSE HER ROLE WITH YOUR HIGHNESS.
OF COURSE! TWO MONTHS! I CAN WAIT. NO PROBLEM.

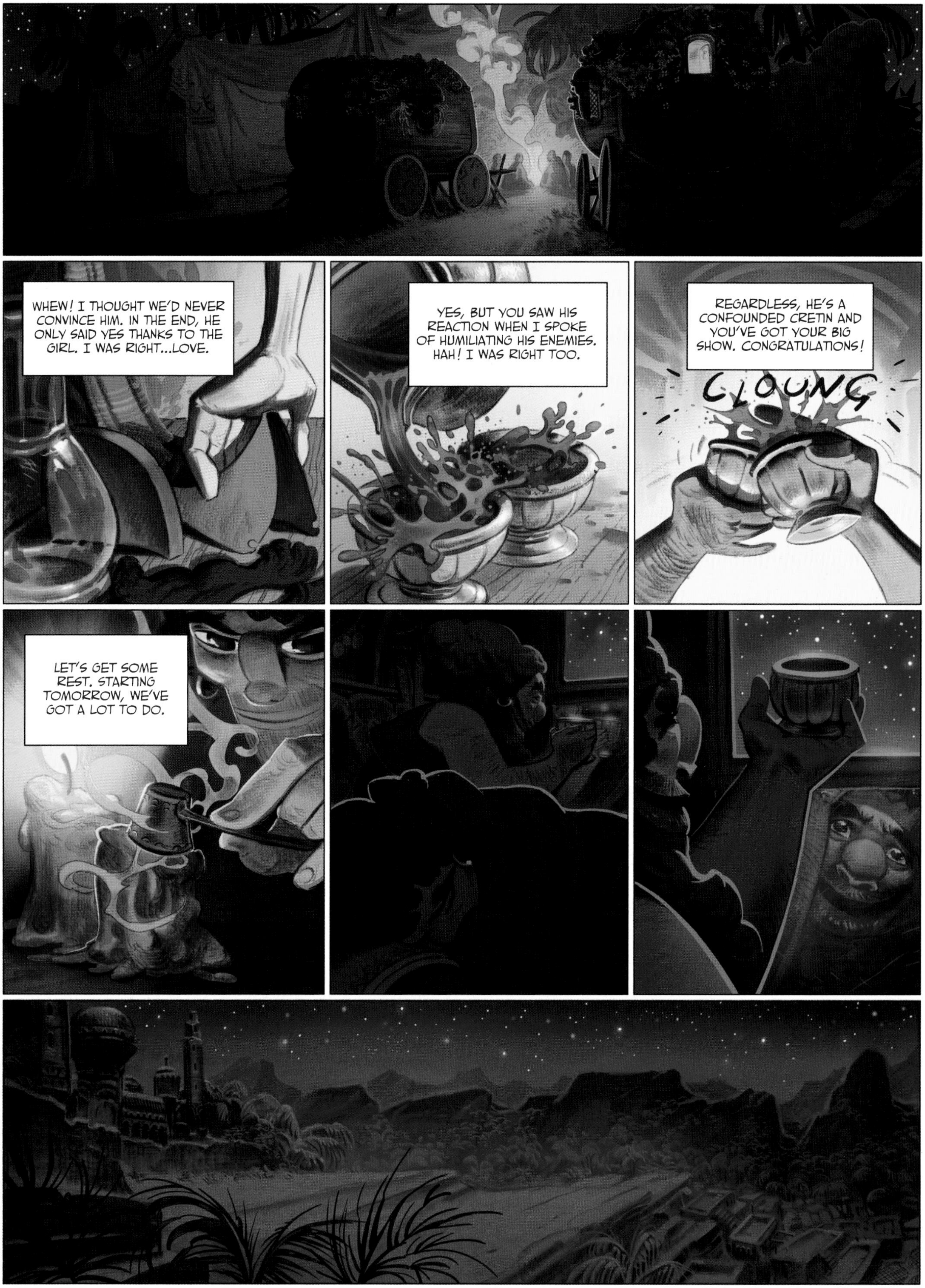
WHEW! I THOUGHT WE'D NEVER CONVINCE HIM. IN THE END, HE ONLY SAID YES THANKS TO THE GIRL. I WAS RIGHT...LOVE.
YES, BUT YOU SAW HIS REACTION WHEN I SPOKE OF HUMILIATING HIS ENEMIES. HAH! I WAS RIGHT TOO.
REGARDLESS, HE'S A CONFOUNDED CRETIN AND YOU'VE GOT YOUR BIG SHOW. CONGRATULATIONS!
CLOUNG
LET'S GET SOME REST. STARTING TOMORROW, WE'VE GOT A LOT TO DO.

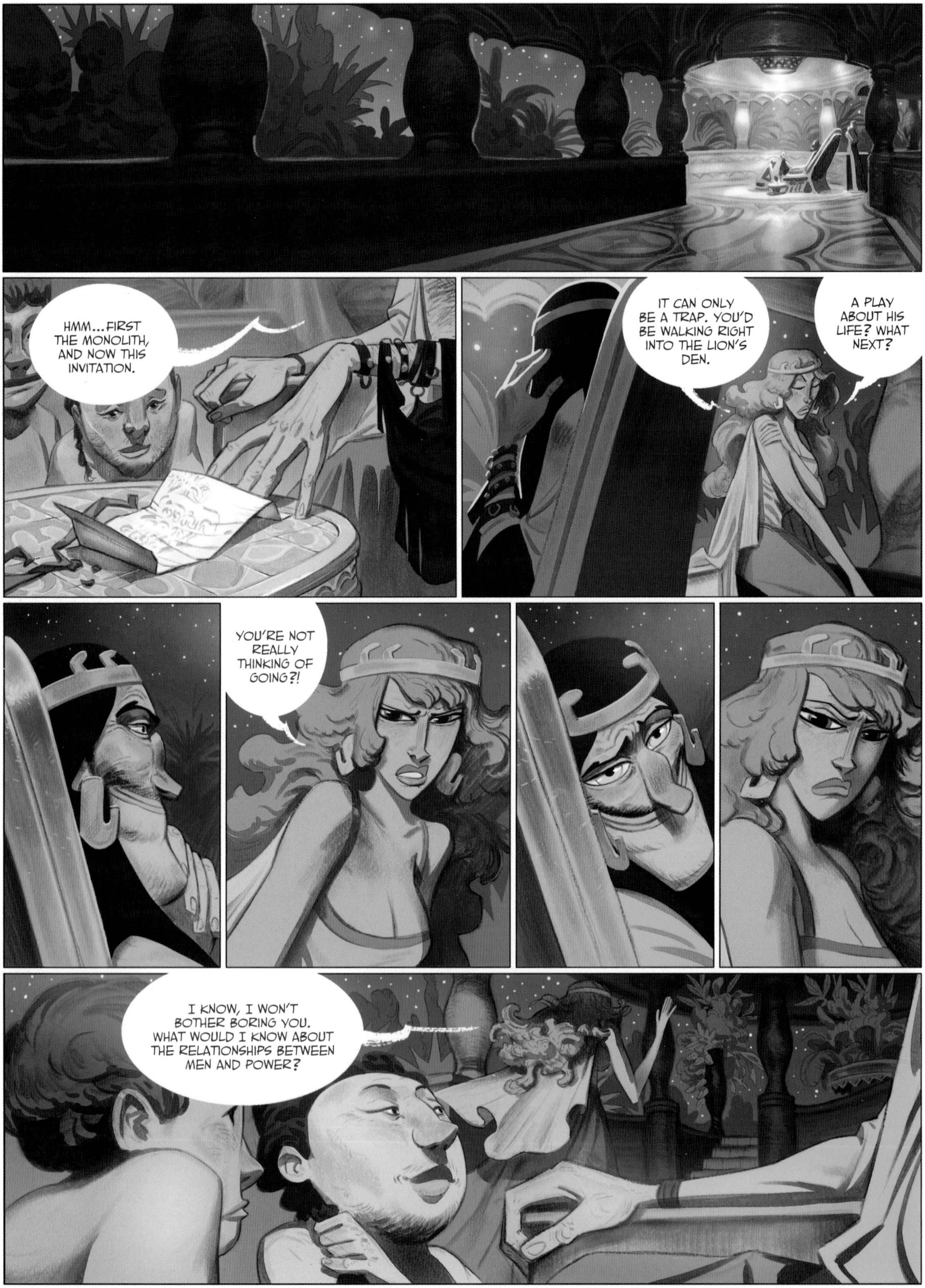
HMM...FIRST THE MONOLITH, AND NOW THIS INVITATION.
IT CAN ONLY BE A TRAP. YOU'D BE WALKING RIGHT INTO THE LION'S DEN.
A PLAY ABOUT HIS LIFE? WHAT NEXT?
YOU'RE NOT REALLY THINKING OF GOING?!
I KNOW, I WON'T BOTHER BORING YOU. WHAT WOULD I KNOW ABOUT THE RELATIONSHIPS BETWEEN MEN AND POWER?

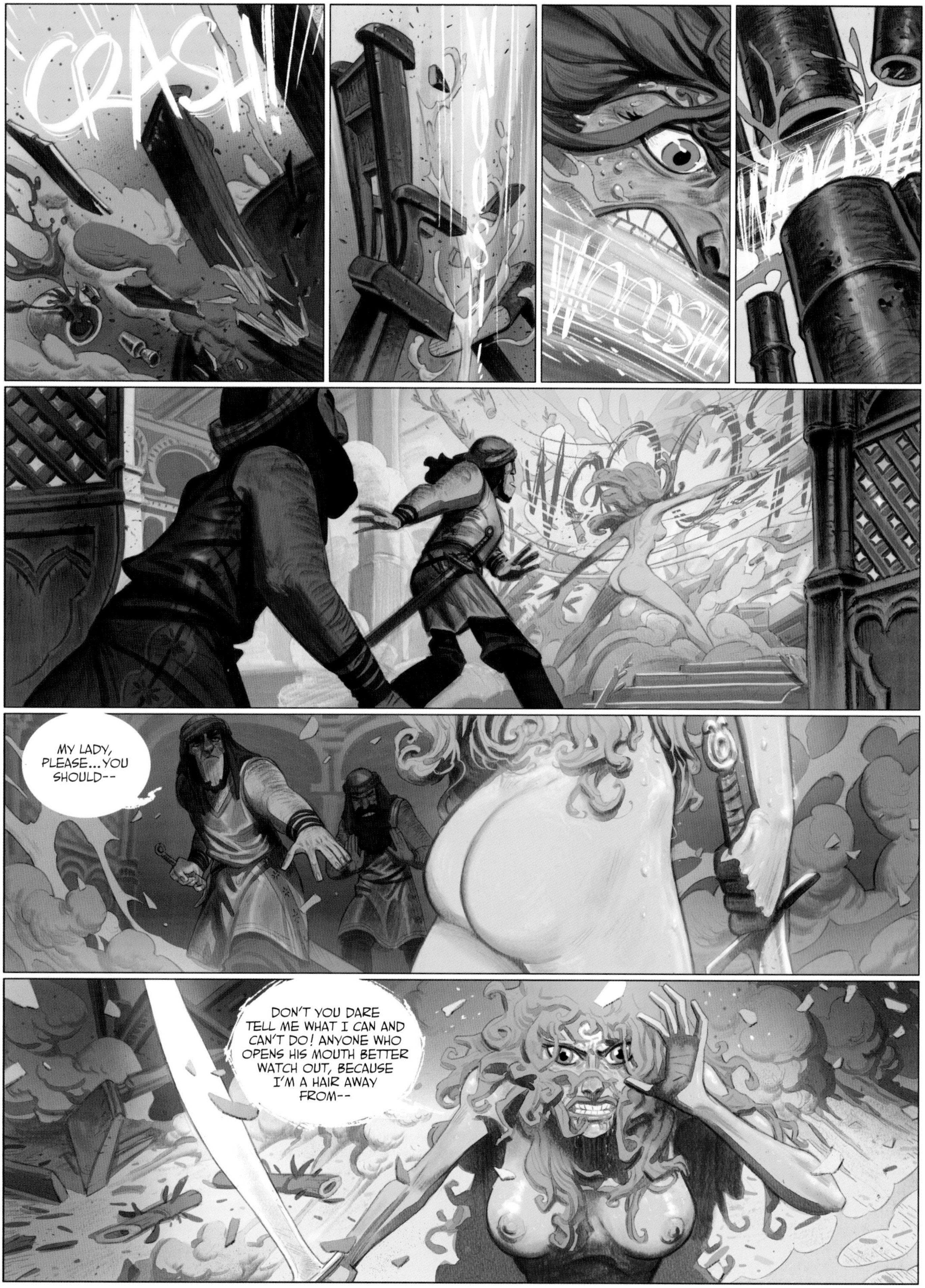
CRASH!
WOOOSH
WOOOSH!
WOOOSH!
WOOOSH!
MY LADY, PLEASE...YOU SHOULD--
DON'T YOU DARE TELL ME WHAT I CAN AND CAN'T DO! ANYONE WHO OPENS HIS MOUTH BETTER WATCH OUT, BECAUSE I'M A HAIR AWAY FROM--

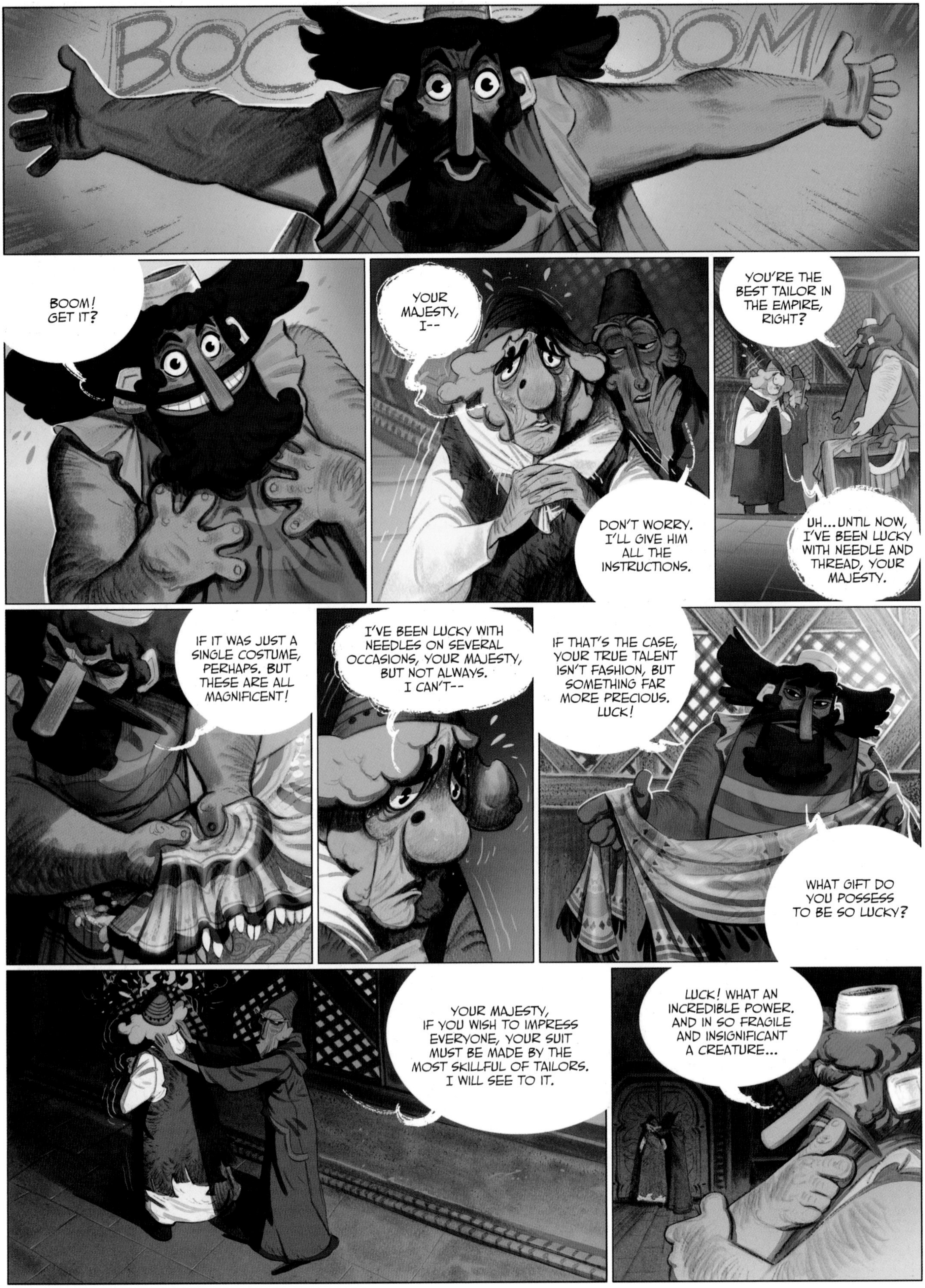
BOO OOM
BOOM! GET IT?
YOUR MAJESTY, I--
DON'T WORRY. I'LL GIVE HIM ALL THE INSTRUCTIONS.
YOU'RE THE BEST TAILOR IN THE EMPIRE, RIGHT?
UH... UNTIL NOW, I'VE BEEN LUCKY WITH NEEDLE AND THREAD, YOUR MAJESTY.
IF IT WAS JUST A SINGLE COSTUME, PERHAPS. BUT THESE ARE ALL MAGNIFICENT!
I'VE BEEN LUCKY WITH NEEDLES ON SEVERAL OCCASIONS, YOUR MAJESTY, BUT NOT ALWAYS. I CAN'T--
IF THAT'S THE CASE, YOUR TRUE TALENT ISN'T FASHION, BUT SOMETHING FAR MORE PRECIOUS. LUCK!
WHAT GIFT DO YOU POSSESS TO BE SO LUCKY?
YOUR MAJESTY, IF YOU WISH TO IMPRESS EVERYONE, YOUR SUIT MUST BE MADE BY THE MOST SKILLFUL OF TAILORS. I WILL SEE TO IT.
LUCK! WHAT AN INCREDIBLE POWER. AND IN SO FRAGILE AND INSIGNIFICANT A CREATURE...

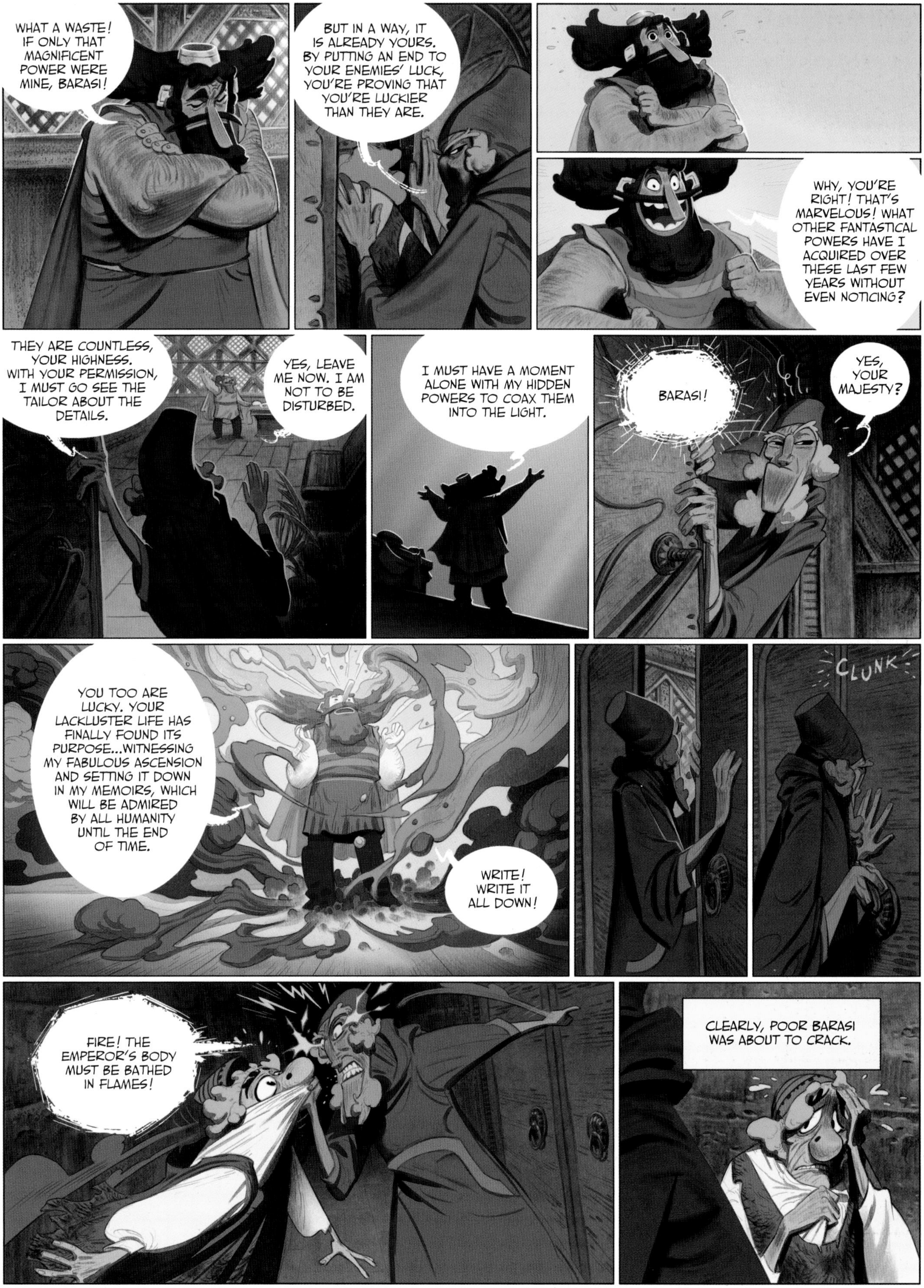
WHAT A WASTE! IF ONLY THAT MAGNIFICENT POWER WERE MINE, BARASI!
BUT IN A WAY, IT IS ALREADY YOURS. BY PUTTING AN END TO YOUR ENEMIES' LUCK, YOU'RE PROVING THAT YOU'RE LUCKIER THAN THEY ARE.
WHY, YOU'RE RIGHT! THAT'S MARVELOUS! WHAT OTHER FANTASTICAL POWERS HAVE I ACQUIRED OVER THESE LAST FEW YEARS WITHOUT EVEN NOTICING?
THEY ARE COUNTLESS, YOUR HIGHNESS. WITH YOUR PERMISSION, I MUST GO SEE THE TAILOR ABOUT THE DETAILS.
YES, LEAVE ME NOW. I AM NOT TO BE DISTURBED.
I MUST HAVE A MOMENT ALONE WITH MY HIDDEN POWERS TO COAX THEM INTO THE LIGHT.
BARASI!
YES, YOUR MAJESTY?
YOU TOO ARE LUCKY. YOUR LACKLUSTER LIFE HAS FINALLY FOUND ITS PURPOSE...WITNESSING MY FABULOUS ASCENSION AND SETTING IT DOWN IN MY MEMOIRS, WHICH WILL BE ADMIRED BY ALL HUMANITY UNTIL THE END OF TIME.
WRITE! WRITE IT ALL DOWN!
CLUNK
FIRE! THE EMPEROR'S BODY MUST BE BATHED IN FLAMES!
CLEARLY, POOR BARASI WAS ABOUT TO CRACK.

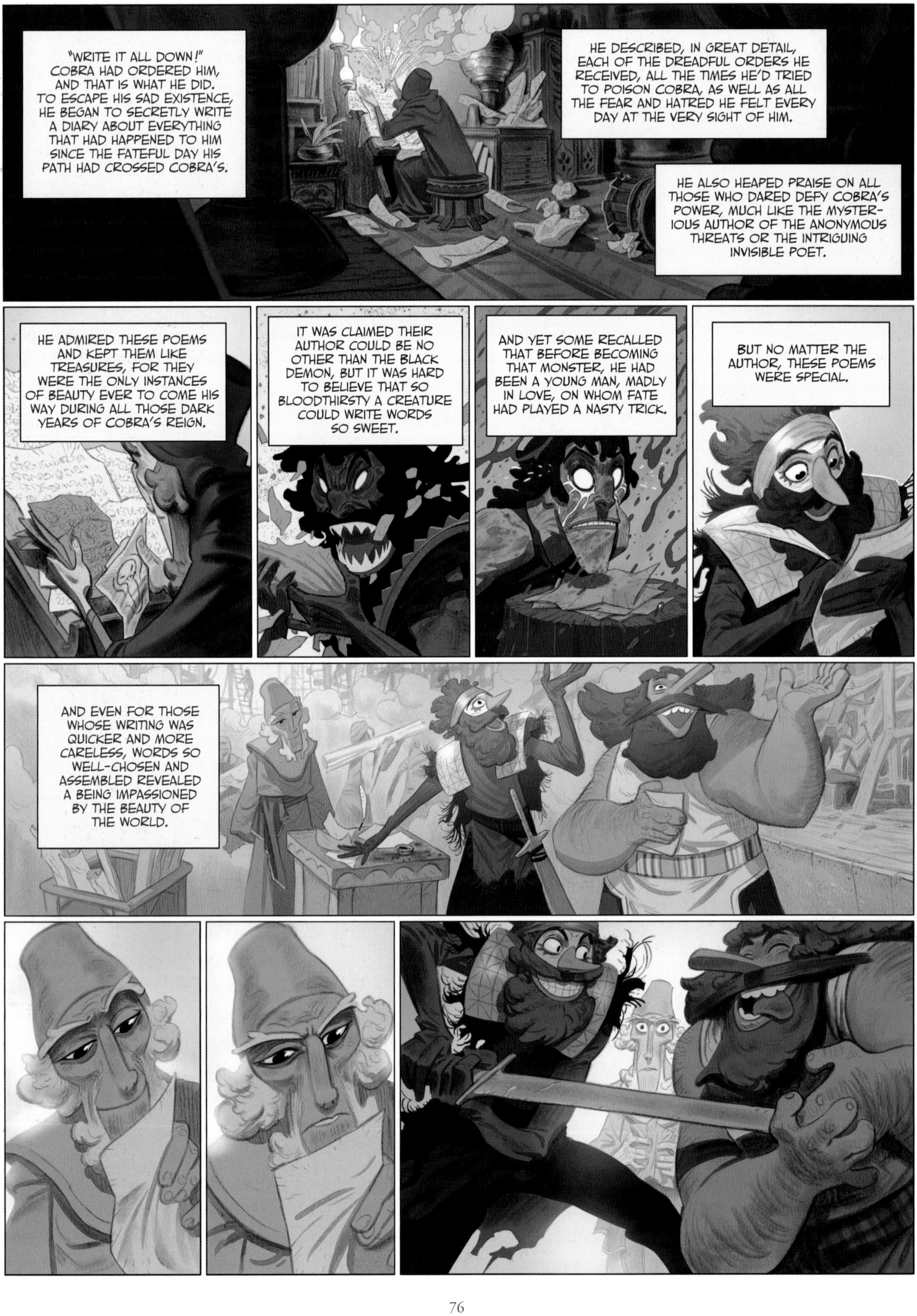
"WRITE IT ALL DOWN!" COBRA HAD ORDERED HIM, AND THAT IS WHAT HE DID. TO ESCAPE HIS SAD EXISTENCE, HE BEGAN TO SECRETLY WRITE A DIARY ABOUT EVERYTHING THAT HAD HAPPENED TO HIM SINCE THE FATEFUL DAY HIS PATH HAD CROSSED COBRA'S.
HE DESCRIBED, IN GREAT DETAIL, EACH OF THE DREADFUL ORDERS HE RECEIVED, ALL THE TIMES HE'D TRIED TO POISON COBRA, AS WELL AS ALL THE FEAR AND HATRED HE FELT EVERY DAY AT THE VERY SIGHT OF HIM.
HE ALSO HEAPED PRAISE ON ALL THOSE WHO DARED DEFY COBRA'S POWER, MUCH LIKE THE MYSTERIOUS AUTHOR OF THE ANONYMOUS THREATS OR THE INTRIGUING INVISIBLE POET.
HE ADMIRED THESE POEMS AND KEPT THEM LIKE TREASURES, FOR THEY WERE THE ONLY INSTANCES OF BEAUTY EVER TO COME HIS WAY DURING ALL THOSE DARK YEARS OF COBRA'S REIGN.
IT WAS CLAIMED THEIR AUTHOR COULD BE NO OTHER THAN THE BLACK DEMON, BUT IT WAS HARD TO BELIEVE THAT SO BLOODTHIRSTY A CREATURE COULD WRITE WORDS SO SWEET.
AND YET SOME RECALLED THAT BEFORE BECOMING THAT MONSTER, HE HAD BEEN A YOUNG MAN, MADLY IN LOVE, ON WHOM FATE HAD PLAYED A NASTY TRICK.
BUT NO MATTER THE AUTHOR, THESE POEMS WERE SPECIAL.
AND EVEN FOR THOSE WHOSE WRITING WAS QUICKER AND MORE CARELESS, WORDS SO WELL-CHOSEN AND ASSEMBLED REVEALED A BEING IMPASSIONED BY THE BEAUTY OF THE WORLD.

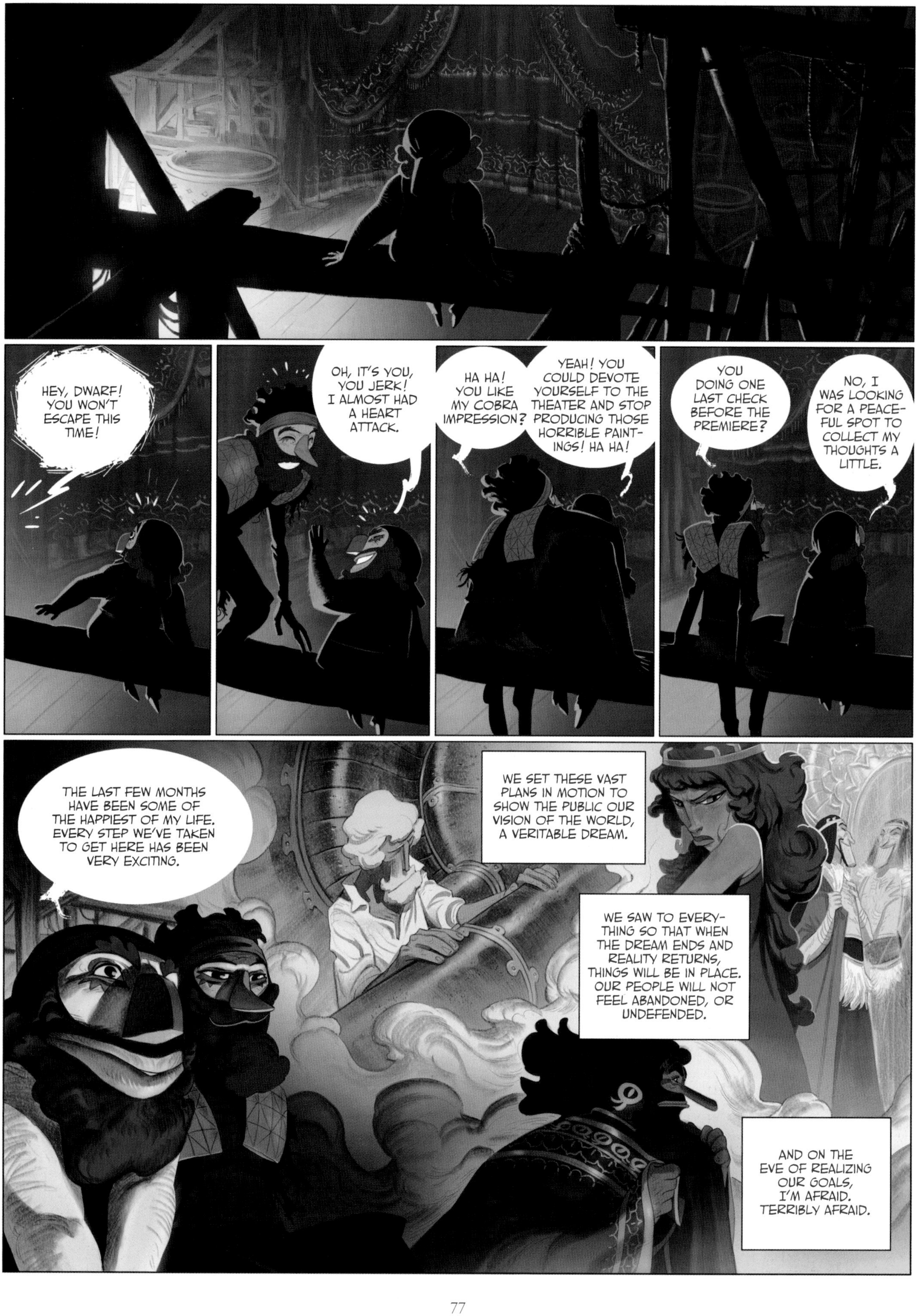
HEY, DWARF! YOU WON'T ESCAPE THIS TIME!
OH, IT'S YOU, YOU JERK! I ALMOST HAD A HEART ATTACK.
HA HA! YOU LIKE MY COBRA IMPRESSION?
YEAH! YOU COULD DEVOTE YOURSELF TO THE THEATER AND STOP PRODUCING THOSE HORRIBLE PAINTINGS! HA HA!
YOU DOING ONE LAST CHECK BEFORE THE PREMIERE?
NO, I WAS LOOKING FOR A PEACEFUL SPOT TO COLLECT MY THOUGHTS A LITTLE.
THE LAST FEW MONTHS HAVE BEEN SOME OF THE HAPPIEST OF MY LIFE. EVERY STEP WE'VE TAKEN TO GET HERE HAS BEEN VERY EXCITING.
WE SET THESE VAST PLANS IN MOTION TO SHOW THE PUBLIC OUR VISION OF THE WORLD, A VERITABLE DREAM.
WE SAW TO EVERYTHING SO THAT WHEN THE DREAM ENDS AND REALITY RETURNS, THINGS WILL BE IN PLACE. OUR PEOPLE WILL NOT FEEL ABANDONED, OR UNDEFENDED.
AND ON THE EVE OF REALIZING OUR GOALS, I'M AFRAID. TERRIBLY AFRAID.

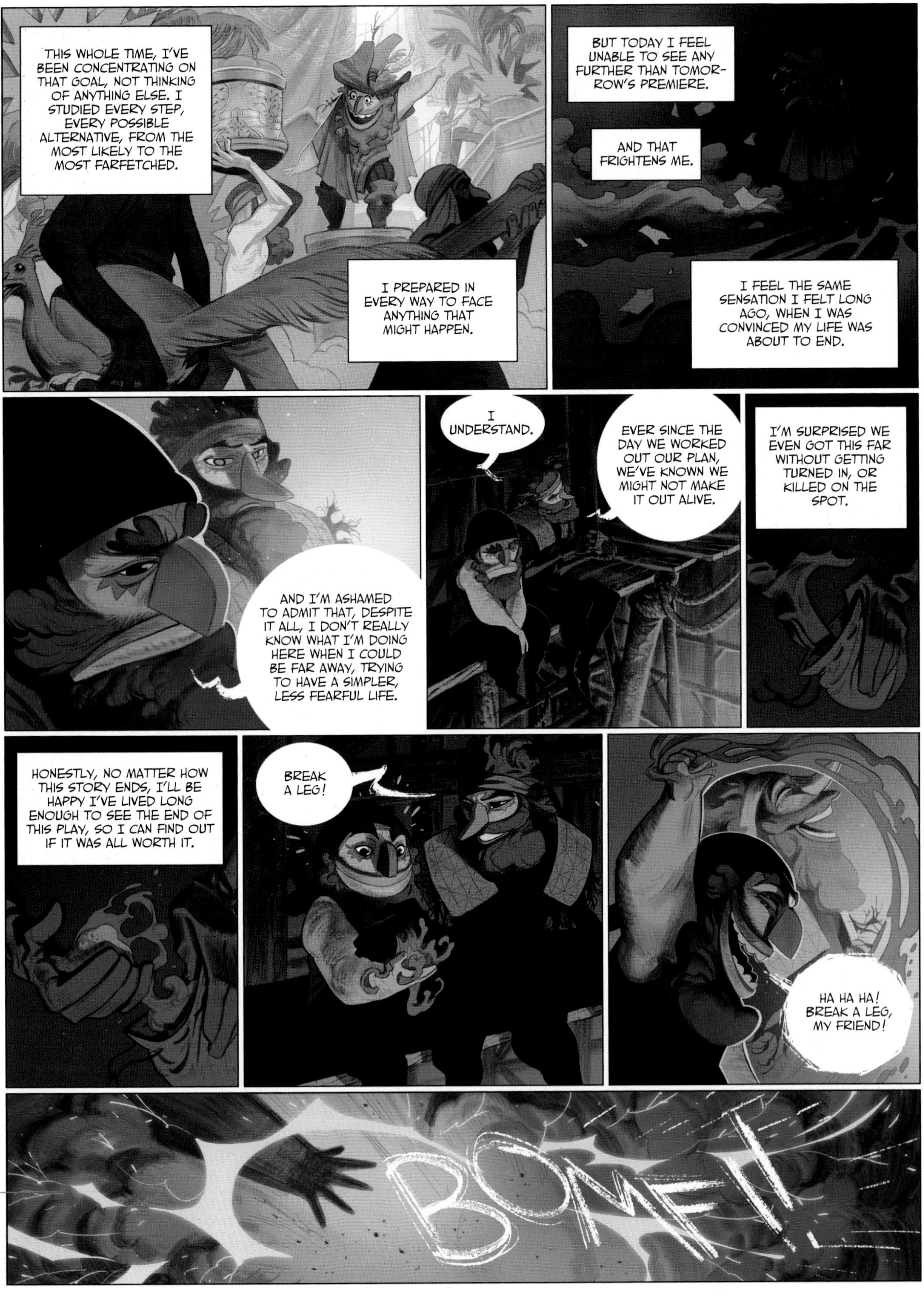
THIS WHOLE TIME, I'VE BEEN CONCENTRATING ON THAT GOAL, NOT THINKING OF ANYTHING ELSE. I STUDIED EVERY STEP, EVERY POSSIBLE ALTERNATIVE, FROM THE MOST LIKELY TO THE MOST FARFETCHED.
I PREPARED IN EVERY WAY TO FACE ANYTHING THAT MIGHT HAPPEN.
BUT TODAY I FEEL UNABLE TO SEE ANY FURTHER THAN TOMORROW'S PREMIERE.
AND THAT FRIGHTENS ME.
I FEEL THE SAME SENSATION I FELT LONG AGO, WHEN I WAS CONVINCED MY LIFE WAS ABOUT TO END.
AND I'M ASHAMED TO ADMIT THAT, DESPITE IT ALL, I DON'T REALLY KNOW WHAT I'M DOING HERE WHEN I COULD BE FAR AWAY, TRYING TO HAVE A SIMPLER, LESS FEARFUL LIFE.
I UNDERSTAND.
EVER SINCE THE DAY WE WORKED OUT OUR PLAN, WE'VE KNOWN WE MIGHT NOT MAKE IT OUT ALIVE.
I'M SURPRISED WE EVEN GOT THIS FAR WITHOUT GETTING TURNED IN, OR KILLED ON THE SPOT.
HONESTLY, NO MATTER HOW THIS STORY ENDS, I'LL BE HAPPY I'VE LIVED LONG ENOUGH TO SEE THE END OF THIS PLAY, SO I CAN FIND OUT IF IT WAS ALL WORTH IT.
BREAK A LEG!
HA HA HA! BREAK A LEG, MY FRIEND!
BOMF!!

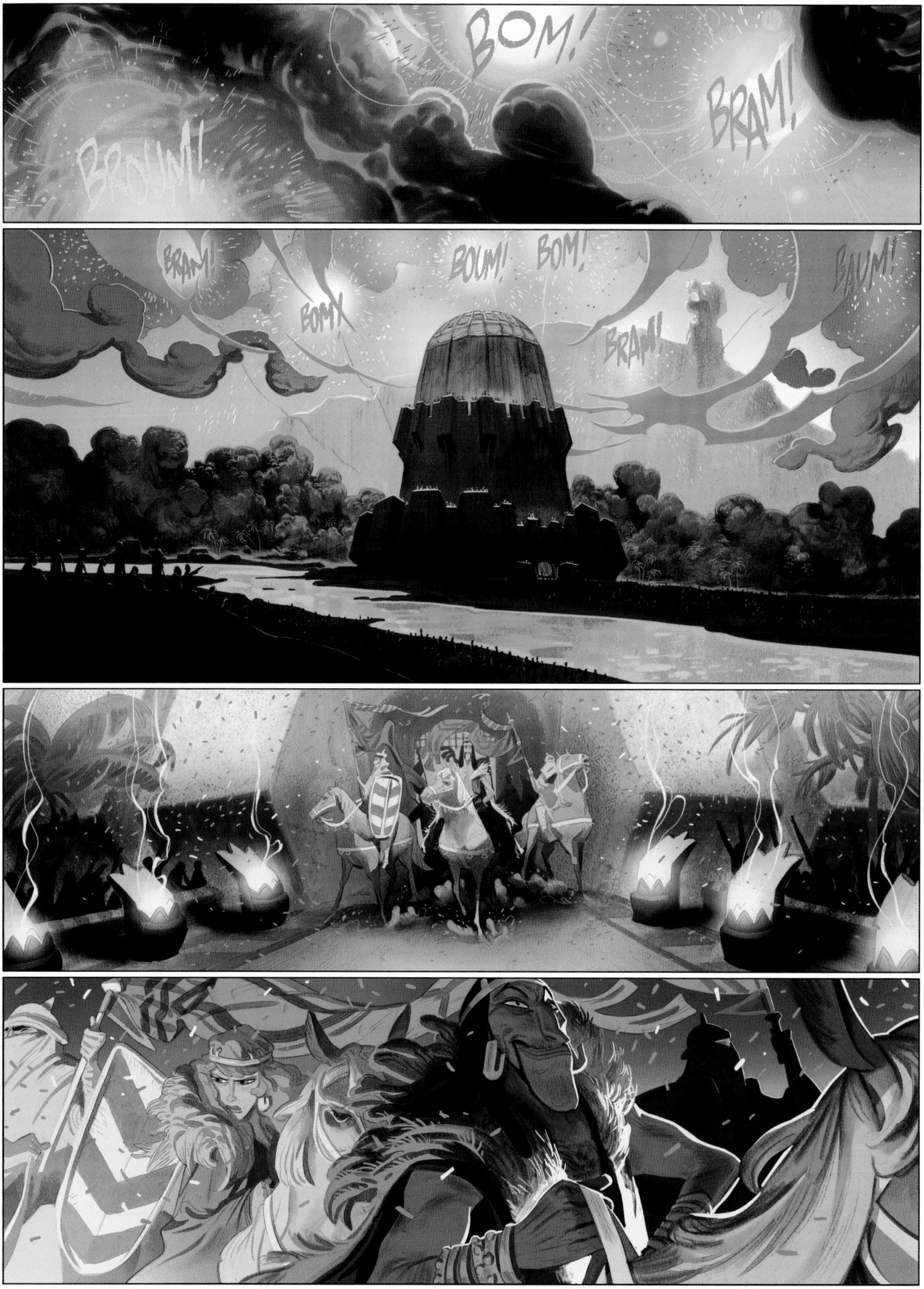
BOM!
BRAM!
BROUM!
BRAM!
BOM!
BOUM!
BOM!
BRAM!
BAUM!

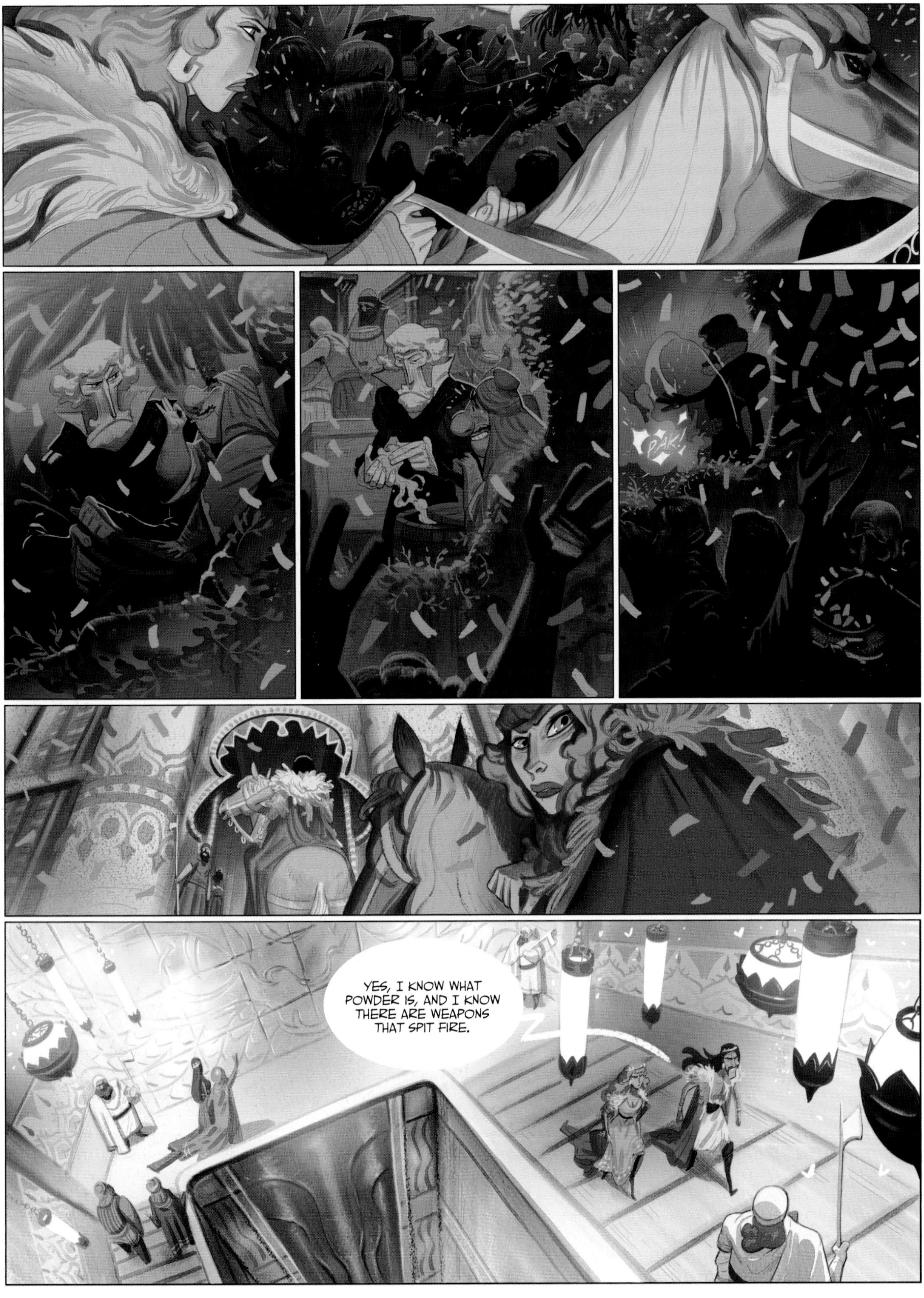
PAK!
YES, I KNOW WHAT POWDER IS, AND I KNOW THERE ARE WEAPONS THAT SPIT FIRE.

I ALSO KNOW HOW LONG THEY TAKE TO LOAD AGAIN, AND WHAT HAPPENS WHEN THEY JAM AND PUT AN END TO THE COWARDS WHO WEREN'T BRAVE ENOUGH TO FIGHT HAND TO HAND.

AND SINCE WE'RE TALKING ABOUT BRAVERY, KNOW THIS... I COULDN'T BE ANY BRAVER IF I WALKED THROUGH THAT DOOR COMPLETELY NUDE, WITHOUT MY ARMY WAITING A STONE'S THROW FROM THE CITADEL.

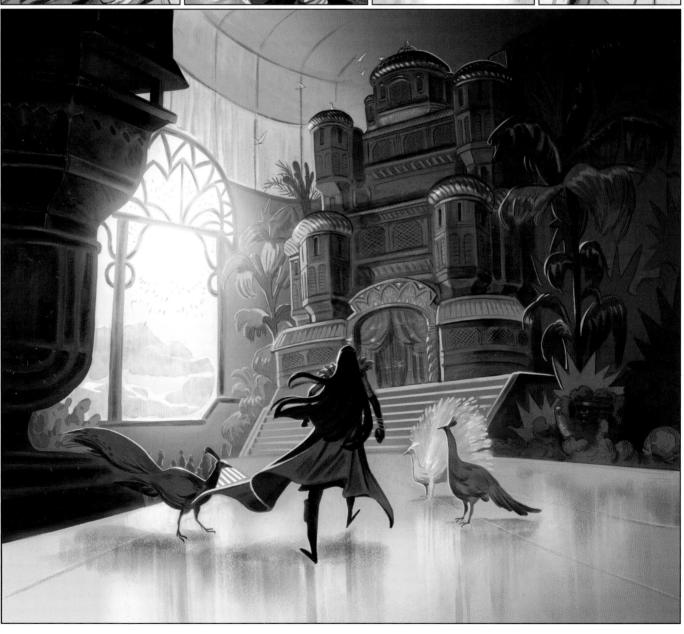

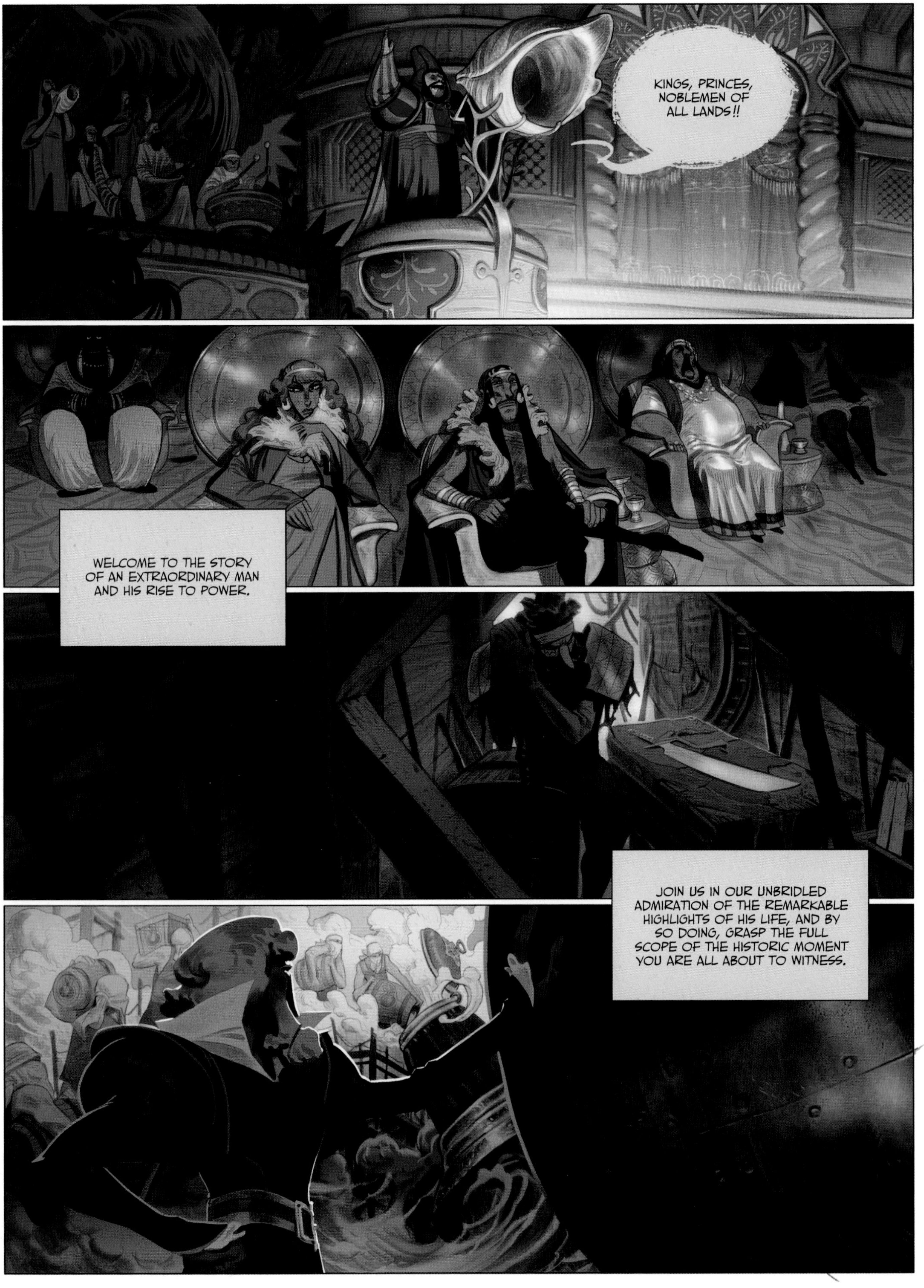
KINGS, PRINCES, NOBLEMEN OF ALL LANDS!!
WELCOME TO THE STORY OF AN EXTRAORDINARY MAN AND HIS RISE TO POWER.
JOIN US IN OUR UNBRIDLED ADMIRATION OF THE REMARKABLE HIGHLIGHTS OF HIS LIFE, AND BY SO DOING, GRASP THE FULL SCOPE OF THE HISTORIC MOMENT YOU ARE ALL ABOUT TO WITNESS.

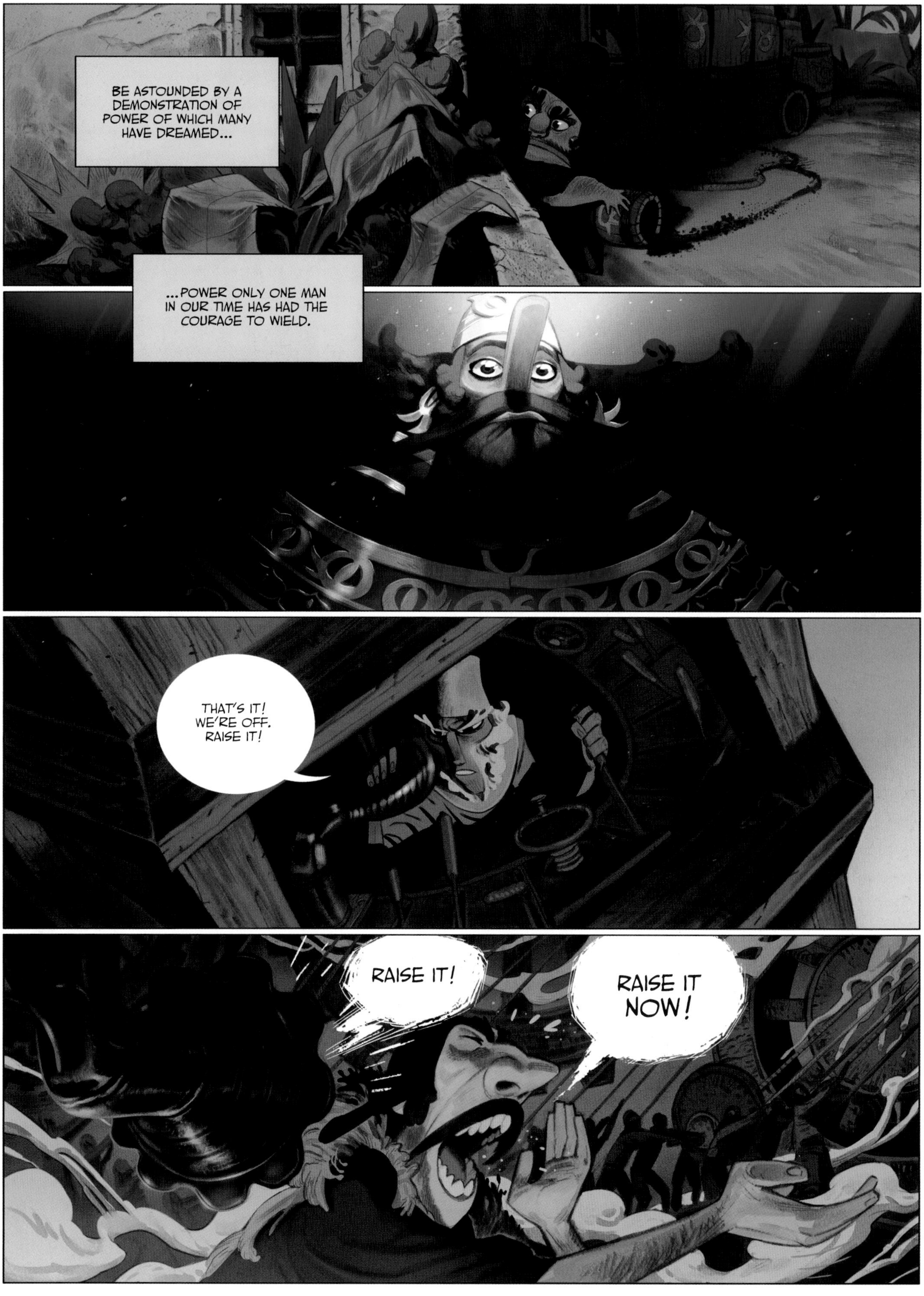
BE ASTOUNDED BY A DEMONSTRATION OF POWER OF WHICH MANY HAVE DREAMED...
...POWER ONLY ONE MAN IN OUR TIME HAS HAD THE COURAGE TO WIELD.
THAT'S IT! WE'RE OFF. RAISE IT!
RAISE IT!
RAISE IT NOW!

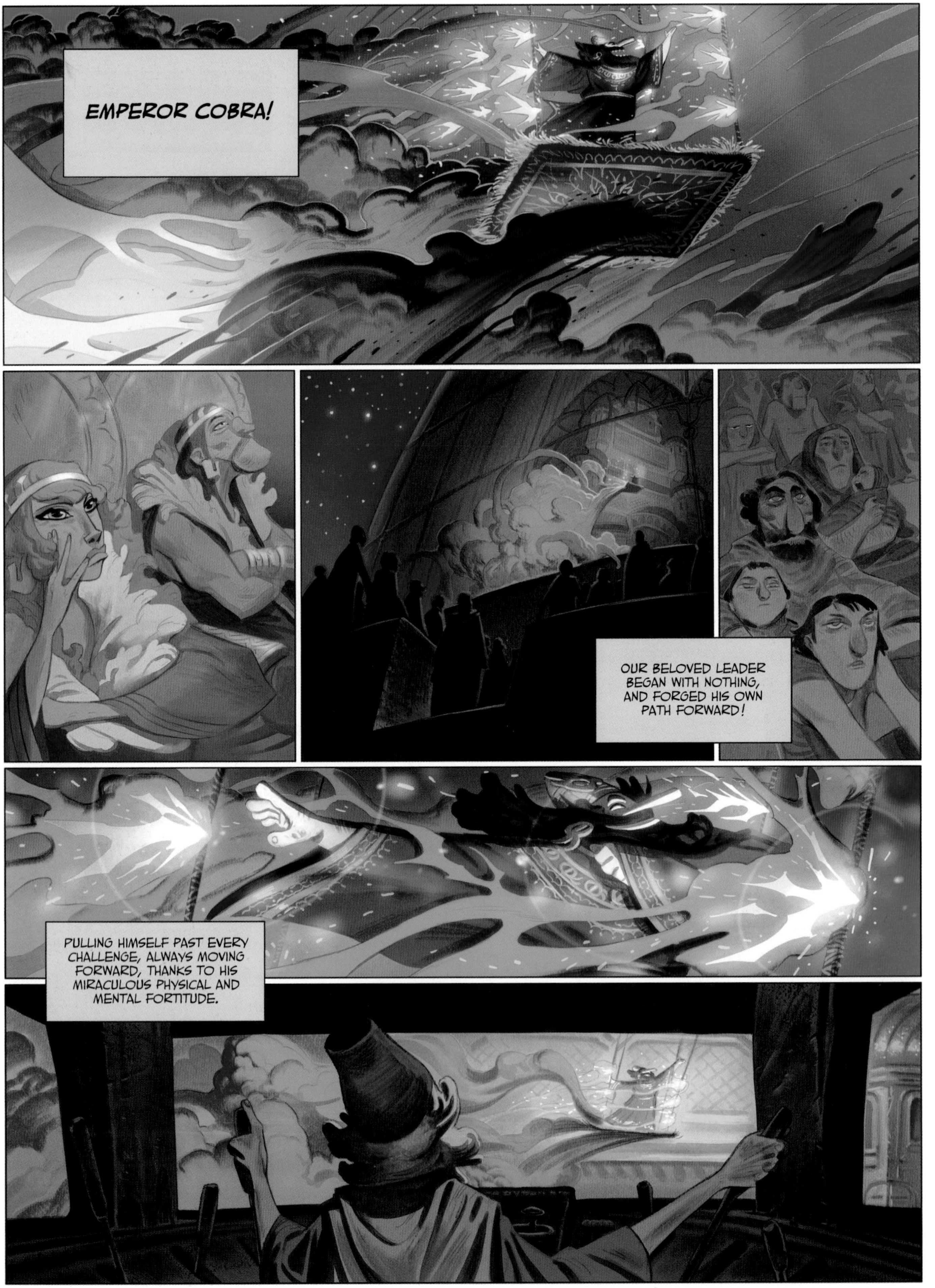
EMPEROR COBRA!
OUR BELOVED LEADER BEGAN WITH NOTHING, AND FORGED HIS OWN PATH FORWARD!
PULLING HIMSELF PAST EVERY CHALLENGE, ALWAYS MOVING FORWARD, THANKS TO HIS MIRACULOUS PHYSICAL AND MENTAL FORTITUDE.

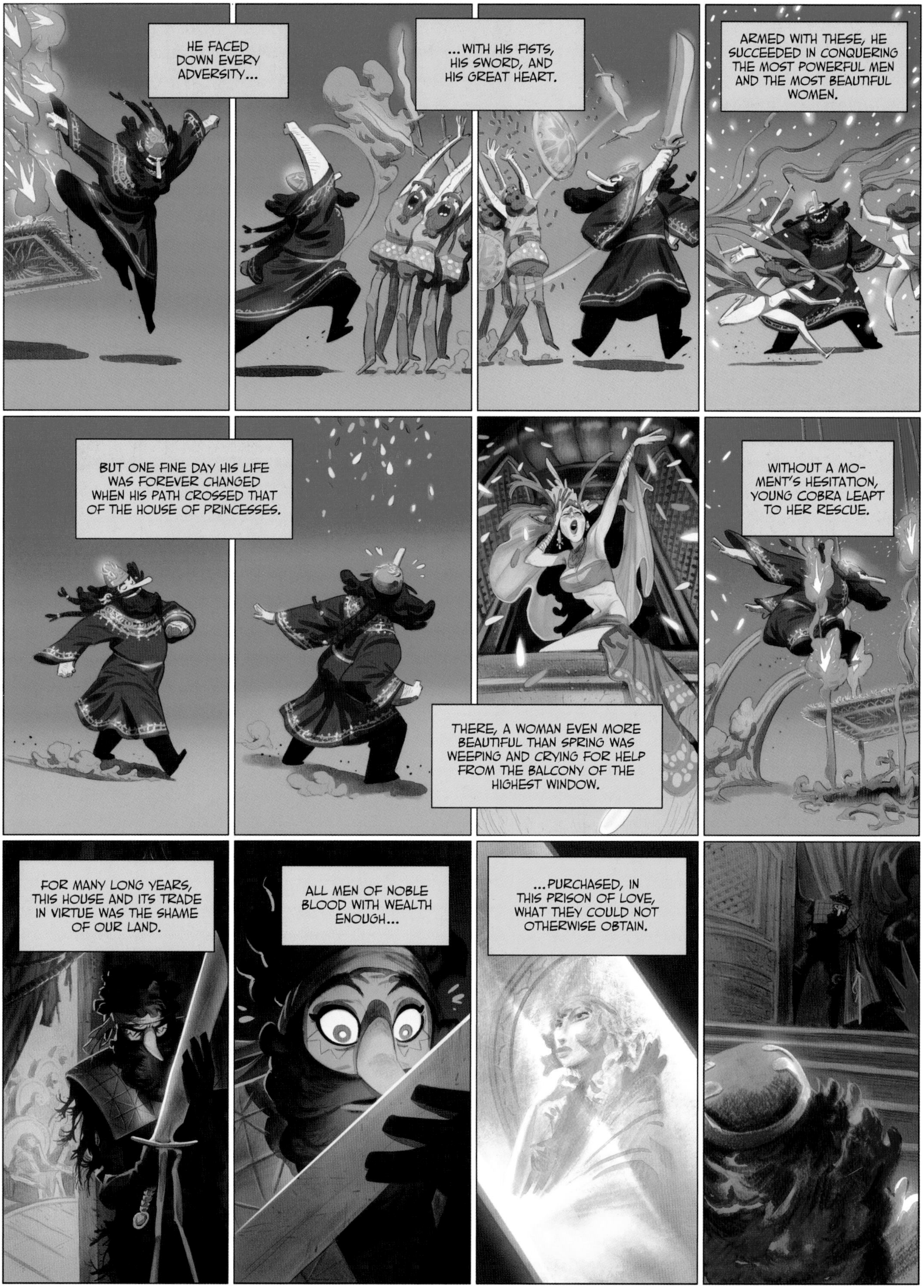
HE FACED DOWN EVERY ADVERSITY...
...WITH HIS FISTS, HIS SWORD, AND HIS GREAT HEART.
ARMED WITH THESE, HE SUCCEEDED IN CONQUERING THE MOST POWERFUL MEN AND THE MOST BEAUTIFUL WOMEN.
BUT ONE FINE DAY HIS LIFE WAS FOREVER CHANGED WHEN HIS PATH CROSSED THAT OF THE HOUSE OF PRINCESSES.
THERE, A WOMAN EVEN MORE BEAUTIFUL THAN SPRING WAS WEEPING AND CRYING FOR HELP FROM THE BALCONY OF THE HIGHEST WINDOW.
WITHOUT A MO-MENT'S HESITATION, YOUNG COBRA LEAPT TO HER RESCUE.
FOR MANY LONG YEARS, THIS HOUSE AND ITS TRADE IN VIRTUE WAS THE SHAME OF OUR LAND.
ALL MEN OF NOBLE BLOOD WITH WEALTH ENOUGH...
...PURCHASED, IN THIS PRISON OF LOVE, WHAT THEY COULD NOT OTHERWISE OBTAIN.

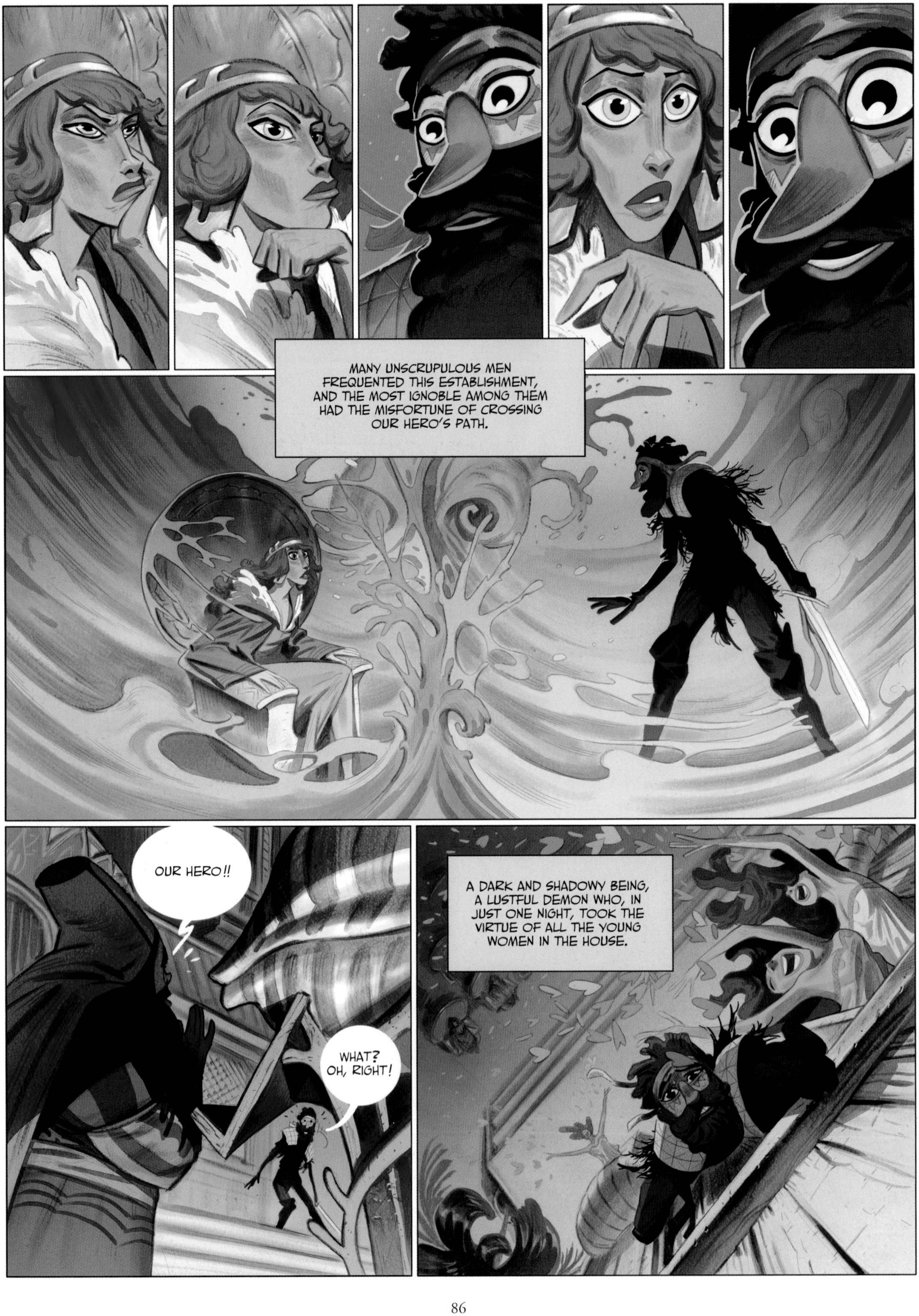
MANY UNSCRUPULOUS MEN FREQUENTED THIS ESTABLISHMENT, AND THE MOST IGNOBLE AMONG THEM HAD THE MISFORTUNE OF CROSSING OUR HERO'S PATH.
OUR HERO!!
WHAT? OH, RIGHT!
A DARK AND SHADOWY BEING, A LUSTFUL DEMON WHO, IN JUST ONE NIGHT, TOOK THE VIRTUE OF ALL THE YOUNG WOMEN IN THE HOUSE.

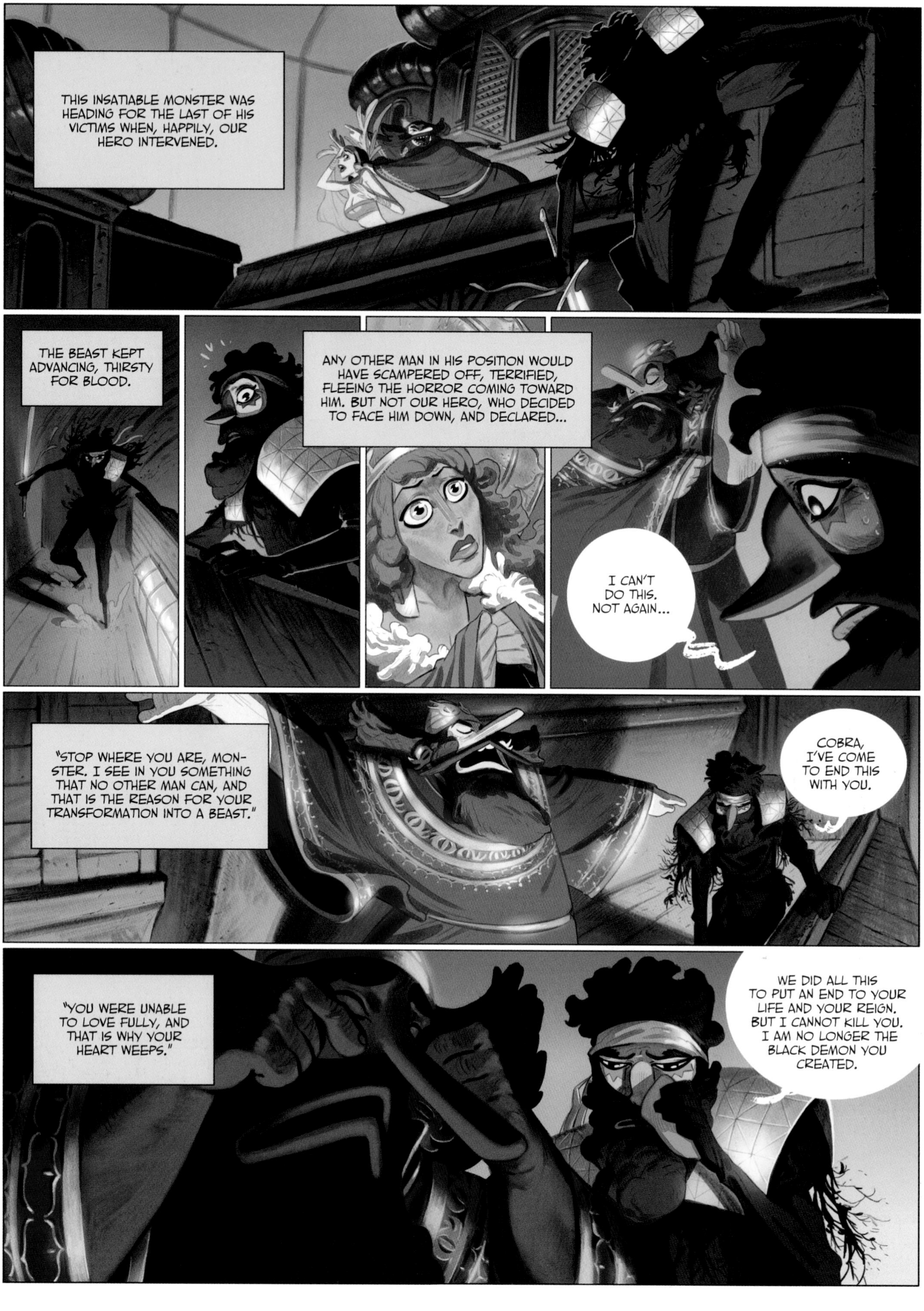

THIS INSATIABLE MONSTER WAS HEADING FOR THE LAST OF HIS VICTIMS WHEN, HAPPILY, OUR HERO INTERVENED.
THE BEAST KEPT ADVANCING, THIRSTY FOR BLOOD.
ANY OTHER MAN IN HIS POSITION WOULD HAVE SCAMPERED OFF, TERRIFIED, FLEEING THE HORROR COMING TOWARD HIM. BUT NOT OUR HERO, WHO DECIDED TO FACE HIM DOWN, AND DECLARED...
I CAN'T DO THIS. NOT AGAIN...
"STOP WHERE YOU ARE, MON-STER. I SEE IN YOU SOMETHING THAT NO OTHER MAN CAN, AND THAT IS THE REASON FOR YOUR TRANSFORMATION INTO A BEAST."
COBRA, I'VE COME TO END THIS WITH YOU.
"YOU WERE UNABLE TO LOVE FULLY, AND THAT IS WHY YOUR HEART WEEPS."
WE DID ALL THIS TO PUT AN END TO YOUR LIFE AND YOUR REIGN. BUT I CANNOT KILL YOU. I AM NO LONGER THE BLACK DEMON YOU CREATED.

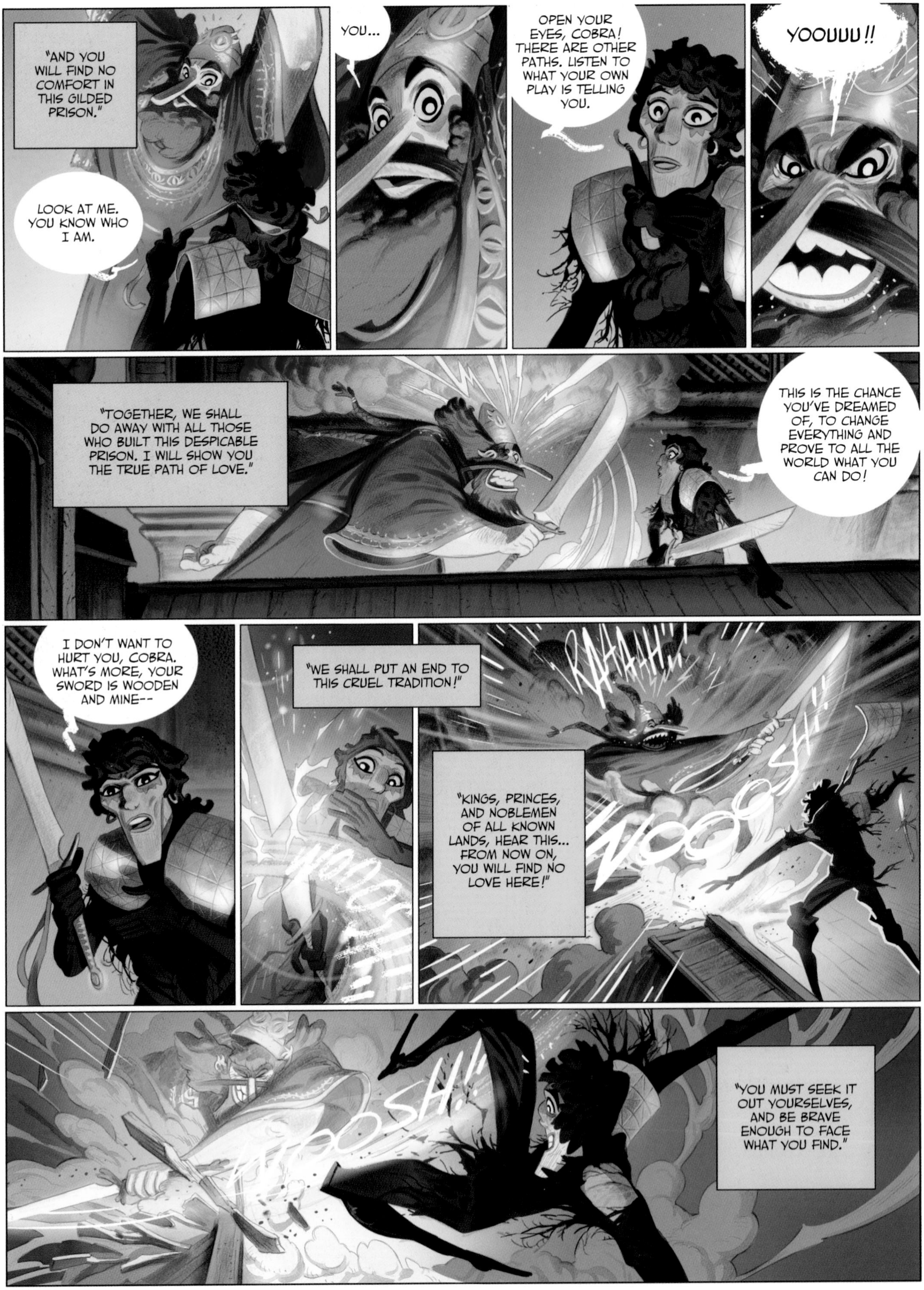
"AND YOU WILL FIND NO COMFORT IN THIS GILDED PRISON."
LOOK AT ME. YOU KNOW WHO I AM.
YOU...
OPEN YOUR EYES, COBRA! THERE ARE OTHER PATHS. LISTEN TO WHAT YOUR OWN PLAY IS TELLING YOU.
YOOUUU!!
"TOGETHER, WE SHALL DO AWAY WITH ALL THOSE WHO BUILT THIS DESPICABLE PRISON. I WILL SHOW YOU THE TRUE PATH OF LOVE."
THIS IS THE CHANCE YOU'VE DREAMED OF, TO CHANGE EVERYTHING AND PROVE TO ALL THE WORLD WHAT YOU CAN DO!
I DON'T WANT TO HURT YOU, COBRA. WHAT'S MORE, YOUR SWORD IS WOODEN AND MINE--
"WE SHALL PUT AN END TO THIS CRUEL TRADITION!"
WOOOSH!!
RAAAAH!!
"KINGS, PRINCES, AND NOBLEMEN OF ALL KNOWN LANDS, HEAR THIS... FROM NOW ON, YOU WILL FIND NO LOVE HERE!"
WOOOOSH!!
WOOOSH!!
"YOU MUST SEEK IT OUT YOURSELVES, AND BE BRAVE ENOUGH TO FACE WHAT YOU FIND."

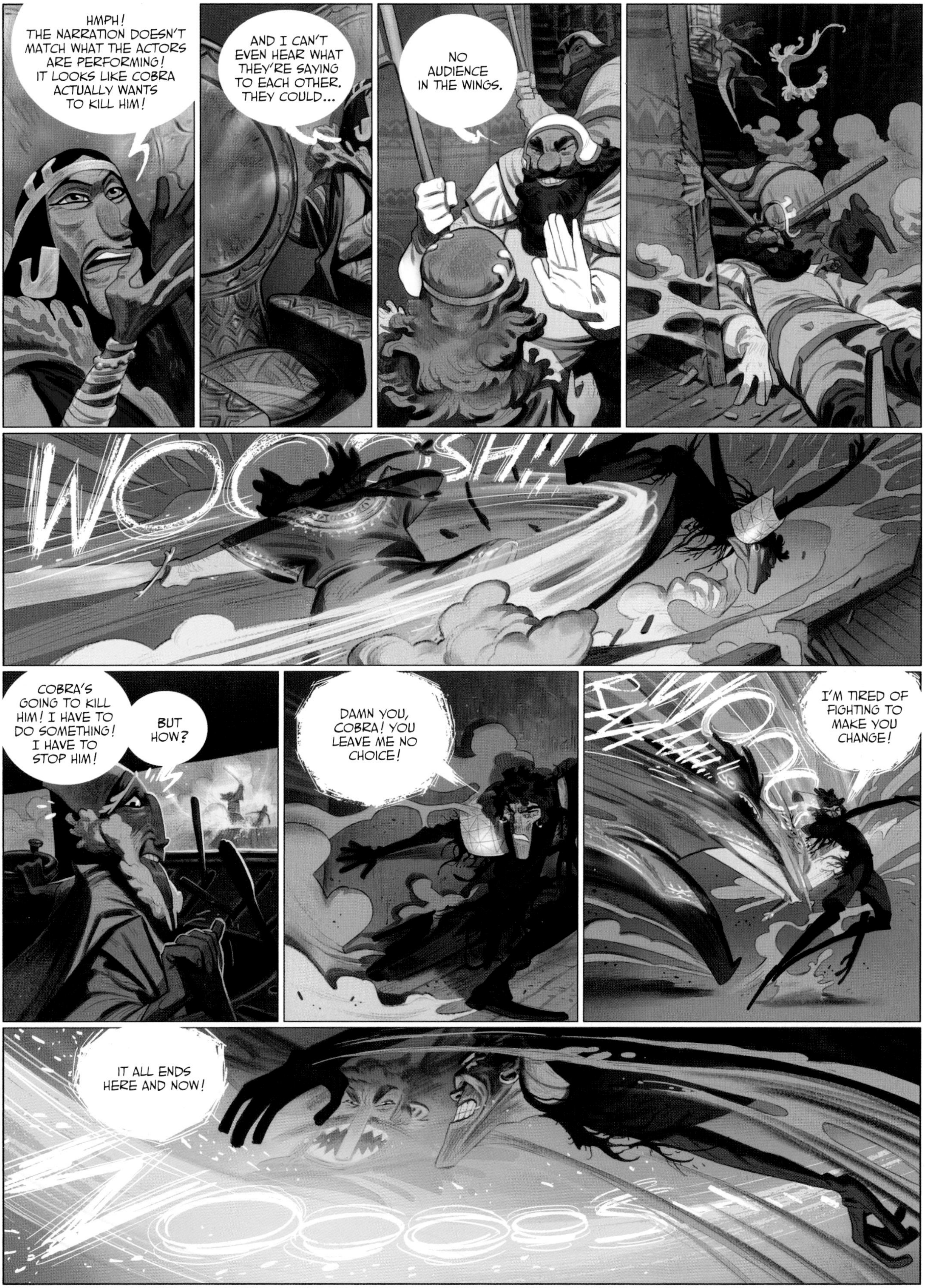
HMPH! THE NARRATION DOESN'T MATCH WHAT THE ACTORS ARE PERFORMING! IT LOOKS LIKE COBRA ACTUALLY WANTS TO KILL HIM!
AND I CAN'T EVEN HEAR WHAT THEY'RE SAYING TO EACH OTHER. THEY COULD...
NO AUDIENCE IN THE WINGS.
COBRA'S GOING TO KILL HIM! I HAVE TO DO SOMETHING! I HAVE TO STOP HIM!
BUT HOW?
DAMN YOU, COBRA! YOU LEAVE ME NO CHOICE!
I'M TIRED OF FIGHTING TO MAKE YOU CHANGE!
IT ALL ENDS HERE AND NOW!

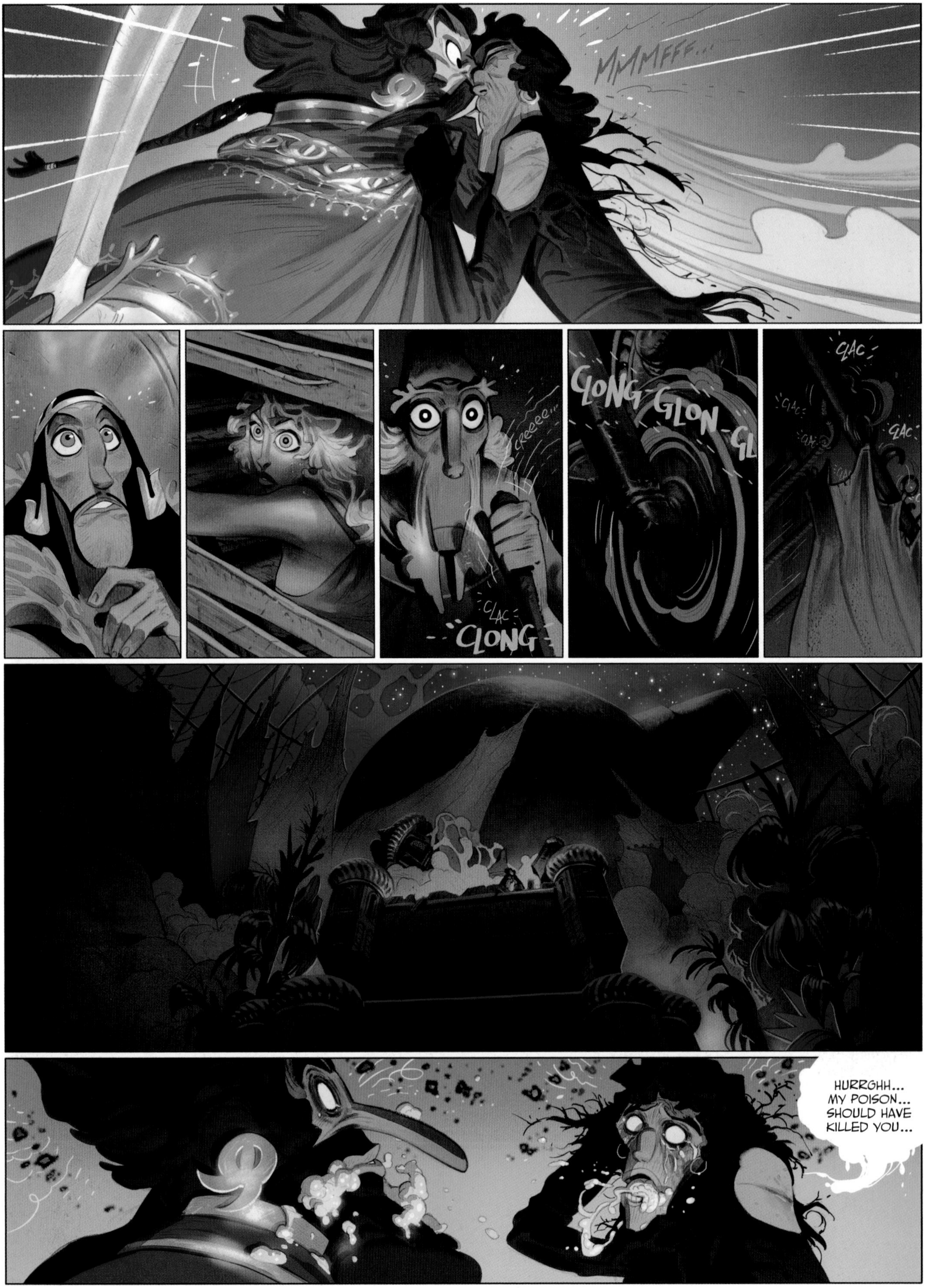
MMMFFF...
creeee...
CLAC
CLONG
CLONG GLON GL
CLAC
CLAC
HURRGHH... MY POISON... SHOULD HAVE KILLED YOU...

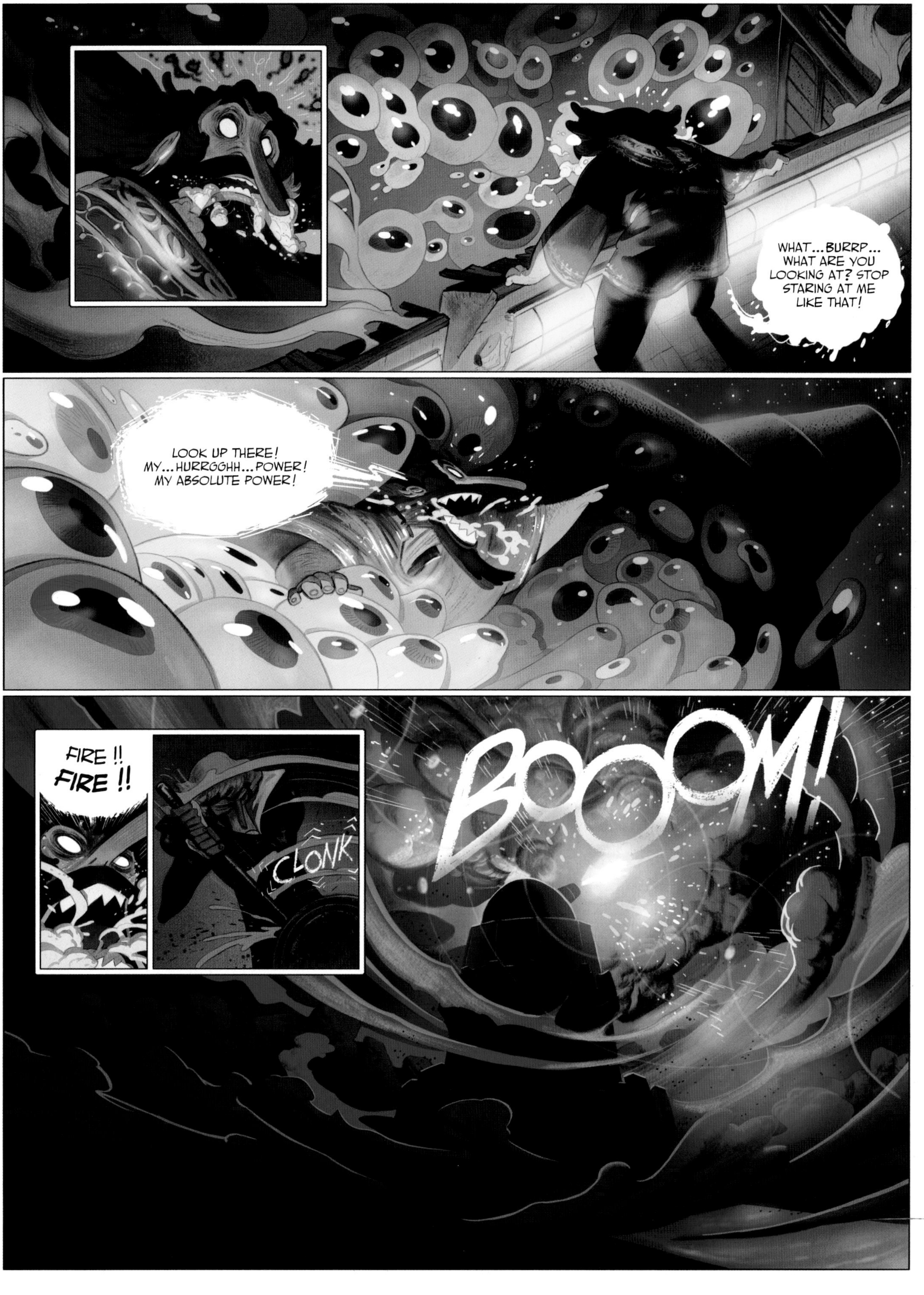
WHAT...BURRP... WHAT ARE YOU LOOKING AT? STOP STARING AT ME LIKE THAT!
LOOK UP THERE! MY...HURRGGHH...POWER! MY ABSOLUTE POWER!
FIRE !! FIRE !!
CLONK
BOOOOM!

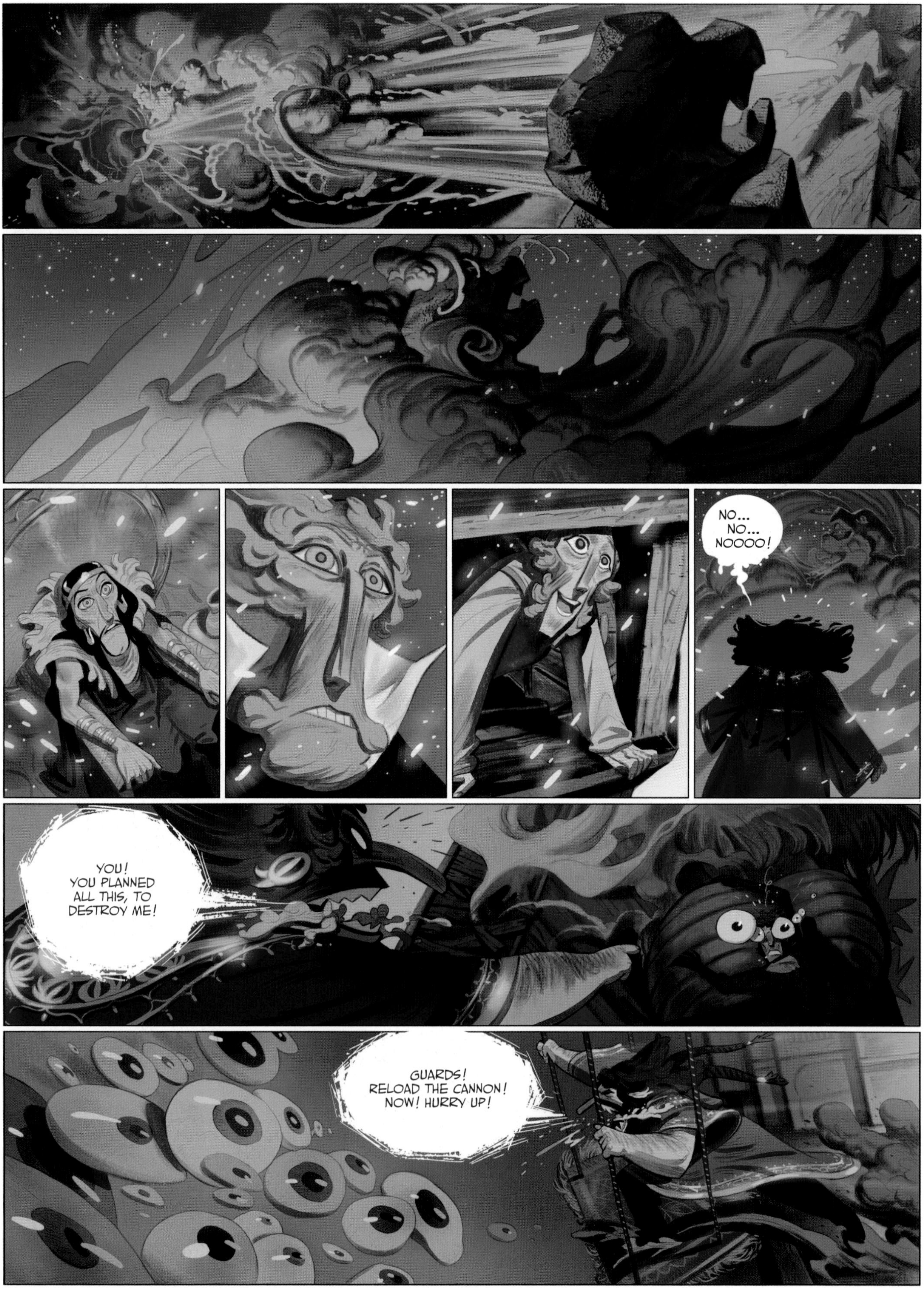
NO...
NO...
NOOOO!
YOU! YOU PLANNED ALL THIS, TO DESTROY ME!
GUARDS! RELOAD THE CANNON! NOW! HURRY UP!

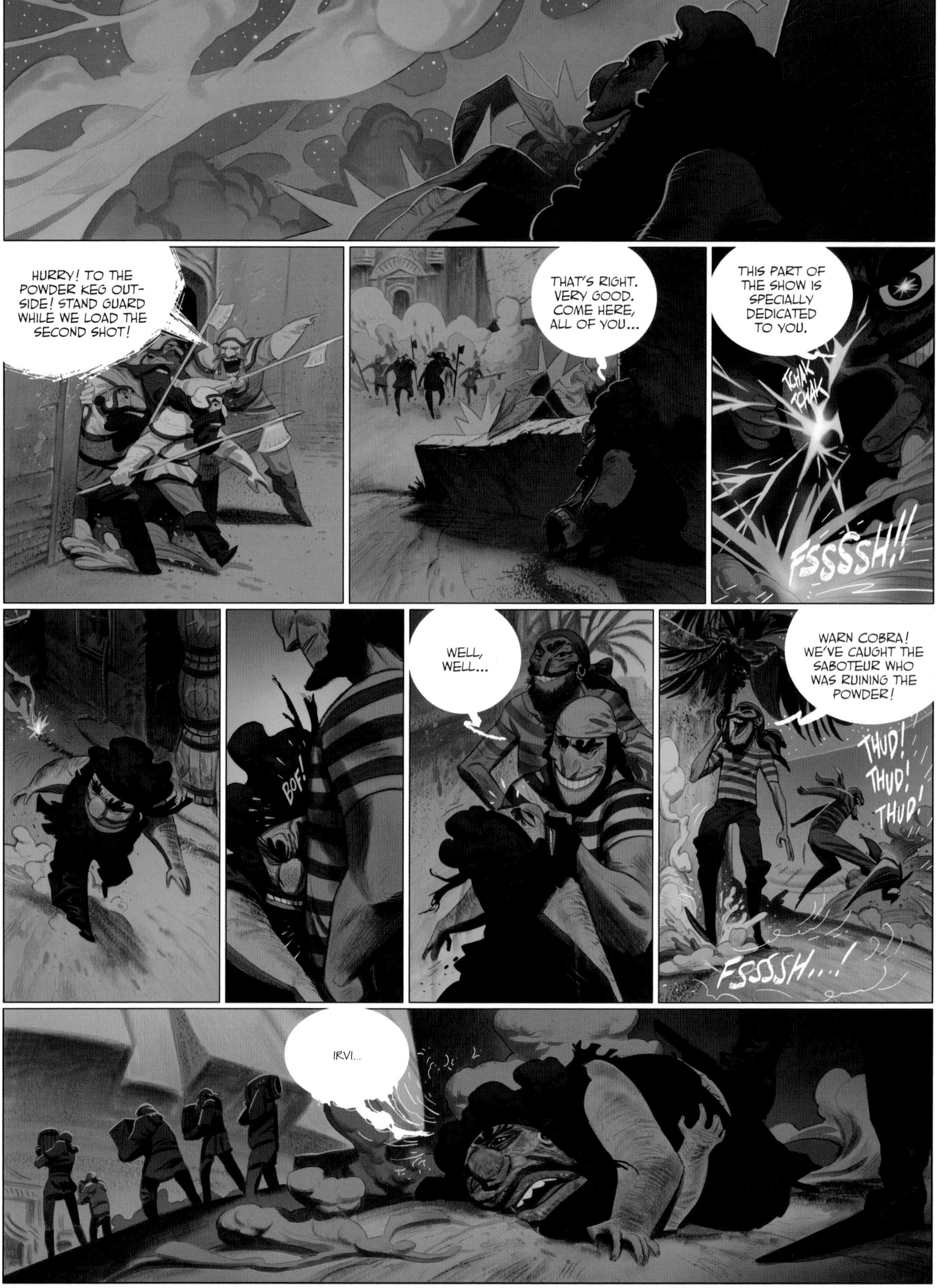
HURRY! TO THE POWDER KEG OUT-SIDE! STAND GUARD WHILE WE LOAD THE SECOND SHOT!
THAT'S RIGHT. VERY GOOD. COME HERE, ALL OF YOU...
THIS PART OF THE SHOW IS SPECIALLY DEDICATED TO YOU.
TCHAK TCHAK
FSSSSH!!
BOF!
WELL, WELL...
WARN COBRA! WE'VE CAUGHT THE SABOTEUR WHO WAS RUINING THE POWDER!
THUD! THUD! THUD!
FSSSSH...!
IRVI...

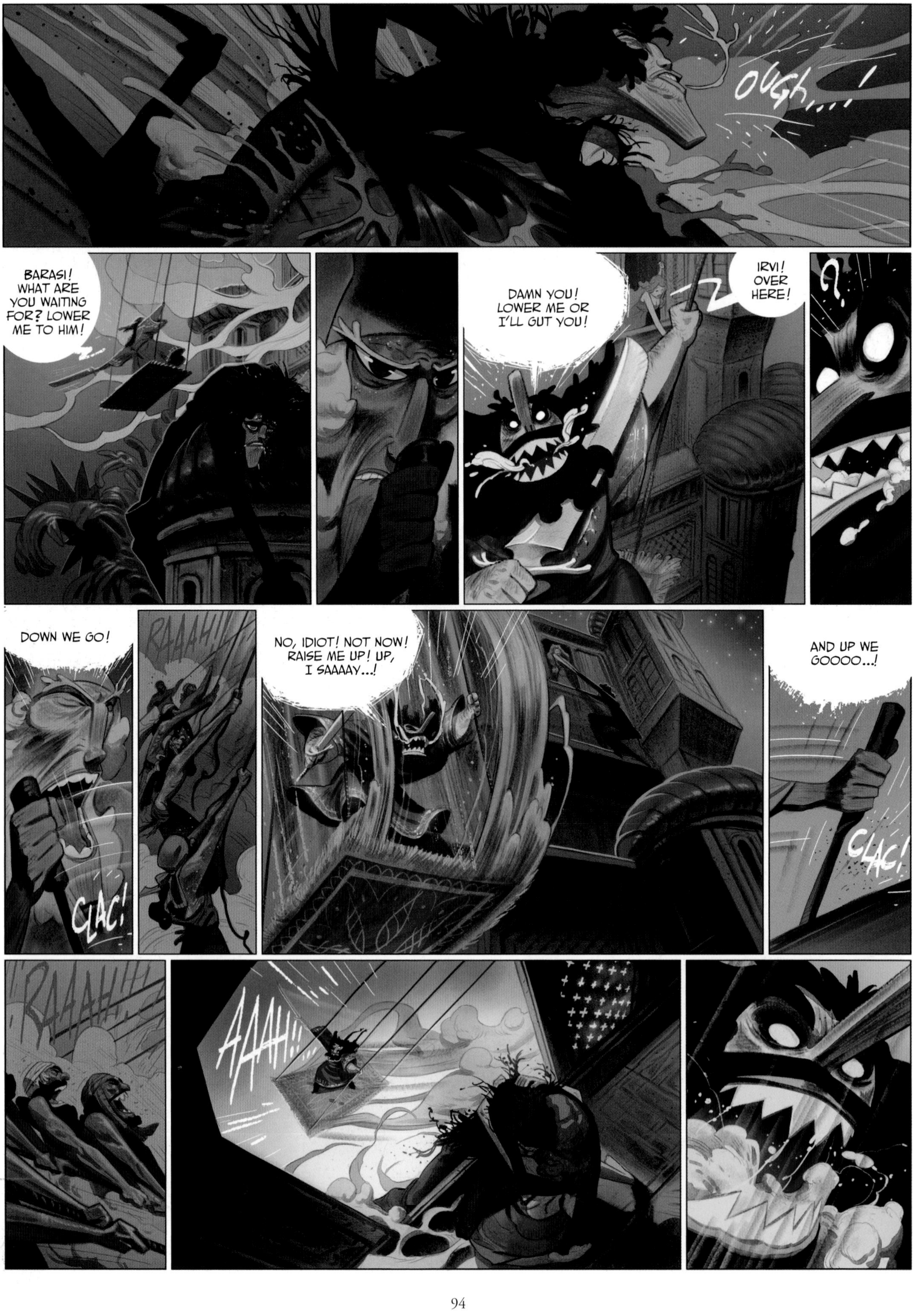
OUGH...!
BARASI! WHAT ARE YOU WAITING FOR? LOWER ME TO HIM!
DAMN YOU! LOWER ME OR I'LL GUT YOU!
IRVI! OVER HERE!
?
DOWN WE GO!
CLAC!
RAAAH!!
NO, IDIOT! NOT NOW! RAISE ME UP! UP, I SAAAAY...!
AND UP WE GOOOO...!
CLAC!
RAAAH!!
AAAH!!

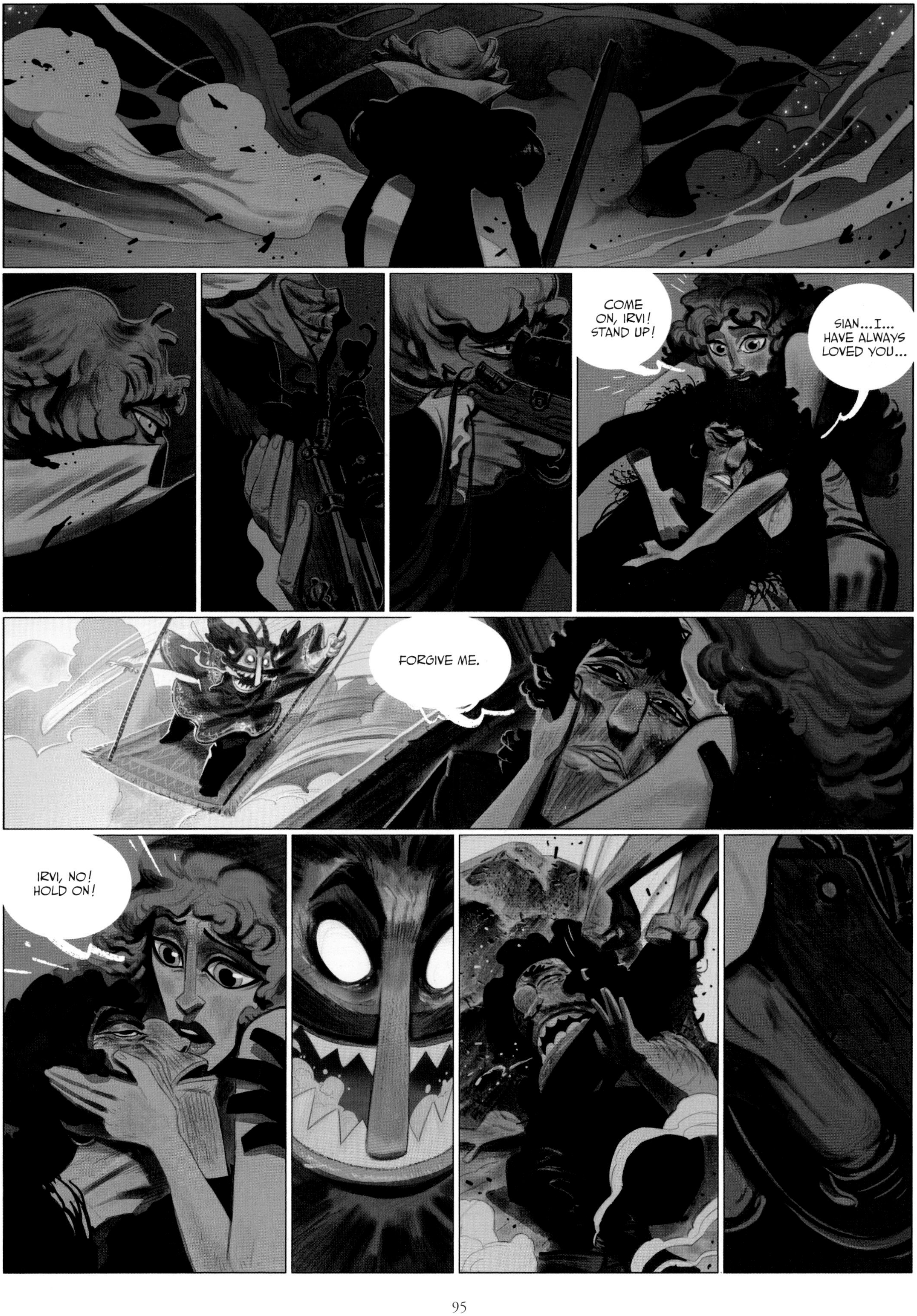
COME ON, IRVI! STAND UP!
SIAN... I... HAVE ALWAYS LOVED YOU...
FORGIVE ME.
IRVI, NO! HOLD ON!

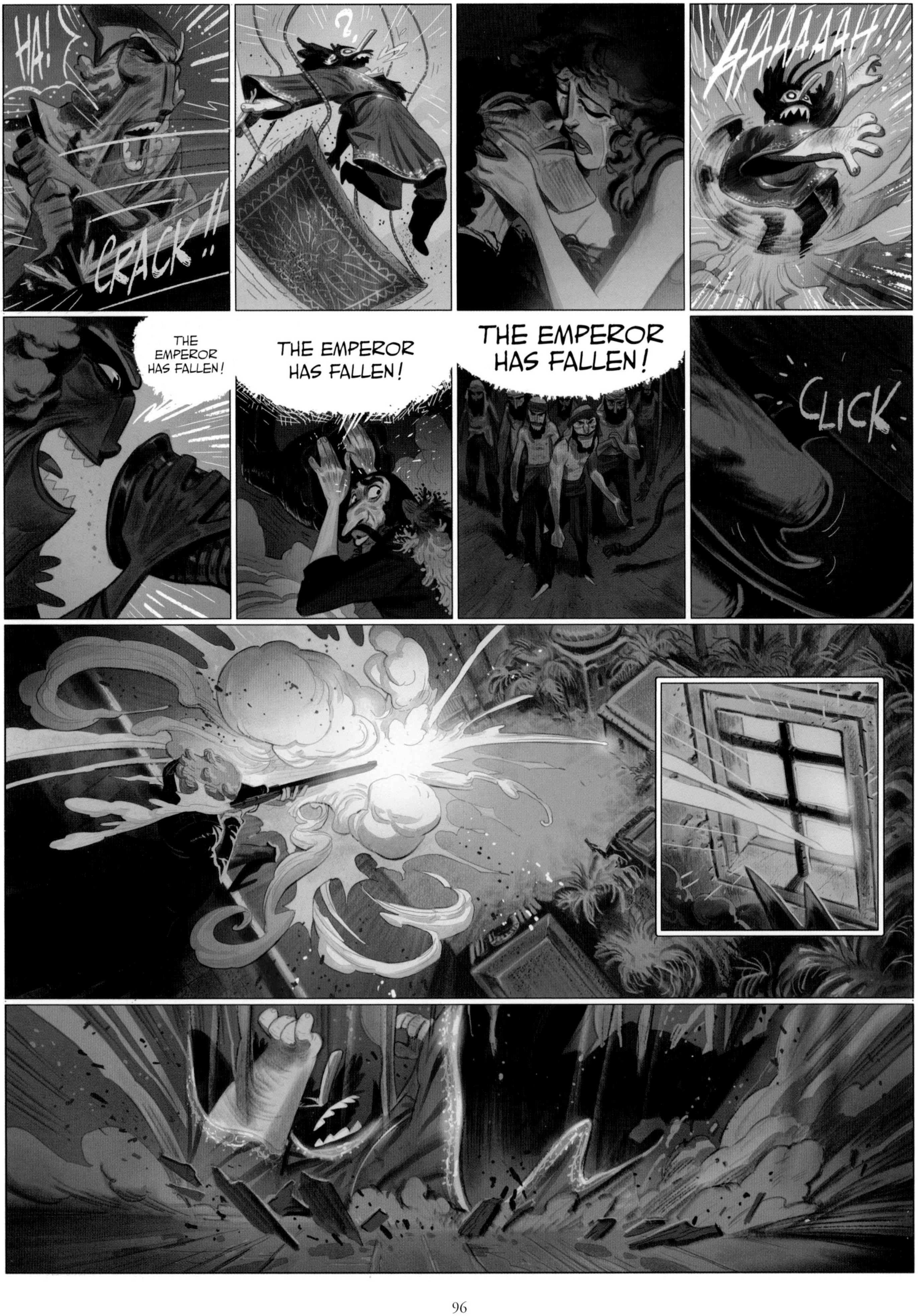
HA!
CRACK!!
?
AAAAAAH!!
THE EMPEROR HAS FALLEN!
THE EMPEROR HAS FALLEN!
THE EMPEROR HAS FALLEN!
CLICK

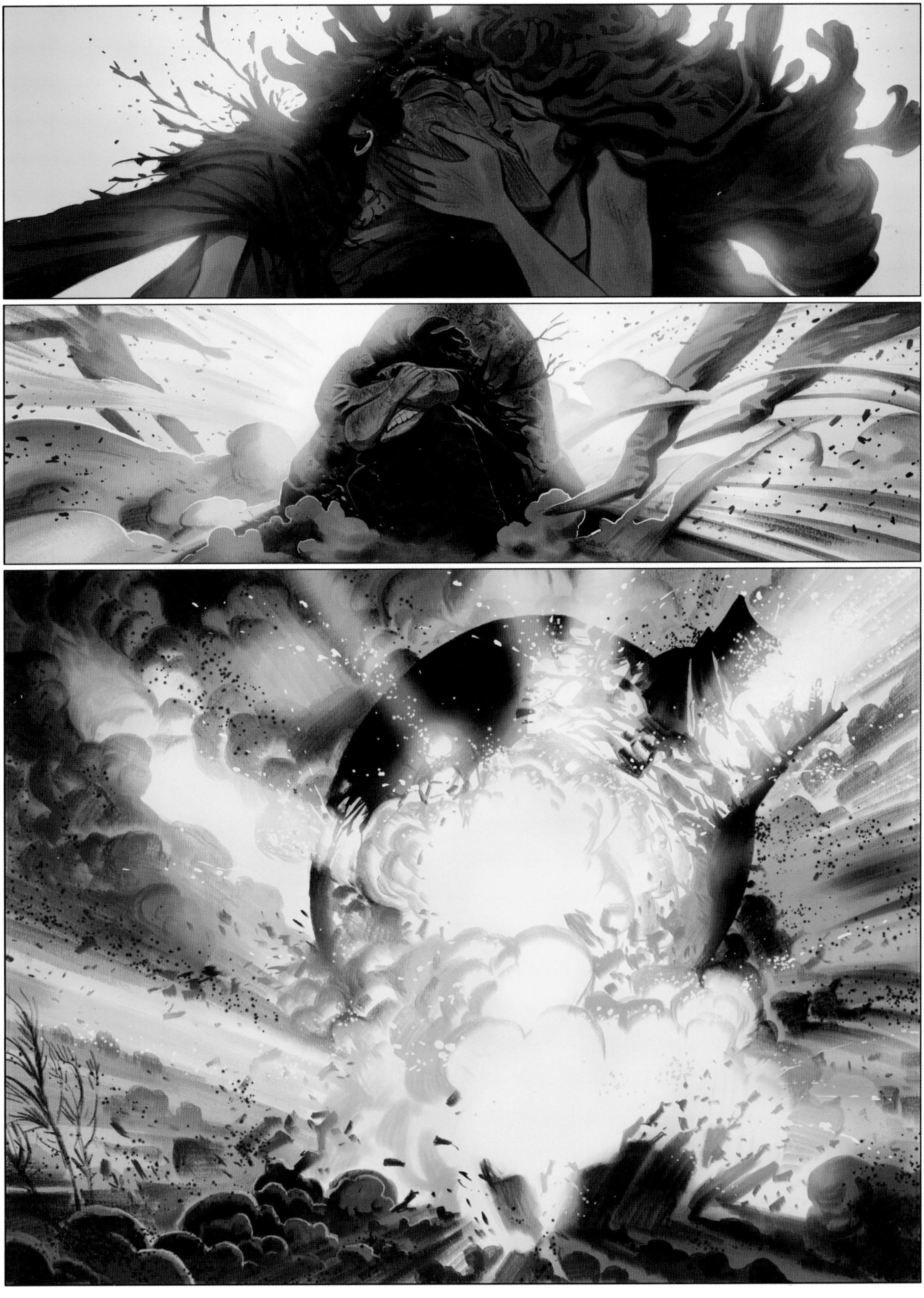

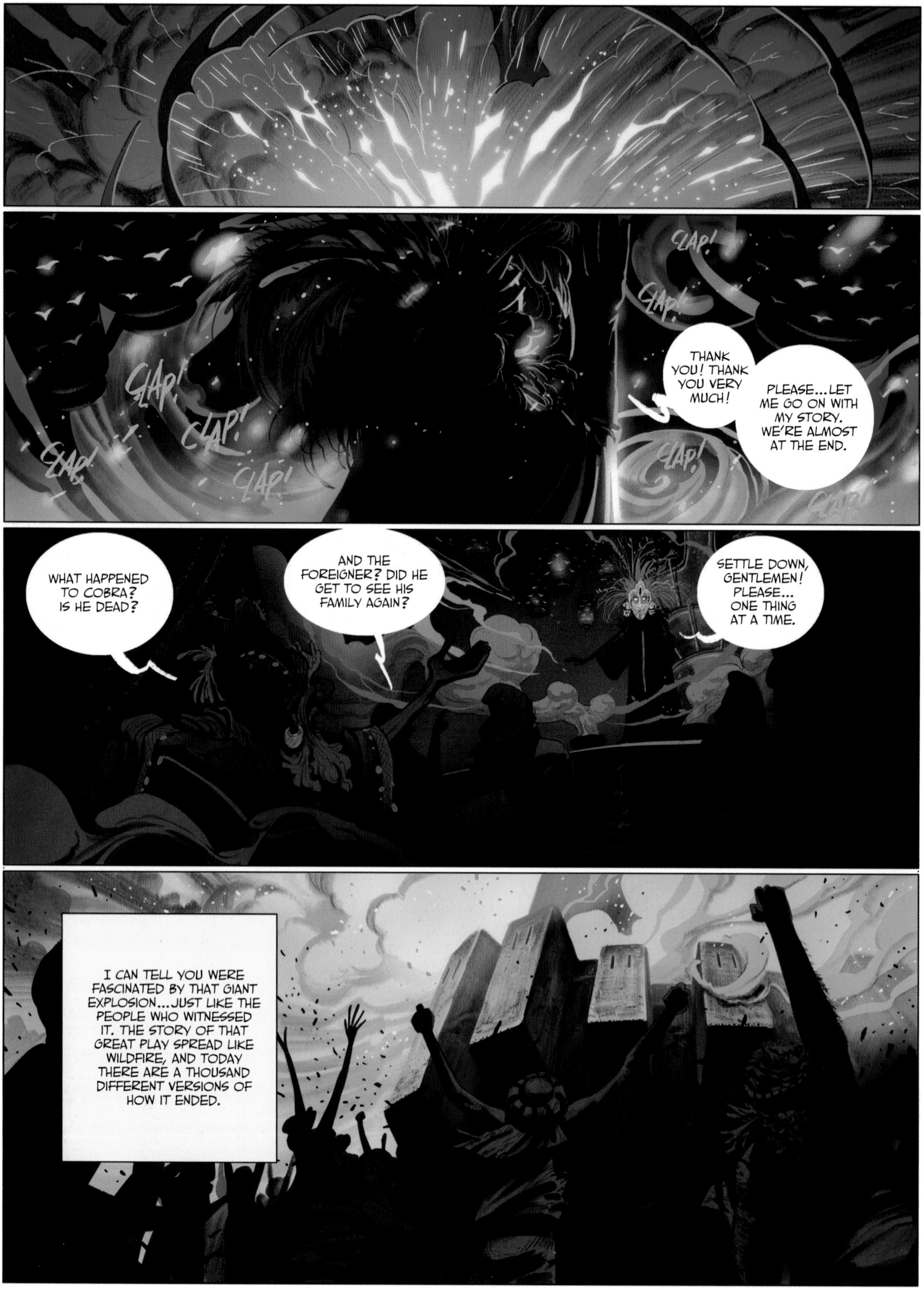
CLAP!
CLAP!
CLAP!
CLAP!
CLAP!
CLAP!
CLAP!
CLAP!
CLAP!
THANK YOU! THANK YOU VERY MUCH!
PLEASE...LET ME GO ON WITH MY STORY. WE'RE ALMOST AT THE END.
WHAT HAPPENED TO COBRA? IS HE DEAD?
AND THE FOREIGNER? DID HE GET TO SEE HIS FAMILY AGAIN?
SETTLE DOWN, GENTLEMEN! PLEASE... ONE THING AT A TIME.
I CAN TELL YOU WERE FASCINATED BY THAT GIANT EXPLOSION...JUST LIKE THE PEOPLE WHO WITNESSED IT. THE STORY OF THAT GREAT PLAY SPREAD LIKE WILDFIRE, AND TODAY THERE ARE A THOUSAND DIFFERENT VERSIONS OF HOW IT ENDED.

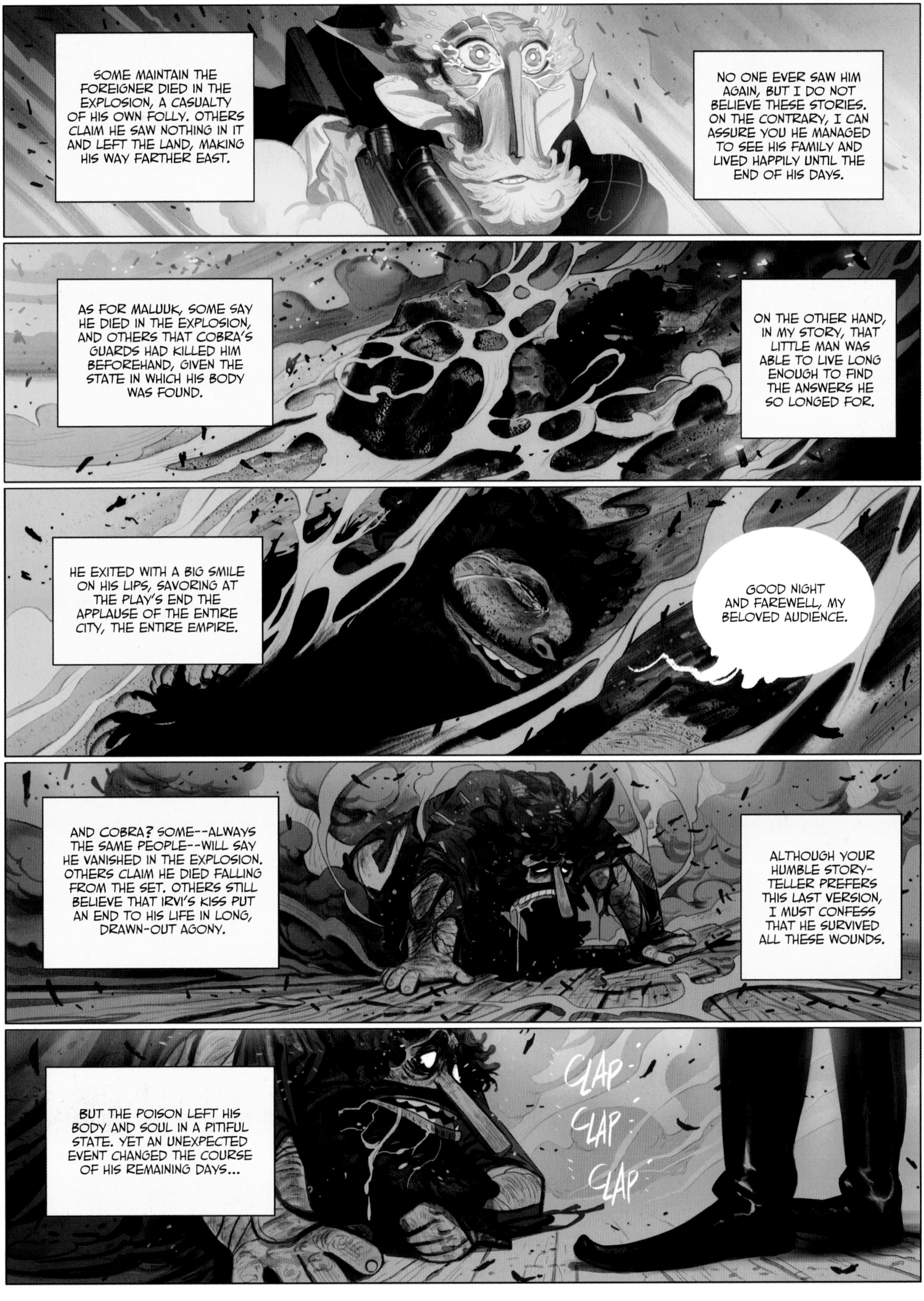
SOME MAINTAIN THE FOREIGNER DIED IN THE EXPLOSION, A CASUALTY OF HIS OWN FOLLY. OTHERS CLAIM HE SAW NOTHING IN IT AND LEFT THE LAND, MAKING HIS WAY FARTHER EAST.
NO ONE EVER SAW HIM AGAIN, BUT I DO NOT BELIEVE THESE STORIES. ON THE CONTRARY, I CAN ASSURE YOU HE MANAGED TO SEE HIS FAMILY AND LIVED HAPPILY UNTIL THE END OF HIS DAYS.
AS FOR MALUUK, SOME SAY HE DIED IN THE EXPLOSION, AND OTHERS THAT COBRA'S GUARDS HAD KILLED HIM BEFOREHAND, GIVEN THE STATE IN WHICH HIS BODY WAS FOUND.
ON THE OTHER HAND, IN MY STORY, THAT LITTLE MAN WAS ABLE TO LIVE LONG ENOUGH TO FIND THE ANSWERS HE SO LONGED FOR.
HE EXITED WITH A BIG SMILE ON HIS LIPS, SAVORING AT THE PLAY'S END THE APPLAUSE OF THE ENTIRE CITY, THE ENTIRE EMPIRE.
GOOD NIGHT AND FAREWELL, MY BELOVED AUDIENCE.
AND COBRA? SOME--ALWAYS THE SAME PEOPLE--WILL SAY HE VANISHED IN THE EXPLOSION. OTHERS CLAIM HE DIED FALLING FROM THE SET. OTHERS STILL BELIEVE THAT IRVI'S KISS PUT AN END TO HIS LIFE IN LONG, DRAWN-OUT AGONY.
ALTHOUGH YOUR HUMBLE STORY-TELLER PREFERS THIS LAST VERSION, I MUST CONFESS THAT HE SURVIVED ALL THESE WOUNDS.
BUT THE POISON LEFT HIS BODY AND SOUL IN A PITIFUL STATE. YET AN UNEXPECTED EVENT CHANGED THE COURSE OF HIS REMAINING DAYS...
CLAP
CLAP
CLAP

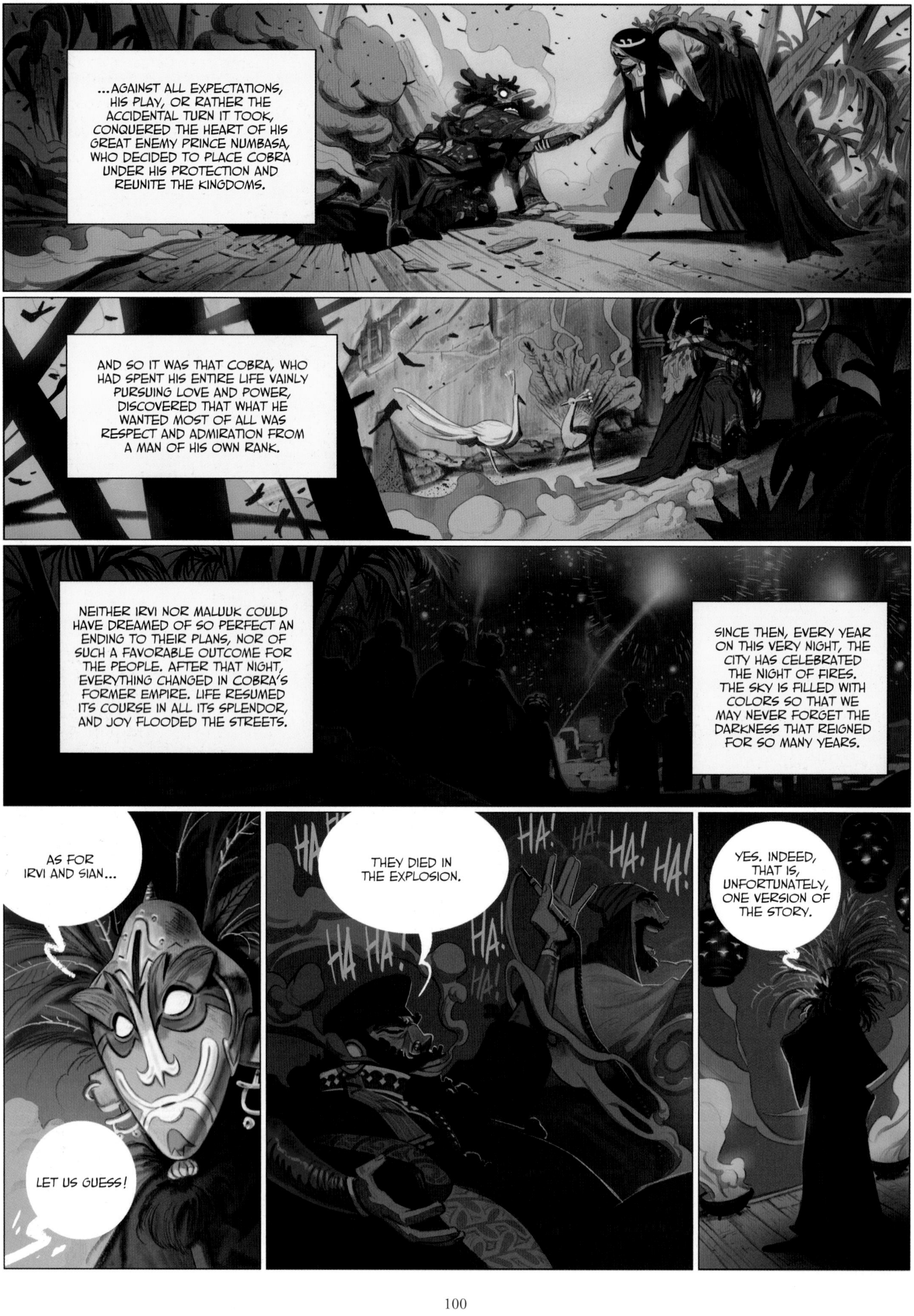
...AGAINST ALL EXPECTATIONS, HIS PLAY, OR RATHER THE ACCIDENTAL TURN IT TOOK, CONQUERED THE HEART OF HIS GREAT ENEMY PRINCE NUMBASA, WHO DECIDED TO PLACE COBRA UNDER HIS PROTECTION AND REUNITE THE KINGDOMS.
AND SO IT WAS THAT COBRA, WHO HAD SPENT HIS ENTIRE LIFE VAINLY PURSUING LOVE AND POWER, DISCOVERED THAT WHAT HE WANTED MOST OF ALL WAS RESPECT AND ADMIRATION FROM A MAN OF HIS OWN RANK.
NEITHER IRVI NOR MALUUK COULD HAVE DREAMED OF SO PERFECT AN ENDING TO THEIR PLANS, NOR OF SUCH A FAVORABLE OUTCOME FOR THE PEOPLE. AFTER THAT NIGHT, EVERYTHING CHANGED IN COBRA'S FORMER EMPIRE. LIFE RESUMED ITS COURSE IN ALL ITS SPLENDOR, AND JOY FLOODED THE STREETS.
SINCE THEN, EVERY YEAR ON THIS VERY NIGHT, THE CITY HAS CELEBRATED THE NIGHT OF FIRES. THE SKY IS FILLED WITH COLORS SO THAT WE MAY NEVER FORGET THE DARKNESS THAT REIGNED FOR SO MANY YEARS.
AS FOR IRVI AND SIAN...
LET US GUESS!
THEY DIED IN THE EXPLOSION.
HA HA! HA! HA! HA! HA! HA HA! HA! HA!
YES. INDEED, THAT IS, UNFORTUNATELY, ONE VERSION OF THE STORY.

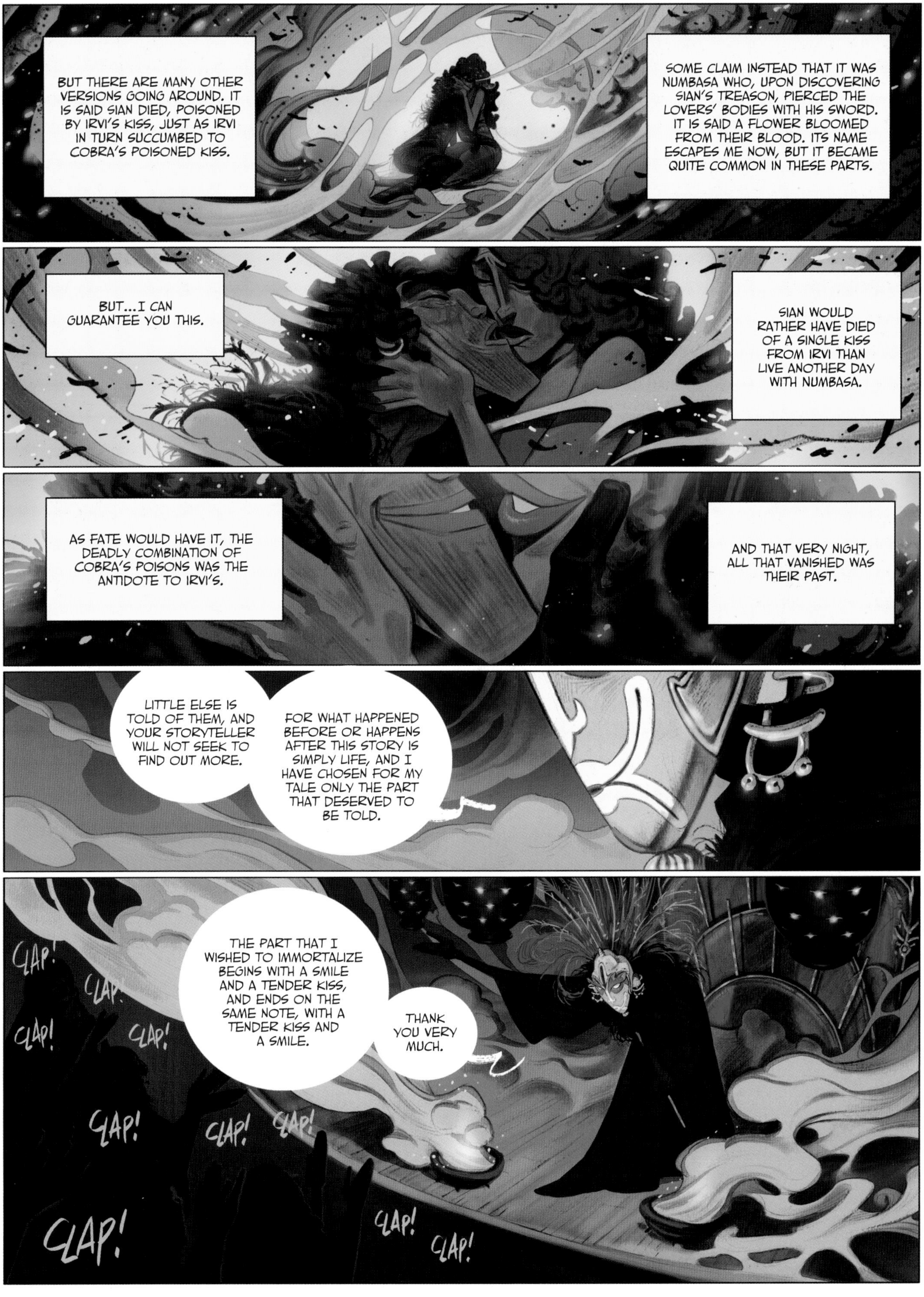
BUT THERE ARE MANY OTHER VERSIONS GOING AROUND. IT IS SAID SIAN DIED, POISONED BY IRVI'S KISS, JUST AS IRVI IN TURN SUCCUMBED TO COBRA'S POISONED KISS.
SOME CLAIM INSTEAD THAT IT WAS NUMBASA WHO, UPON DISCOVERING SIAN'S TREASON, PIERCED THE LOVERS' BODIES WITH HIS SWORD. IT IS SAID A FLOWER BLOOMED FROM THEIR BLOOD. ITS NAME ESCAPES ME NOW, BUT IT BECAME QUITE COMMON IN THESE PARTS.
BUT...I CAN GUARANTEE YOU THIS.
SIAN WOULD RATHER HAVE DIED OF A SINGLE KISS FROM IRVI THAN LIVE ANOTHER DAY WITH NUMBASA.
AS FATE WOULD HAVE IT, THE DEADLY COMBINATION OF COBRA'S POISONS WAS THE ANTIDOTE TO IRVI'S.
AND THAT VERY NIGHT, ALL THAT VANISHED WAS THEIR PAST.
LITTLE ELSE IS TOLD OF THEM, AND YOUR STORYTELLER WILL NOT SEEK TO FIND OUT MORE.
FOR WHAT HAPPENED BEFORE OR HAPPENS AFTER THIS STORY IS SIMPLY LIFE, AND I HAVE CHOSEN FOR MY TALE ONLY THE PART THAT DESERVED TO BE TOLD.
CLAP! CLAP! CLAP! CLAP!
THE PART THAT I WISHED TO IMMORTALIZE BEGINS WITH A SMILE AND A TENDER KISS, AND ENDS ON THE SAME NOTE, WITH A TENDER KISS AND A SMILE.
THANK YOU VERY MUCH.
CLAP! CLAP! CLAP! CLAP! CLAP! CLAP!

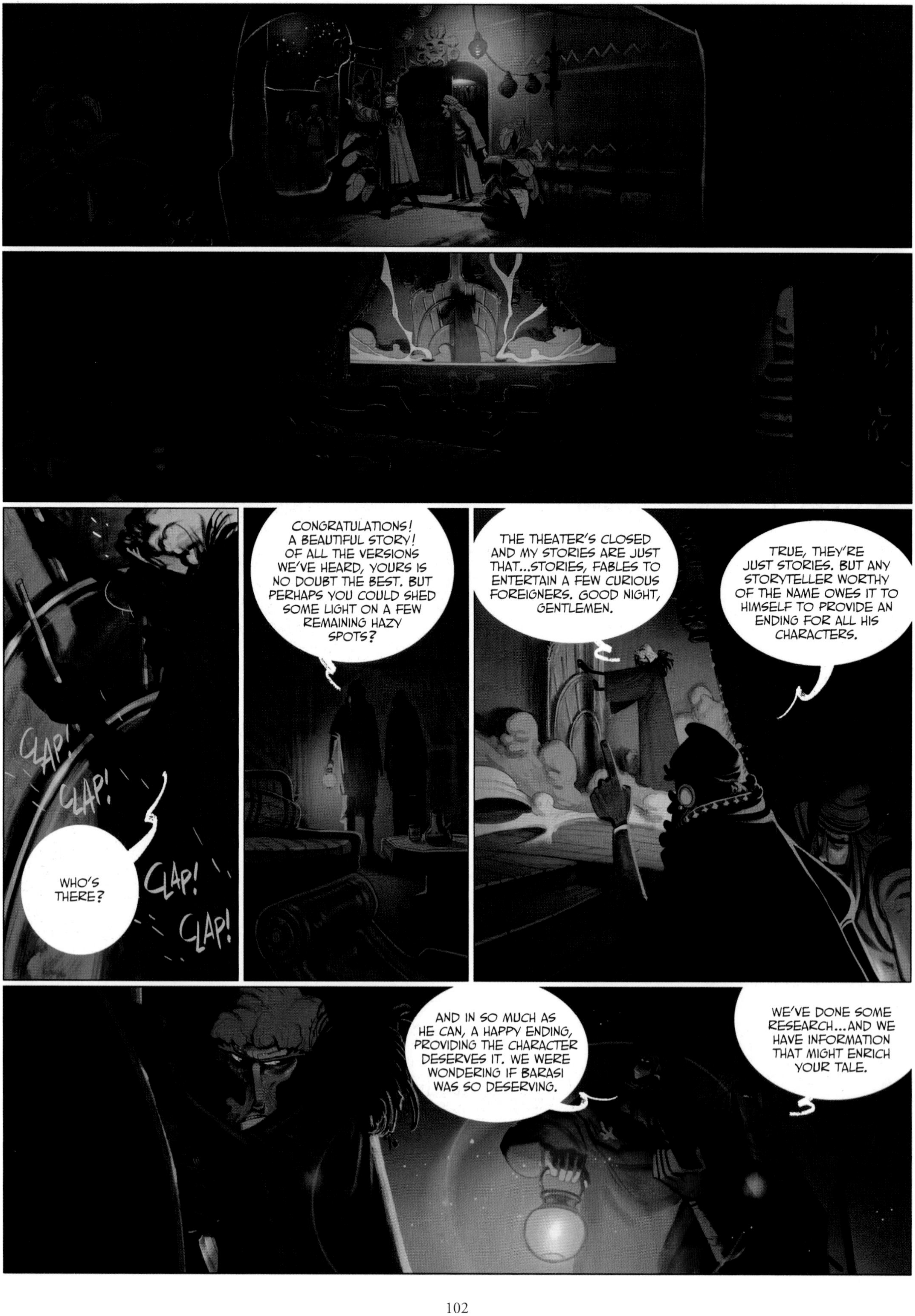
CLAP!
CLAP!
CLAP!
CLAP!
WHO'S THERE?
CONGRATULATIONS! A BEAUTIFUL STORY! OF ALL THE VERSIONS WE'VE HEARD, YOURS IS NO DOUBT THE BEST. BUT PERHAPS YOU COULD SHED SOME LIGHT ON A FEW REMAINING HAZY SPOTS?
THE THEATER'S CLOSED AND MY STORIES ARE JUST THAT...STORIES, FABLES TO ENTERTAIN A FEW CURIOUS FOREIGNERS. GOOD NIGHT, GENTLEMEN.
TRUE, THEY'RE JUST STORIES. BUT ANY STORYTELLER WORTHY OF THE NAME OWES IT TO HIMSELF TO PROVIDE AN ENDING FOR ALL HIS CHARACTERS.
AND IN SO MUCH AS HE CAN, A HAPPY ENDING, PROVIDING THE CHARACTER DESERVES IT. WE WERE WONDERING IF BARASI WAS SO DESERVING.
WE'VE DONE SOME RESEARCH...AND WE HAVE INFORMATION THAT MIGHT ENRICH YOUR TALE.

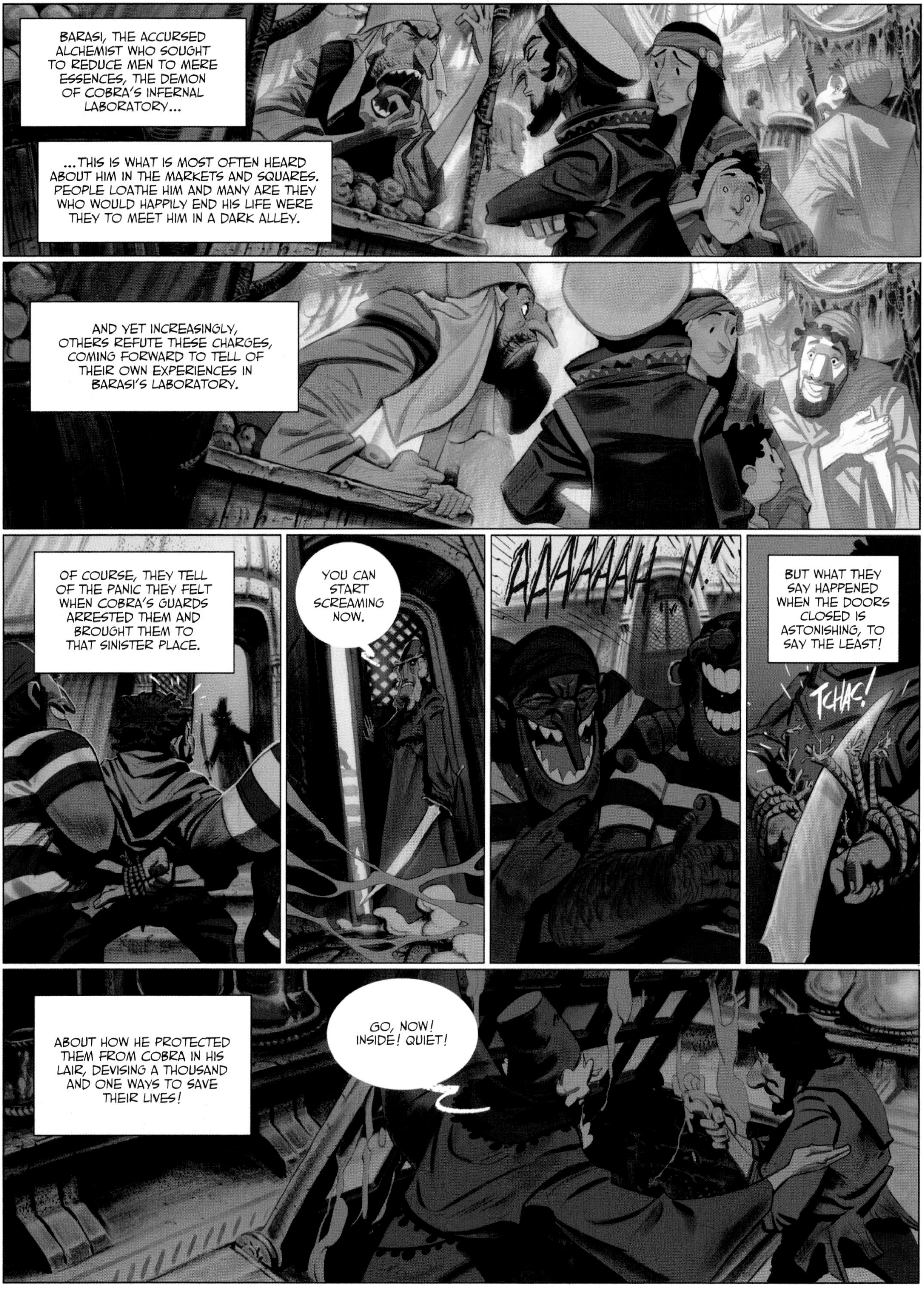
BARASI, THE ACCURSED ALCHEMIST WHO SOUGHT TO REDUCE MEN TO MERE ESSENCES, THE DEMON OF COBRA'S INFERNAL LABORATORY...
...THIS IS WHAT IS MOST OFTEN HEARD ABOUT HIM IN THE MARKETS AND SQUARES. PEOPLE LOATHE HIM AND MANY ARE THEY WHO WOULD HAPPILY END HIS LIFE WERE THEY TO MEET HIM IN A DARK ALLEY.
AND YET INCREASINGLY, OTHERS REFUTE THESE CHARGES, COMING FORWARD TO TELL OF THEIR OWN EXPERIENCES IN BARASI'S LABORATORY.
OF COURSE, THEY TELL OF THE PANIC THEY FELT WHEN COBRA'S GUARDS ARRESTED THEM AND BROUGHT THEM TO THAT SINISTER PLACE.
YOU CAN START SCREAMING NOW.
AAAAAAH !!
BUT WHAT THEY SAY HAPPENED WHEN THE DOORS CLOSED IS ASTONISHING, TO SAY THE LEAST!
TCHAC!
ABOUT HOW HE PROTECTED THEM FROM COBRA IN HIS LAIR, DEVISING A THOUSAND AND ONE WAYS TO SAVE THEIR LIVES!
GO, NOW! INSIDE! QUIET!

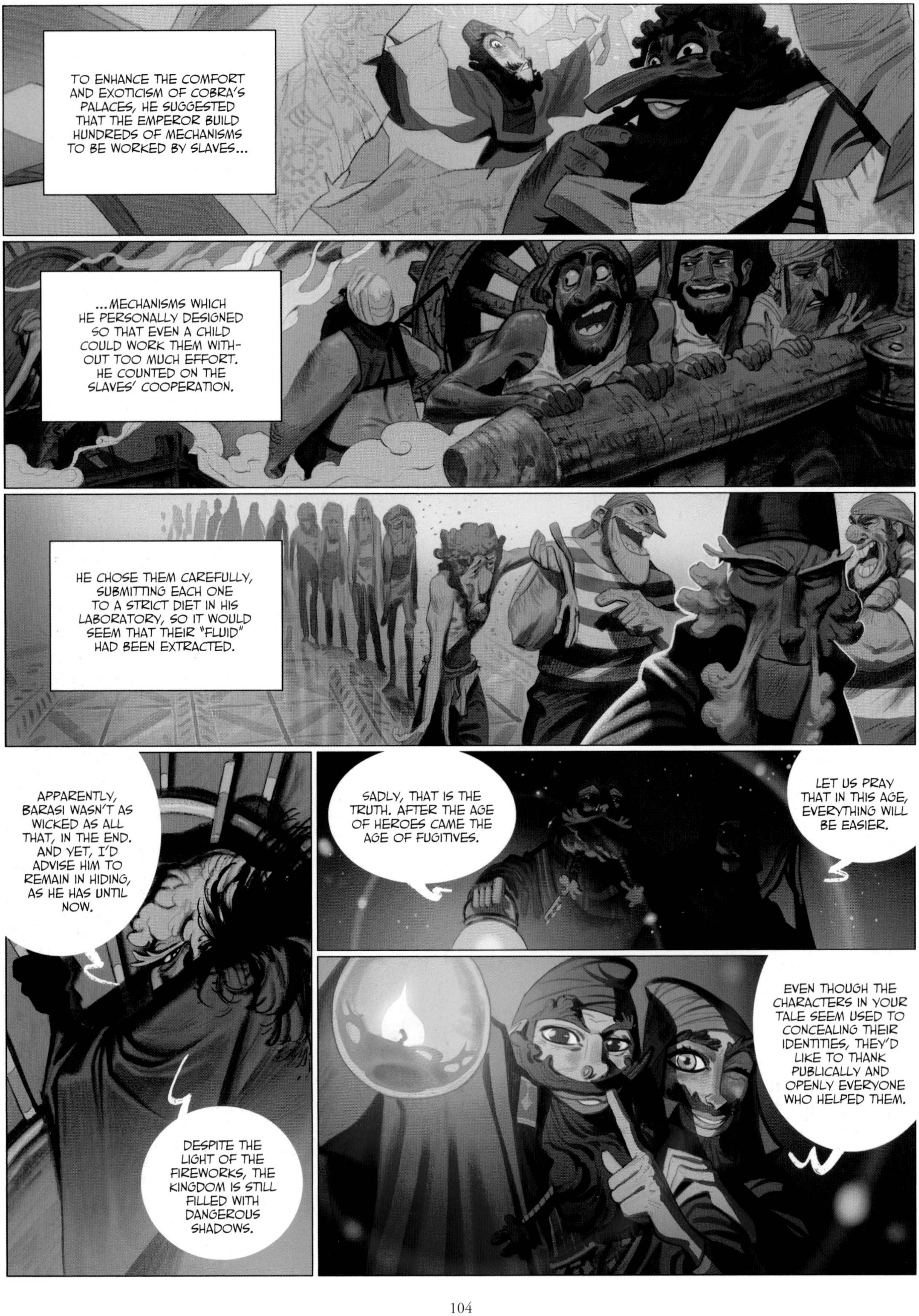

TO ENHANCE THE COMFORT AND EXOTICISM OF COBRA'S PALACES, HE SUGGESTED THAT THE EMPEROR BUILD HUNDREDS OF MECHANISMS TO BE WORKED BY SLAVES...
...MECHANISMS WHICH HE PERSONALLY DESIGNED SO THAT EVEN A CHILD COULD WORK THEM WITHOUT TOO MUCH EFFORT. HE COUNTED ON THE SLAVES' COOPERATION.
HE CHOSE THEM CAREFULLY, SUBMITTING EACH ONE TO A STRICT DIET IN HIS LABORATORY, SO IT WOULD SEEM THAT THEIR "FLUID" HAD BEEN EXTRACTED.
APPARENTLY, BARASI WASN'T AS WICKED AS ALL THAT, IN THE END. AND YET, I'D ADVISE HIM TO REMAIN IN HIDING, AS HE HAS UNTIL NOW.
SADLY, THAT IS THE TRUTH. AFTER THE AGE OF HEROES CAME THE AGE OF FUGITIVES.
LET US PRAY THAT IN THIS AGE, EVERYTHING WILL BE EASIER.
DESPITE THE LIGHT OF THE FIREWORKS, THE KINGDOM IS STILL FILLED WITH DANGEROUS SHADOWS.
EVEN THOUGH THE CHARACTERS IN YOUR TALE SEEM USED TO CONCEALING THEIR IDENTITIES, THEY'D LIKE TO THANK PUBLICALLY AND OPENLY EVERYONE WHO HELPED THEM.

WE, WHO LOVED YOUR TALE SO MUCH, SHALL MAKE DO FOR NOW WITH THIS ALMOST CLANDESTINE DEMONSTRATION OF GRATITUDE.

AND WE WILL TRY TO COME BACK AS OFTEN AS POSSIBLE.

BUT WE WOULD ALSO LIKE TO SUPPORT YOU, HELP YOU THROUGH HARD TIMES, SO THAT YOUR STORY SPREADS AND YOU WRITE IT DOWN, LIKE BARASI, WHO MUST BE PRECIOUSLY GUARDING HIS WORK.

Tchink

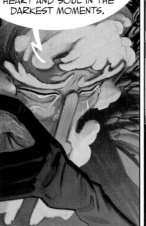

I'M SURE HE IS, AND I CAN ALSO GUARANTEE THAT BARASI STILL KEEPS IRVI'S POEMS BESIDE HIM. HE WOULD LIKE TO GIVE THEM BACK BY WAY OF THANKS FOR HAVING SAVED HIS HEART AND SOUL IN THE DARKEST MOMENTS.

WE ARE COUNTING ON BARASI TO KEEP THOSE POEMS AND INCLUDE THEM IN HIS BOOK, FOR THAT IS WHERE THEY MUST STAY FOREVER.

IRVI WILL BE HAPPY TO LEARN THAT AFTER SO MANY EFFORTS TO PASS THEM ON, HIS POEMS WILL FINALLY HAVE BEEN OF SOME USE.

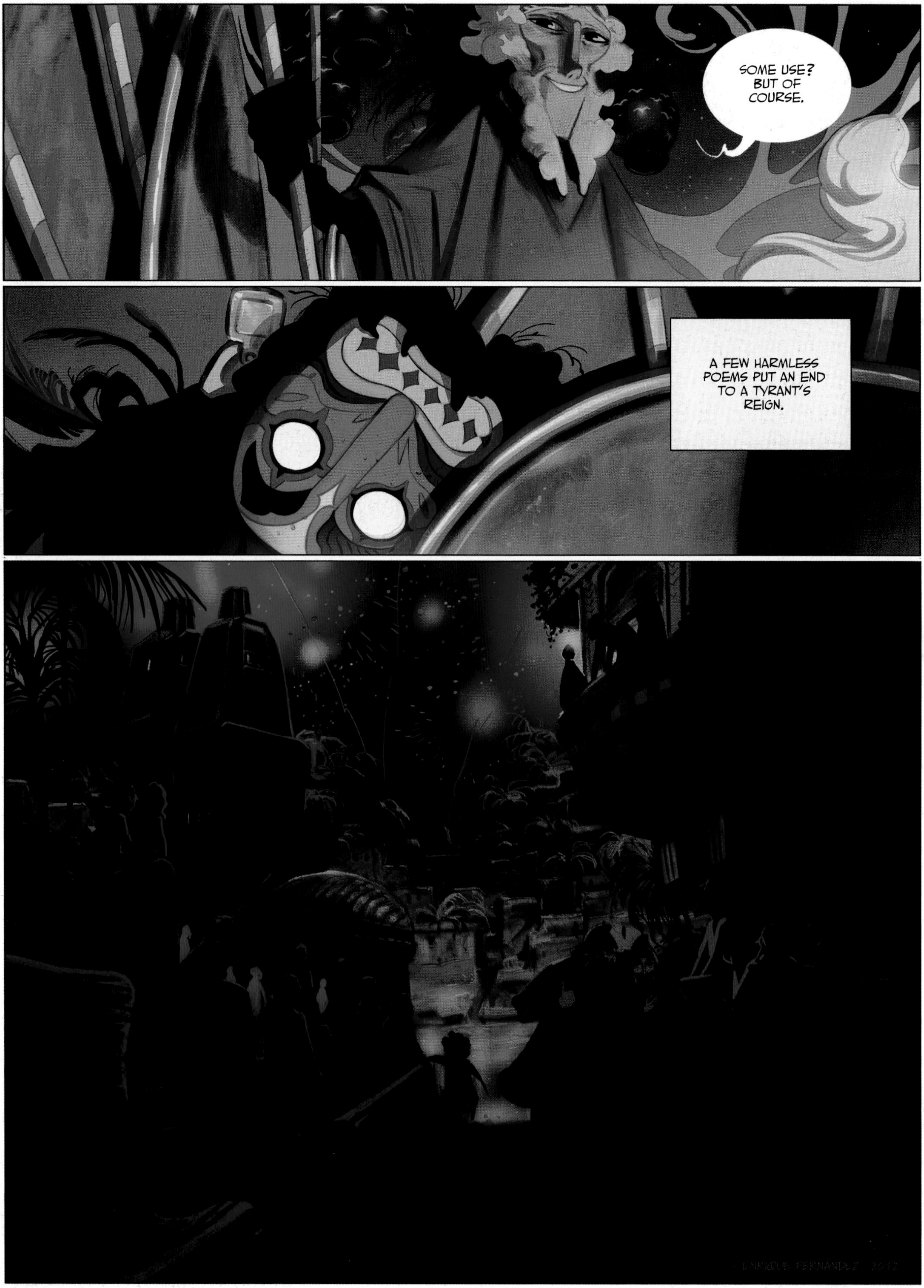
SOME USE? BUT OF COURSE.
A FEW HARMLESS POEMS PUT AN END TO A TYRANT'S REIGN.
ENRIQUE FERNANDEZ 2012

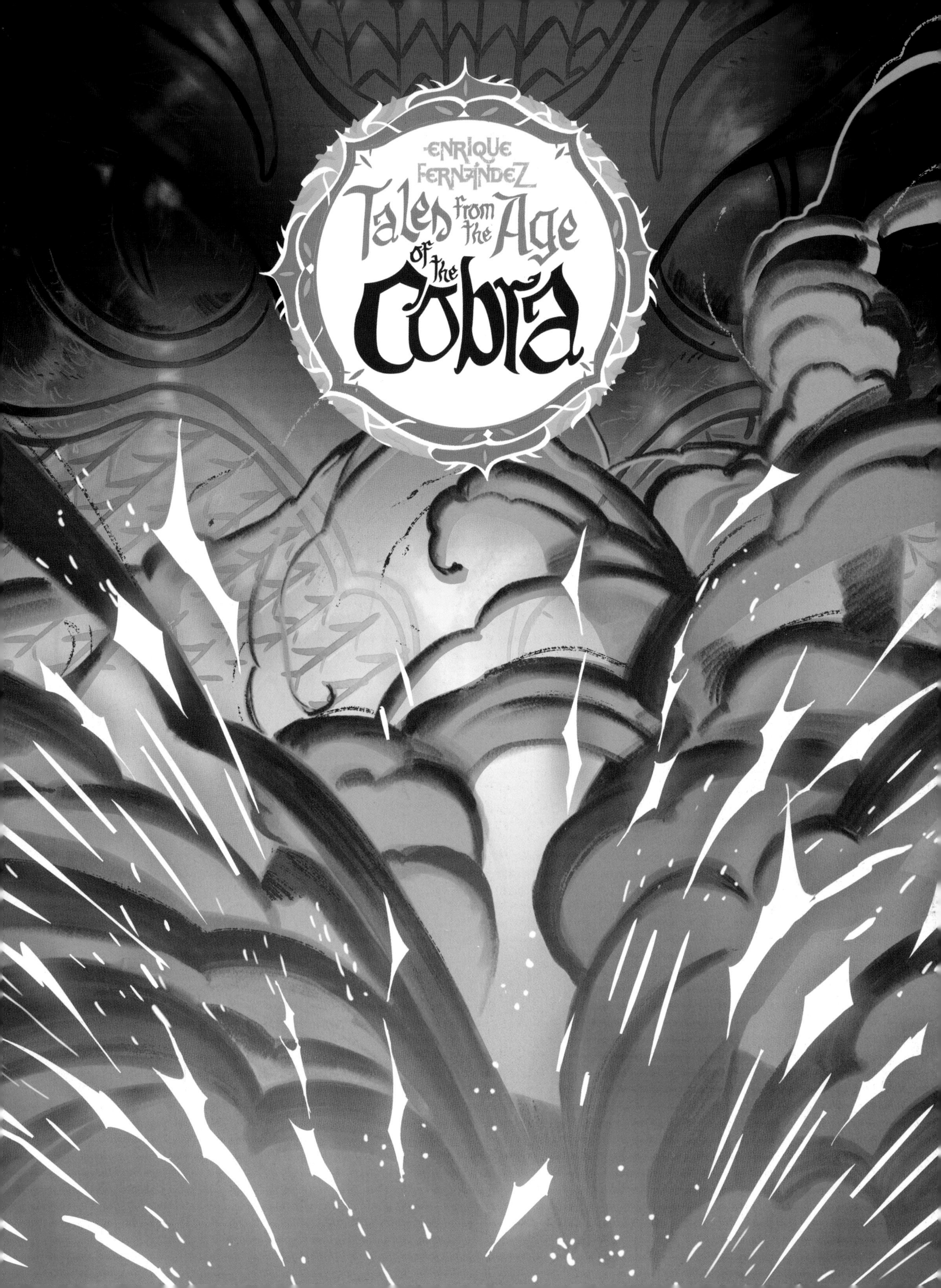

ENRIQUE
FERNÁNDEZ
Tales from the Age of the Cobra

OTHER BOOKS FROM EuroComics/IDW

CORTO MALTESE BY HUGO PRATT

THE ADVENTURES OF DIETER LUMPEN
BY JORGE ZENTNER & RUBÉN PELLEJERO

PARACUELLOS BY CARLOS GIMÉNEZ

FLIGHT OF THE RAVEN BY JEAN-PIERRE GIBRAT

ALACK SINNER BY CARLOS SAMPAYO & JOSÉ MUÑOZ

JEROME K. JEROME BLOCHE BY ALAIN DODIER

LIGHTS OF THE AMALOU
BY CHRISTOPHE GIBELIN & CLAIRE WENDLING

ONE MAN, ONE ADVENTURE:
THE MAN FROM THE GREAT NORTH
BY HUGO PRATT